The
Special Collections
Handbook

The Special Collections Handbook

Alison Cullingford

facet publishing

Published by Facet Publishing
7 Ridgmount Street, London WC1E 7AE
www.facetpublishing.co.uk

Facet Publishing is wholly owned by CILIP: the
Chartered Institute of Library and Information
Professionals.

British Library Cataloguing in Publication Data
A catalogue record for this book is available from the
British Library.

ISBN 978-1-85604-757-9

First published 2011
Reprinted digitally thereafter

Text printed on FSC accredited material.

Typeset from author's files in
10/13 pt Garamond and Frutiger by Facet Publishing.
Printed and made in Great Britain by
MPG Books Group, UK.

Contents

Preface and acknowledgements

In 2000, I became the first ever Special Collections Librarian at the University of Bradford. I took charge of collections that were truly hidden: little known, uncatalogued, unused, neglected and vulnerable to damage. Thanks to a great deal of help from colleagues at Bradford and in the profession, I have been able to make many of these materials available for the first time. I was thrilled to be asked by Facet Publishing to write this book to share my experience and knowledge of developing Special Collections from scratch with few resources.

Far too many people have helped directly or indirectly in the creation of this book to begin to thank them all, notably colleagues in the CILIP Rare Books and Special Collections Group. I would particularly like to mention here my colleagues at Bradford who gave me the opportunity to manage and transform a wonderful set of Special Collections, and above all the Special Collections Assistant, John Brooker. On a personal note, many, many thanks to Simon and to my parents for all their support.

Alison Cullingford

Introduction

Introducing Special Collections

So what are Special Collections, and where are they to be found? Special Collections are everywhere!

1 They are held by all kinds of organizations: research libraries, universities, colleges, schools, national libraries, public libraries, museums, art galleries, archives, historic houses, cathedrals, subscription libraries, learned societies …
2 They include many kinds of material: early printed books, manuscripts, pamphlets, ephemera, maps, photographs, archives, newspapers, digital files and much more.

The term 'Special Collections' can refer to the collections themselves, the staff who care for them, the physical and virtual spaces they occupy, and the administrative department in a larger library that manages all these entities. In this Handbook, the context should make it clear which meaning is intended.

The term also implies other, non-special collections: a distinction between a main library service and the special material, typical of university and research libraries. However, much Special Collections work takes place in libraries that contain mostly special materials, though staff may not use the term in describing their collections.

Until relatively recently, Special Collections were seen as special because they needed special care: they were too old, valuable, rare, unique or fragile to be stored on open library shelves. As we will see in Chapter 1, this remains true: Special Collections materials need particular care if they are to survive, and their well-being should be at the heart of all management activities.

However, Special Collections librarians are making this rather negative definition positive: Special Collections are special also because of their potential relevance to people outside the library service and in the long term. They can be the most exciting, appealing and useful materials in a library.

Exactly which historic materials are part of the 'Special Collections' administrative structure, and which are not, varies between libraries. In larger services, the term 'Special

Collections' is often reserved for modern, unpublished rare material, with rare books, archives and/or manuscripts managed separately.

To make this book as useful as possible, I apply the widest definition of 'Special Collections', covering any material that is managed by any Special Collections service, including rare books, manuscripts and archives. In doing so I follow the Association of College and Research Libraries (2003) definition: 'Special collections materials: The entire range of textual, graphic and artefact primary source materials in analog and digital formats, including printed books, manuscripts, photographs, maps, artworks, audiovisual materials, and realia.'

Using *The Special Collections Handbook*

The Handbook is written for professional librarians working with Special Collections, or those aspiring to do so, especially library school students and new professionals. It will also be useful to anyone who needs an introduction to the subject, including managers of Special Collections staff, archivists and museum professionals, paraprofessional library staff or volunteers. For convenience, I generally refer to the individual professional as a 'librarian' and their organization as a 'library'.

The book takes a pragmatic approach to the management of Special Collections. The main chapters cover all aspects of Special Collections work, taking the reader from the basics of collections care to reaching out to new audiences and funding sources. Issues in the management of digital Special Collections are discussed in the appropriate chapter. The appendices focus on key resources and skills required for Special Collections work.

Look out for the examples and case studies! This book is packed with useful information, but managing Special Collections effectively is not just about information but is also about judgement and balance. I have therefore included many real examples for readers to consider. I have anonymized the libraries involved where the story may reflect badly on them, but note that all these stories came to me from public sources on the web or in print.

Each chapter includes a list of useful websites, web citations for the examples and case studies, and suggestions for further reading. The bibliography at the end of the book includes all bibliographic citations and other titles that readers may find helpful. The references are not intended to form a comprehensive review of the academic and professional literature on Special Collections, which is beyond the scope of this work.

Mindful of the time and financial pressures faced by so many Special Collections librarians, I have cited resources that are freely available on the internet or readily available in print wherever possible. As web addresses change and new resources become available, I will create and maintain indefinitely an online list of these citations on the website for this book: http://specialcollectionshandbook.com/.

The Handbook does not include:

- instructions on how to use particular software
- generic management skills

- records management; aspects of managing archives are covered in a Special Collections context.

Please note that:

1 The occasional mention of commercial companies is there to help readers; it should not be seen as an endorsement of a particular firm by Facet Publishing, CILIP or the University of Bradford.
2 In Chapter 6 and throughout the book, legal issues are discussed from a Special Collections management perspective. Libraries are advised to seek expert advice before taking any action that may have legal consequences.

Special Collections in a Cold Climate ...

The book is written in difficult and uncertain times for higher education and public institutions worldwide, a time of budget cuts and threats to the very existence of libraries. Meanwhile, audiences expect quicker replies and more online material. Special Collections librarians, like their colleagues throughout the information and heritage sectors, face the challenge of having to do much more with less.

However, there is hope:

1 New technologies offer free, fun ways to reach out to audiences, and to communicate and learn from colleagues.
2 Parent organizations are beginning to understand that Special Collections are priceless assets that can help them achieve their missions: such collections are distinctive, full of stories and human incident, unique, rich and real.

This book cannot solve the problems faced by Special Collections librarians, but I hope it will help them to understand these problems, to set priorities, to manage effectively and, above all, to try new ideas.

Companion website

For more information, resources and links please visit the author's companion website at http://specialcollectionshandbook.com.

Some essential websites

Association for Manuscripts and Archives in Research Collections, www.amarc.org.uk
Association of Research Libraries Special Collections, www.arl.org/rtl/speccoll
CILIP Rare Books and Special Collections Group, www.cilip.org.uk/get-involved/special-
    interest-groups/rare-books/pages/default.aspx
Historic Libraries Forum, www.historiclibrariesforum.org.uk
Rare Books and Manuscripts Section of the Association of College and Research Libraries (part
    of the American Library Association), www.rbms.info

Rare Books in Scotland, www.nls.uk/about-us/working-with-others/rare-books-in-scotland

Research Libraries UK, www.rluk.ac.uk

Useful listservs and blogs

Archives-nra, https://www.jiscmail.ac.uk/cgi-bin/webadmin?A0=archives-nra

Collections in a Cold Climate, http://alisoncullingford.wordpress.com (includes links to many more blogs on archives and rare books management).

Ex Libris, https://listserv.indiana.edu/cgi-bin/wa-iub.exe?A0=exlibris-l

Lis-rarebooks, https://www.jiscmail.ac.uk/cgi-bin/webadmin?A0=lis-rarebooks

1
The care of Special Collections

Introducing collections care

As stated in the Introduction, the care of collections is the basis of Special Collections work. Librarians need to decide what to preserve and why, and to what extent the information and the artefact can be separated. The choices made in caring for collections have long-term, often irreversible effects.

This chapter will:

1 Outline threats to collections and how to manage them. Threats include the physical composition of the objects themselves, environmental factors, pests and mould, buildings and storage, and handling.
2 Discuss how to bring all these ideas together in a preservation policy.
3 Examine three key issues in more detail: conservation and the role of the conservator, preservation reformatting, and digital preservation.

The care of Special Collections has much in common with care of archives and museum objects, hence this chapter draws on resources concerning all aspects of heritage.

A note on terminology

Conservation and preservation are easily confused, and have different meanings in other professional areas. These definitions are usual in Special Collections practice, quoted here from National Preservation Office (n.d.):

- **Preservation** 'includes all the managerial and financial considerations including storage and accommodation provisions, staffing levels, policies, techniques and methods involved in preserving library and archive materials and the information contained in them'.
- **Conservation** is one approach to dealing with damaged materials, as part of a preservation programme. It 'denotes those specific treatments and techniques applied in protecting library and archive materials from deterioration which involves

intervention with the object itself'. Modern conservation ethics demand respect for the historical integrity of an item.

- **Restoration** 'denotes those techniques used in reconstructing damaged library and archive materials to what is perceived to be their original form', which may not necessarily take conservation ethics into account. It would therefore seldom be an appropriate treatment for Special Collections materials.

A note on standards

The importance of collections care means many standards and guidelines exist, although libraries may have difficulty meeting these because of building constraints and lack of funding. The most relevant were created for archives services, which have in common with Special Collections types of material, concern with the long-term survival of items, and similar access methods. These standards include BS 5454:2000 (British Standards Institution 2000) for storage and exhibition, BS 4971:2002 (British Standards Institution 2002) for conservation work and the National Archives (2004) standard for record repositories. Kitching, Edgar and Milford (2001) offer guidance on implementing BS 5454.

This chapter picks out some of the key points in the standards, while the survey and audit methods covered below will help librarians set priorities for improvement. Any new build or refurbishment for Special Collections should aim to meet the highest standards of collection care.

Understanding the physical nature of Special Collections

To preserve materials in Special Collections, it is essential to understand their physical composition. Special Collections contain many physical formats, created over millennia to record and share knowledge. For example the John Rylands Library in Manchester, which, like other large Special Collections departments, holds material from the third century BC to the present, including clay tablets, papyri, bamboo, bark, bone and palm leaf, alongside vellum and other animal products, paper from various eras, photographic material, sound recordings and other audiovisual media, and, increasingly, digital formats. Even smaller libraries holding only printed book collections have different kinds of paper, ink, glue and binding materials to consider.

Chapter 3 explores Special Collections objects in more detail. For collections care, what matters most is the chemical stability of materials:

1 **Chemically stable** materials, with proper care as outlined below, will last indefinitely. Early printed books printed on durable rag paper have lasted 500 years.
2 **Chemically unstable** materials, even with good care, will deteriorate within a short period of time. Newsprint, produced by quick, cheap processes to meet the needs of the moment, has a high lignin content, which promotes quick acidification and eventual destruction. Many plastics, such as polyvinylchloride or acetates, are unstable. Such materials are said to have **inherent vice**. A few materials are

hazardous to health as they decompose, notably cellulose nitrate base film, which was used until the 1950s. At high temperatures, in closed conditions, such film can spontaneously burst into flames.

Understanding chemical stability is complicated by:

1 **Complex artefacts.** Items in Special Collections are usually made of more than one substance. An early printed book consists of paper (made of linen rags dipped in **size**, a gelatine mix that made it less permeable), ink, and the various materials used in binding it. There may also be notes in different inks and later inserts made of other substances. Each of these materials will have different characteristics and decay at different rates.
2 **Other instability.** Chemically stable materials still respond to changes in their environment, for example parchment and vellum are chemically stable but hygroscopic: they absorb moisture from the atmosphere. Exposed to fluctuating levels of humidity, they will stretch and shrink repeatedly in irregular patterns, leading to the distinctive crinkled effect known as **cockling**.
3 **Modern media** pose additional problems. Audiovisual formats (from wax cylinders to videocassettes) require equipment to read them. This will have to be preserved alongside the media or the material will have to be reformatted (see 'Understanding preservation reformatting and digitization').

The guidance below will help preserve all kinds of materials for as long as possible.

Understanding the impact of the environment on Special Collections

The following environmental factors contribute to the decay of Special Collections materials: light, temperature and relative humidity (RH), air pollution, mould and pests. To help readers understand them, they are discussed separately, but they do of course interact, for example high RH encourages mould growth. Fortunately, good practice in minimizing one factor usually reduces others, for example keeping collections in **archival quality boxes** limits exposure to light, and also prevents pollutant and mechanical damage (more on archival quality materials below).

Archival/museum suppliers offer a range of data loggers and meters to monitor these factors. Henderson (2010) offers useful guidance on choosing the right device for a particular library and situation.

Understanding the impact of light

Exposure to light speeds up the deterioration of Special Collections materials, as light energy encourages chemical reactions (**photochemical deterioration**). Ultraviolet (UV) light is particularly harmful. Light damage is cumulative and irreversible: cellulose becomes weakened and brittle, paper bleaches or darkens, and dyes fade.

Special Collections therefore should be exposed to as little light as possible, though some kinds of light are required for essential activities:

1 **UV light** should be eliminated where possible.
2 **Visible light** cannot be eliminated completely, as users and staff need to be able to see materials and move around, but it should be controlled as much as possible.
3 **Natural light**, especially sunlight, is more harmful than artificial light, and should be eliminated from storage areas. However, natural light (though not direct sunlight) is desirable in areas such as reading rooms because it creates a more pleasant environment for people.

Some specific recommendations:

1 **Windows**. Ideally, storage areas should be windowless. Skylights or windows in these areas should be covered with UV screening film or painted with titanium dioxide paint.
2 **Artificial lighting** should be in use only when actually needed, and UV filtered if necessary.
3 **Archival quality boxes** or other enclosures for materials in storage cut exposure to light.
4 **Exhibitions of original materials** should be designed to keep lighting as low as possible. If it is desired to exhibit a particular 'treasure' indefinitely, damage must be kept to a minimum by maintaining very low light levels and (if the treasure is in book form) turning the pages regularly.

Understanding the impact of temperature and relative humidity

Relative humidity (RH) depends on temperature, so they are considered together. These factors damage collections as follows:

1 **Heat**, like light, speeds up the rate of chemical reactions that lead to deterioration of materials (the rate is approximately doubled by each 10°C increase in temperature).
2 **High relative humidity** encourages chemical reactions, mould growth and infestation by insects.
3 **Low relative humidity** dries out paper, vellum and parchment and other materials, leaving them brittle.
4 **Fluctuations** in temperature and relative humidity are particularly harmful, causing materials to expand and contract repeatedly, as they absorb and then release moisture. This will speed up chemical deterioration and cause physical damage: parchment and paper will cockle, as mentioned above, and photographic emulsions may crack.

BS 5454:2000 (British Standards Institution 2000) recommends the following levels of temperature and RH for safe storage of paper and parchment:

1 **Temperature** should be kept at a fixed point between 13°C and 16°C with a tolerance of 1°C on either side.
2 **Relative humidity** should be at a fixed point between 45% and 60% with a tolerance of 5% on either side.

The recommended temperature is too low for human comfort when doing sedentary tasks such as consulting Special Collections; reading rooms should be kept at 20–22°C. To lessen the impact on materials of moving from the cold storage area to the warmer reading room, the Standard recommends that **frequently handled material** should be kept at a fixed point between 16°C and 19°C with a tolerance of 1°C on either side. Photographic and other modern media benefit from even lower temperatures.

Many libraries will find it difficult to achieve these standards without specialist heating/air-conditioning systems. However, some improvements may be possible, for example Henderson (2010) suggests moving the most vulnerable material to the coldest and driest storage areas and that the conservation heating approach used by the National Trust be considered for historic buildings: the heating system is activated by RH levels. The Preservation Index, available from the Image Permanence Institute, provides a measurement of the lifetime impact of particular conditions on collections, enabling management decisions to be made.

Understanding the impact of air pollution

Air pollution is probably less well known and less dramatic than other threats to Special Collections, but can still cause significant damage.

1 **Particulates** (e.g. soot, dirt or dust) abrade materials, scratching or rubbing at surfaces, doing particular harm to modern media. They encourage mould growth and harmful chemical reactions. The risk from particulates will increase during building work, as will the risk of damage to collections from vibration.
2 **Gases** (e.g. sulphur dioxide) come from the burning of certain fuels (e.g. in vehicle exhausts), are produced by some photocopiers or are given off by unstable materials, for example certain woods or paints. They catalyse chemical reactions leading to the formation of acid in materials, making paper brittle. Air pollution is thought to play a key role in the phenomenon of **red rot**, in which tannins in leather bindings decay to a fine red powder that can be hazardous to health.

Cut exposure to air pollution by:

1 **Filtering external air** entering storage areas, or, if this is not possible, using seals on windows and doors to exclude pollutants.
2 **Improving air circulation**, thereby removing off-gassing (and preventing mould growth).
3 **Restricting the kinds of materials used or permitted in the building**, for example use metal shelving rather than wooden unless there are particular historic or aesthetic considerations, as wooden shelving gives off gases.
4 **Using archival quality boxes or other enclosures** for storage to create clean microclimates.
5 **Cleaning routines** that prevent dust build-up. Bendix and Walker (2011) offer practical advice.

Understanding moulds
Mould basics
Moulds (molds in US spelling) are fungi, which feed on organic material such as Special Collections objects. Items attacked by moulds will be stained, softened, lose images and text, and eventually destroyed. Moulds are also harmful to people, affecting the lungs (especially of people with asthma and other allergies), skin, eyes and other organs. Some kinds are highly toxic.

Mould spores are always present in the air. They remain dormant until temperature and humidity levels are right for them to become active, whereupon spores burst, become filaments (hyphae), which develop by feeding on organic materials; masses of filaments (mycelia) then produce more spores. Temperatures over 22°C and RH over 70% are ideal for mould growth, though it can happen at lower levels.

If a flood or water leak soaks materials, mould is likely to become active within a couple of days. Emergency plans, discussed in Chapter 2, need to take this into account and plan to use the small window of opportunity, for example by freezing materials.

Foxing, the brown spots seen on 19th century paper, may be caused by fungi, often interacting with metal traces in the paper. However, not all spots and stains on paper are fungal in origin. Foxing can be removed by conservation treatments.

Preventing the growth of moulds
As the above account suggests, if temperature and RH are controlled, mould is far less likely to grow. Levels should be monitored using appropriate loggers so that action can be taken if mould-friendly changes happen. Keeping air circulating will also limit mould growth.

It is essential to **quarantine** new acquisitions. Materials accepted by Special Collections, particularly from private individuals, have often been stored in damp conditions favourable to mould growth, in attics, basements, garages or sheds. They should be stored separately from other collections, and closely monitored until definitely free of active moulds (see below).

Coping with mould outbreaks

The key question: is the mould **active or inactive**? Active moulds are growing and feeding and therefore a concern; inactive moulds are dormant. Active moulds are usually colourful, feel damp, and have a strong smell. Inactive moulds are dull in colour and feel powdery. Items bearing inactive moulds should be cleaned as below.

If mould is active:

1 **Seek expert help** as necessary, from mycologists, conservators, and buildings staff.
2 **Isolate the mouldy items:** they should not be allowed to contaminate clean stock. If only a few items are affected, they can be stored in plastic bags.
3 **Establish the cause and fix it.** Unless the stock has just arrived, a mould outbreak will almost certainly be the result of changes in environmental conditions, for example a sudden rise in RH, a water leak or a problem in the heating and air conditioning systems.
4 **Make the mould inactive** by freezing, air drying or use of a low oxygen environment.
5 **Clean the affected items** with a HEPA filter vacuum (with cloth or a screen over the nozzle) or a soft brush – outdoors!
6 **Clean the storage area** (shelves, walls, etc.) using appropriate cleaning solutions. Items should only be re-shelved when they and the area are clean.

Note that the use of cleaning materials and respiratory masks should conform to safety standards: see 'Further reading' (below) for more details, and seek advice from health and safety colleagues.

Dealing with a mould outbreak in this way is to be preferred to chemical interventions. Chemicals used to treat moulds are highly toxic, and there is little point in treating books that are then returned to the conditions that caused the mould growth in the first place.

Understanding pests
Pest basics

Alongside moulds, Special Collections can be damaged by many other creatures, known as **pests**. Insect pests include beetles, silverfish, booklice and cockroaches. Other pests include rodents (rats, mice, squirrels) and birds. Insects do harm by eating materials: they are particularly drawn to sizes (mentioned above) and glues, but will also devour cellulose-based material and animal skins such as parchment. Excreting, tunnelling and nesting also harm collections. Larger creatures are less likely to eat collections, but can do great harm by excreting, chewing electrical wires or blocking drainpipes with nests. Historic buildings containing period furnishings, usually made of organic materials, are particularly at risk, because they offer so many potential foodstuffs.

Preventing infestation

The historic practice of spraying buildings and collections regularly with pesticides is now considered unsafe and unnecessary. As with mould, museums, libraries and archives are turning to **integrated pest management (IPM)**: instead of reacting to infestations when they occur, prevent them by:

1 **Knowing** the life cycles and food sources of the pests most likely to occur in the area and be attracted by particular collections (see 'Further reading' (below) for advice). Once these are understood, action can be taken to deter the pests, as below.
2 **Monitoring. Sticky traps** (also known as **blunder traps**), cardboard foldout traps containing sticky substances that appeal to insects and trap them, are recommended and cheap. Traps should be placed in locations likely to attract insects and checked regularly. Staff should also watch out for sightings of pests, and for evidence of their presence such as damaged materials or excretions.
3 **Eliminating environmental factors** that encourage pests. Materials in dirty, damp, neglected conditions are more attractive to pests, so good housekeeping is essential. Possible routes of entry to the building such as cracks, vents and badly sealed windows can be closed. The levels of temperature and relative humidity recommended above will also deter pests.
4 **Eliminating/reducing potential food sources**, for example live or dead plants and flowers, organic mulch, food, food waste and rubbish.
5 **Quarantining** new acquisitions, as for moulds.

Coping with an infestation

* **identify the pests**
* **establish and tackle environmental factors**, as above.

This may be sufficient to remove the pests. If not, the action then taken depends on the kinds of pests: specialist help will be needed, for example rodent control or use of insecticides.

Understanding buildings, storage and Special Collections

As the discussion of environmental factors suggests, the buildings and storage areas used for Special Collections are key to their survival. The basics are simple to state, though harder to achieve: 'The essential requirements for a building used to house library and archive collections are that it should be soundly constructed, watertight and well-ventilated. It should also have a stable internal climate with temperatures and relative humidity (RH) levels varying only gradually over the seasons' Hughes (2002).

These needs are elaborated in the standards, notably BS 5454:2000 (British Standards Institution 2000).

It is best to store collections away from spaces used by people. Preferred light levels, temperatures and so on for people are different from safe levels for collections storage.

As security is also a concern, it is best practice to store the collections separately in **strong rooms**, bringing out only what is needed by users. Historic foundations such as cathedrals and colleges sometimes use the term **muniment room**, the space used to store records such as charters and deeds.

While many of the recommendations are difficult to achieve in existing spaces, there are many ways to improve collections storage. For example:

1 **Air circulation** is important, as we have seen, for avoiding mould growth. Bookshelves should not be directly against a wall, and items within cabinets should not touch the back wall.

2 **Shelving layout** should avoid mechanical damage to collections, for example items can be crushed on overcrowded shelves or distorted by the proximity of different sized items. Items should not protrude beyond the edges of shelves, especially in mobile shelving, where they could easily be damaged.

3 **Books:** large heavy books should be stored lying flat. Bookends should be used when shelves are not full, but should not be damaging in their design. Boxes are invaluable in protecting fragile or special bindings, limiting mechanical damage from other volumes. Where the appearance of book spines is important, for example in a historic library, using **book shoes** (see North East Document Conservation Centre 2007) protects volumes while keeping beautiful spines on show.

4 **Materials used with Special Collections** should be of **archival quality**, particularly if they will be permanently associated with those items. Archival quality means that the materials are designed to minimize chemical or physical damage. BS 4971:2002 (British Standards Institution 2002) is the relevant standard. For example, boxes should be acid- and lignin-free to avoid chemical damage, paperclips should be brass so that rust damage is eliminated, protective sleeves for photographs should be made of inert polyester film (brand names **Mylar** or **Melinex**).

5 **Storage areas and the collections themselves should be kept clean** as part of a rolling programme of maintenance. This minimizes risk of pests, mould and mechanical damage from dust. This is skilled work requiring training, and specialist equipment needs to be used, for example soft brushes to remove dust, and vacuum cleaners with HEPA filters to catch smaller particulates. Bendix and Walker (2011) offer a practical introduction.

6 **Shelving types**. Wooden or metal? Mobile or static? Wooden may be more combustible and prone to off-gassing, but metal shelving can rust or damage collections with sharp edges. Wooden shelving is usually more aesthetically pleasing, where that is a consideration. Mobile shelving saves space compared to static, but if poorly installed or maintained can cause safety or access problems. Rhys-Lewis (2007) discusses the decisions involved in selecting shelving and other kinds of storage such as chests to store maps, plans and other large documents.

A note on preservation and historic buildings

Many Special Collections are housed in ancient buildings such as cathedrals, university colleges or historic houses. These are wonderful, inspiring settings for staff and collections users; the original settings enhance the collections and vice versa. Witness the Chawton House Library, where early modern women's writing is held in the manor house of Jane Austen's brother, or Chethams, the ancient public library in Manchester.

However, there are extra challenges in managing Special Collections in such environments:

1 **Inappropriate spaces**. Buildings may not have been designed for Special Collections and may have suffered poor maintenance. Collections often outgrow their original shelving, and may have to be kept in unsuitable overflow storage.
2 **Constraints**. It may not be possible to take the best actions to preserve collections because of planning constraints associated with a listed building, or its visual appeal to visitors. For example, the original shelving is unlikely to be ideal from a collections care perspective, but historic and aesthetic reasons will outweigh this concern.
3 As a **visitor attraction**, the premises are likely to have a higher footfall than other Special Collections, leading to greater wear and tear, and extra risks such as fire in catering services.
4 Historic buildings and furnishings may be more difficult to **clean and maintain** than modern materials, and, as already mentioned, more vulnerable to pest infestation.
5 The library may be in demand for **hospitality** or **broadcast filming**. It is easy for the demands of these users to take precedence over the preservation of the materials. Effective policies and procedures based on the experiences of others can make these situations workable for both sides (more on income generation in Chapter 10).
6 Increased **fire risk** because of the materials and design of historic buildings and limitations on preventive measures (more on fire in Chapter 2).

Handling Special Collections safely

Users or librarians with the best intentions can inadvertently harm collections if they have not been properly trained in handling. Fortunately this aspect of collection care can be greatly improved at relatively low cost. Some typical examples of poor handling, and suggested practices to eliminate them:

1 **Problems with opening materials**, for example opening a volume without support strains the spine, eventually causing it to break and exposing the book to more damage. Propping volumes or rolled materials open with unsuitable objects may stain or mechanically damage materials. Equipment to help hold materials open

correctly, such as book pillows, foam supports, book snakes and weights, should be readily available to readers, helping them follow the rules easily.

2 **Damage from inappropriate substances, for example ink, food or drink**. These should not be permitted in Special Collections areas. Pencils only should be used. Even if food or drink are not actually spilled on collections items, other spillage or smells encourage pests.

3 **Inappropriate repairs**, such as the use of adhesive tape, laminators or unstable plastics. Such materials should never be used on Special Collections objects.

4 **Poor working practices**, such as trying to carry too many volumes or using a trolley that does not support the materials. Working practices need to be designed around collections care.

5 It is vital to **educate users and staff** in sensitive handling of Special Collections. Handling should form part of the induction of all staff and volunteers. Such trained individuals can set a good example to users and enforce handling rules in an informed and sensitive way.

How users are trained in handling depends on the size and nature of the library. Ideally such training should be more than issuing a list of rules: it should be about building understanding of materials as artefacts, though in practice, larger organizations may have to rely on detailed rules backed up by supervision. The marketing and communication methods covered in Chapters 8 and 9 offer ideal ways to train users in good handling. Whichever methods are used, handling guidelines can be presented to users in a positive way, about respect for the materials. Many users value the sense of special access that such rules give them.

A note on the glove question

The compulsory wearing of white cotton gloves to handle materials is a classic signifier of Special Collections, an idea users recognize from the media, instant shorthand for precious material. However, gloves are actually more harmful to collections than clean bare hands:

1 They are likely to be dirtier, picking up all kinds of contamination from around the reading room.

2 The extra layer between hand and material makes the hands less sensitive, and therefore users are more likely to damage materials as they handle them.

Gloves separate the reader from the physical reality of the objects handled, and thus mute the experience of using Special Collections.

Baker and Silverman (2005) analyse the problems with gloves and the relatively recent growth of the glove rule. They conclude that 'implementing a universally observed, hand-cleaning policy is a reasonable and effective alternative to glove-use', suggesting that where access to water is a problem, disposable wipes might be made available.

However, gloves should be used when handling certain vulnerable formats, for example to protect photographs, scrapbooks, prints and drawings, and realia such as lead seals or globes from fingerprint damage. When gloves are needed, the white cotton glove is the most comfortable. A range of sizes should be stocked, and regular cleaning in gentle detergent is advised. Latex and other plastic-type gloves should be avoided, as they are unpleasant to wear, particularly in hot weather, and allergies to such materials are common.

As readers may expect to be required to wear gloves, libraries may find it helpful to publicize and explain their policies as the British Library and National Archives do.

A note on reprographics and collections care

Reprographics is the reproduction of materials via various mechanical and electronic means, such as photocopying, digitization and microfilming. **Contact reprographic methods**, where the copy is made by machines touching the original object, such as office photocopiers and scanners, are easy to use in harmful ways, for example forcing the lid of the machine down to make volumes lie flat. If possible, book-friendly machines designed for the safe copying of historic volumes or other specialist material should be used. However these are expensive, probably beyond the budget of smaller libraries.

Even with access to book-friendly machines, contact reprographics should be carried out only by trained staff, and appropriate restrictions imposed. It is usual in Special Collections not to allow copying of oversize or tightly bound volumes or fragile materials. As it is impossible for a list of restrictions to cover every possible problem, such copying is generally at the discretion of staff, who will need either to be trained to make the decisions, or given clear guidelines about when to refer the request to a skilled colleague. National Preservation Office (2000b) is a useful introduction to the practical management of photocopying from a collections care perspective.

The advent of digital photography has relieved some of the pressure on Special Collections, as little or no contact with the item is required to get a legible copy. See Chapter 7 for a service perspective on reprographics and the digital revolution.

A note on packing and moving

Special Collections may be moved for many reasons, for example to new premises or to an external event or exhibition. Outhousing during building work is common to protect collections from increased security and fire risks. However, packing and moving Special Collections exposes them to new risks, for example:

- mechanical damage, for example from careless handling or inappropriate packing
- environmental problems, for example fluctuating temperature
- theft or accidental loss
- re-shelving in wrong order.

Firms specialize in packing, moving and storing heritage collections, but care is needed in choosing and working with such companies. Bendix (2005) offers a practical guide to safe packing and moving. As with so much of collections care, risk assessment and careful planning are essential.

Managing preservation of Special Collections

The above threats may seem overwhelming, but taking a preservation approach helps librarians to cope. Good preservation practice is about establishing workable policies, procedures and aspirations, and regularly reviewing them in the light of changing circumstances and technologies.

Taking audits and surveys

The starting point for preservation planning is the audit or survey, which gives librarians the information they need about their situation to enable them to plan improvements.

Surveys may assess the physical nature of the collections, their condition and stability, or existing standards of collections care. They are often carried out when major new collections are added, before a refurbishment or to support applications for external funding. Repeating a survey later can show the impact of changes to buildings or new funding on collections care. It may be possible to find external funding to support a survey: see Chapter 10.

Depending on finances, and the nature and size of the collections to be surveyed, surveys can be:

1 Commissioned from external experts, individually or using programmes such as the **Preservation Assessment Survey (PAS)** and **Preservation Health Check** offered by British Library Preservation Advisory Centre (BLPAC).
2 Created in-house using toolkits such as:
   — **Benchmarks in Collection Care** (Winsor 2002), which enables libraries to assess their collections care against three levels of benchmarks.
   — **CALIPR** (see 'Useful websites' below), created by the California Preservation Program, is a free website tool that 'leads the user through the design and implementation of a preservation needs assessment survey'.
   — **Columbia Audio/Moving Image Survey** (see 'Useful websites' below): Columbia University Libraries developed a methodology 'to inventory and assess the physical condition and intellectual control of audio and moving image materials', available as an Access database.
   — Patkus (2003), **a self-survey guide** of preservation needs.

A note on mission and strategy

Before looking in detail at the preservation policy, a reminder that the mission and strategy of the service should underlie this and all Special Collections policies and procedures:

Special Collections can contain millions of items in thousands of collections, in hundreds of formats on all kinds of subjects. Each collection contains boundless possibilities for preservation, cataloguing, marketing, etc., which is part of the excitement in working with Special Collections. Managing collections effectively is about making good choices from these possibilities: here, what to preserve and how. These choices can be difficult, have long-term effects and are often irreversible. If they are not made with an understanding of the ultimate purpose and long-term goals of the service, they may well not be the best choices to achieve those ends – wasting vital resources and missing opportunities.

Writing the preservation policy

The preservation policy (or plan) unites all the above in defining the library's intentions for collections care, starting from its mission. It is essential to understand why the organization has Special Collections, what it intends to do with them in future and which are critical to its mission.

The policy should also cover:

- **Aspirations** for collections care, based on priorities from survey findings and outlining the relevant standards, for example BS 5454:2000.
- **Activities** with collections care implications:
  — storage and housekeeping
  — handling (above, and Chapter 7)
  — exhibitions (Chapters 8 and 9)
  — loans – to users, inter-library loans and external exhibitions (Chapters 7 and 8)
  — reprographics (above, and Chapter 7).
- **Resources** for collections care:
  — finances – funding available, fund-raising aspirations and how funding will be spent
  — staff and their training, including volunteers, other library staff and users.
- **Methods** of managing damaged or chemically unstable materials, discussed below.
  — conservation
  — preservation reformatting
  — digital preservation.

Security and emergency planning (see Chapter 2) should be mentioned, but the detail is probably better covered in a separate process. More advice on preservation policy content and writing can be found in Foot (2001). There are many examples of Special Collections preservation policies online especially from national libraries and academic libraries, though it is more difficult to find examples from other organizations. To implement the aspirations of the policy, action plans will be needed, for example to tackle weaknesses found during surveys. Such plans are less commonly found online, as they are matters of internal procedure rather than customer-facing documents, and may reveal security problems and the like that should not be made public.

Understanding conservation and the role of the conservator

As noted above, conservation is one approach to dealing with damaged materials within a Special Collections preservation policy: the treatment of individual items using interventive techniques but with concern for the historic integrity of the structures. How large a part conservation plays in a particular service depends on how much funding is available or can be obtained, the formats in Special Collections, and the kinds of damage they have suffered.

Conservation is a highly skilled activity, which should always be carried out by trained conservators. They 'combine their knowledge of the most up-to-date science with an understanding of the properties of materials and construction techniques to determine the best means of conservation of these objects'. Conservators need to know the 'context of the objects they work with', developing an aesthetic appreciation of 'art history, architecture, changing fashions and lifestyles' to find the most suitable treatment for particular objects (extracts from the Institute of Conservation, www.icon.org.uk).

Larger Special Collections often have their own conservator or conservation department, either as part of the management structure of Special Collections, or as a separate team. Smaller establishments might employ external conservators to carry out specified work. Choosing a conservator is an important decision, financially and for the long-term well-being of the collection being treated. Databases of accredited conservators and advice on choosing and working with them can be found via their professional organizations (see 'Useful websites'); further advice can be found in Paris (2010). Issues to consider include skills, experience, insurance and security.

A good relationship between librarians and conservators is vital for collections care. Special Collections librarians are advised to learn the basic language of conservation and follow developments in the profession, so that they can communicate effectively with conservators and find the best treatments for their collections.

Conservators may use chemical or physical treatments. Here is a selection, based on Ogden (2007):

- **Surface cleaning of book pages**: removing dirt, dust and mould by gentle mechanical means.
- **Removal of old repairs and tape**, using water, moisture, steam or solvents as appropriate.
- **Washing book pages**.
- **Deacidification** of book pages: 'the purpose of the treatment is to neutralize acids and to deposit in paper a buffer that will protect it from the formation of acid in the future'.
- **Mending, filling and guarding book pages**: tears in pages can be mended using Japanese paper or another suitable paper.

- **Sewing book pages**.
- **Rebacking** loose/detached boards or spines of books.
- **Rebinding**: if the original is missing or too badly damaged, various structures are used depending on the nature of the book.
- **Boxing**. There are various kinds of boxes that help protect items: including **book shoes**, **phase boxes**, **drop spine** and **solander boxes**.

Conservation can achieve stunning results, but cannot always solve inherent vice and other issues in complex artefacts, as this story shows.

Case study: mending Mercator's Atlas

The British Library website contains a detailed account of the work of conservators on 'Mercator's Atlas of Europe, a unique item compiled in the early 1570s which contains the only extant remaining parts of Mercator's influential 1554 wall map of Europe, along with two unique manuscript maps attributed to him'. The Atlas was fragile, torn, fractured and distorted by old repairs. The work carried out by the conservators stabilized the paper and binding, so the volume can be displayed and handled with appropriate care. The account gives a vivid picture of the possibilities and philosophy of conservation. Note for instance:

- that the conservators did not remove evidence of the old repairs, as these form part of the Atlas's story
- that the item remains fragile; most public access in future will be through digital methods
- the discussion of decision making, for example why water-based methods were not used.

As with the Mercator Atlas, many conservators are using websites and blogs to show the treatment of individual items in photographic detail. Librarians new to conservation can learn more about its language, ethics and possibilities from such sites.

Conservators can offer much more than conservation work on individual items: they are an important source of advice on all aspects of preservation including storage, handling, disaster control planning and response.

New technologies are helping conservators and librarians to find out more about Special Collections artefacts. For example, multi-spectral imaging techniques make it possible to decipher the original writings on palimpsests (parchments that were recycled: original text was scraped off and a new one overwritten). In the Archimedes Palimpsest project, a 13th-century Byzantine prayer book revealed otherwise unknown works by Archimedes originally written on the parchments.

Understanding preservation reformatting and digitization

Not all damaged materials in Special Collections can be preserved in their original format, even using conservation techniques.

Another approach to damage to consider in a preservation plan is reformatting, also known as **migration, format shifting** or **surrogacy**. This has historically been the solution offered for materials with 'inherent vice'. Such materials would be difficult, expensive, even impossible to preserve in their original format: shifting the information they contain to another format made it possible to keep that information for longer and make it available. Witness the widespread microfilming of newspapers in the 20th century.

Reformatting can be done on any scale, ranging from in-house on an item-by-item basis (fragile items in high demand) to huge projects covering many libraries. Photocopying might be useful for individual objects, but until recently, creating microforms (microfilm or fiche) was the usual choice for larger projects. Microforms are easy to store and reproduce, and the best quality microform (silver halide) is a stable format. However, bulky equipment is needed to read them, they can be tiring to use and the experience is far from that of using the originals.

Not surprisingly, digitization is now the norm for reformatting. This requires only common devices and software and recreates the original experience much more effectively. Above all, it can improve access rather than just replacing the original. Even microforms could be made available to many libraries, but digitized surrogates can not only be made available worldwide, but are searchable in ways that simply were not possible with the original medium or previous methods of surrogacy. For example, the British Library Newspapers Project offers keyword searching on 2 million pages of 19th century newspapers, offering unimaginable possibilities compared to the fragile, bulky, even unusable originals previously available only in physical form at the British Library. Or consider Turning the Pages™ (see 'Examples and case studies' below), adopted by major libraries and museums to highlight their treasures online.

However, reformatting raises further issues, which need to be covered in the preservation and other relevant policies.

Fate of the original

It is attractive to managers faced with large volumes of unusable material to throw it away to make better use of scarce space. However, Special Collections are materials where the original artefact is seen to have value beyond its informational content and would not be discarded even if it had been reformatted. Exceptions might include obsolete audiovisual formats, film which has deteriorated to the point of harm to other materials, or ephemeral press cuttings in collections of historic books. If originals are discarded, then quality control of the surrogacy process becomes even more critical, as does the durability of the copy.

Copyright

Decisions about reformatting are complicated by copyright law. If material is in copyright, it is not necessarily legal for a library to migrate it to a new format even for preservation reasons (see Chapter 6).

Commercial partnerships and the future

A service may not have the resources for mass digitization: often the work is done by commercial firms in partnership with the libraries holding the materials. Such firms need to recoup their investment, so there may be restrictions on access to material (subscription only for example), though it may return to the public domain later. Librarians interested in working with commercial partners should choose firms with relevant experience and evidence of care for collections, and are advised to discuss the implications with librarians who have worked with such firms recently.

The growth of mass digitization of Special Collections has wider implications for Special Collections librarianship. Here are two of the most significant developments:

1 The **Google Books** project takes digitization to a new scale, working with many national and research libraries to digitize millions of books. In a long and complex legal saga, Google have sought to put full text of out of print but in copyright works online: an agreement to this effect whereby Google would pay royalties was thrown out of court in March 2011. The implications of Google Books for access, copyright law and the nature of publishing and creation are huge: librarians need to be aware of developments.

2 **Early English Books Online** (EEBO) and **Eighteenth Century Collections Online** (ECCO), explained more fully in Appendix A. Unlike the rather haphazard interface of Google Books, these resources offer digitized early books supported by rigorous bibliography and other scholarship, making them a serious academic resource.

In light of the above, it seems that Special Collections in future, particularly those whose holdings consist mainly of early books, will have fewer visitors in person needing to examine particular texts, as users will be able to access material remotely. But librarians need to be aware that this may threaten the other services they offer, particularly if senior managers think that because texts of books are online, librarians are not needed. Throughout this book, we discuss the other activities that Special Collections librarians carry out, the value they bring and how to communicate that value.

Understanding digital preservation

The discussion of reformatting leads into considering digital preservation. Special Collections are facing the challenges of preserving collections in digital form. These may be digitized versions of physical collections, created as surrogates or for marketing and access purposes. Increasingly, however, collections are creating or acquiring **born-digital** material: 'items created and managed in digital form' (Erway 2010).

Born-digital material is created in various ways and for various purposes: Erway lists digital cameras, digital documents, web content, digital manuscripts, static data sets, electronic records, dynamic data, digital art and digital media publications. Not all Special Collections are concerned with collecting or preserving all these kinds of material. When discussing the preservation of born-digital material, it is helpful to define which of these types of data are being considered.

Digital preservation is far more than a matter of copying files onto high-quality optical media and managing them like other physical formats (on which, see Finch and Webster 2008). Digital media have distinct qualities from physical media, which require a different attitude to their preservation:

1 Storage media such as CDs or DVDs are particularly vulnerable to **physical degradation**, easily harmed by high humidity or poor handling. Copying readily introduces errors.
2 Commercial imperatives mean that a **huge range of shapes and sizes of digital storage media** have been available, requiring a similar range of equipment to read them. The pace of change has been rapid: 3.5 inch floppy disks were ubiquitous ten years ago but no modern PC or laptop has a drive to read them now.
3 **Software** is required to read digital data, but this has also seen rapid development: new versions of software may not accurately render older versions.

Even more so than the preservation of paper-based materials, digital preservation is about **effective planning and management** from the outset. In any digital project or managing any digital material, the choices of file formats, file naming, metadata, storage and standards will affect whether the material is to survive and be useful into the future.

Preservation of digital media cannot be about keeping one individual physical object. Instead, **'Lots of copies keeps stuff safe!'**. Important files should be stored in different physical places and on different media. The rule of three is often suggested: three copies, three media, three places. Where media such as DVDs are used, they should be regularly checked and copied if problems are found.

However, when copying files, it is important to distinguish between:

• **preservation master generation**: files which remain authentic and high quality and which are duplicated for safe-keeping, and
• **delivery generations**, which can be shared, compressed and made available in whatever formats are helpful to users.

Key techniques for digital preservation include (in order of difficulty):

1 **Refreshment:** copying data onto a newer example of the same format.

2 **Migration:** copying content from one format onto a newer format. It can also include moving files to a more recent version of its software or a different data format.

3 **Emulation:** creating systems that emulate the original system used to access data, because this is no longer available. This is more complex, involving writing new software or rebuilding hardware to enable a modern computer to recreate the appearance and functions of obsolete systems.

Conclusion

Materials in Special Collections face many threats: their physical and chemical instabilities, environmental problems that speed up chemical reactions or cause other harm, attacks by moulds and pests, and damage caused by poor storage and handling. The scale of these threats is daunting, but a preservation approach helps librarians to manage them: improving storage, housekeeping and handling procedures, conservation techniques and preservation reformatting. Digital formats have distinct preservation issues, but also offer new ways to care for physical originals.

In Chapter 2, we consider a further group of threats that pose serious risks to Special Collections: fire, flood, theft and other emergencies. Issues relating to collections care will appear throughout the book, and should be considered in all Special Collections activities.

Further reading

In addition to the works cited, Feather (2004), Forde (2007) and Gorman and Shep (2006) are useful introductions to preservation. See Hughes (2001 and 2002) for preservation in historic buildings and National Preservation Office (2000a) for good advice on handling.

Mould: Nyberg (n.d.) and Child (2011) are useful introductions; Florian (2002) includes more technical detail about species and treatments. See Pinniger (2009) and Kingsley (2001) for detail on understanding and controlling pests.

The sets of guidance notes produced by BLPAC, North East Document Conservation Centre (NEDCC) and the Canadian Conservation Institute (CCI) (some of which are cited in the bibliography) are freely available online and offer practical help with preservation. NEDCC leaflets are available as a print volume (Ogden 1999). The Conservation Online database links to full text of many invaluable resources.

Like preservation of physical materials, the importance of digital preservation means it is an area in which plenty of online advice is available to Special Collections librarians. For instance: Joint Information Systems Committee (JISC) resources (notably the JISC Beginners' Guide to Digital Preservation and JISC Digital Media) and the National Digital Information Infrastructure and Preservation Program. Useful textbooks include Deegan and Tanner (2006). Association of Research Libraries (2010a) and Rieger (2010) offer advice on working with digitization companies.

Examples and case studies

Archimedes Palimpsest, www.archimedespalimpsest.org/digitalproduct1.html

British Library Newspapers Project, http://newspapers.bl.uk

Chawton House Library, www.chawton.org

Chetham's Library, www.chethams.org.uk

John Rylands Library, www.library.manchester.ac.uk/specialcollections

Mercator Atlas, www.bl.uk/aboutus/stratpolprog/ccare/projects/mercatoratlas/index.html

Turning the Pages™, www.armadillosystems.com/ttp_commercial/

White glove policies, British Library and National Archives, www.bl.uk/aboutus/stratpolprog/
ccare/introduction/preservation/usingcollections/whitegloves.pdf;
www.nationalarchives.gov.uk/documents/information-management/what-is-the-policy-on-
wearing-gloves-to-handle-documents.pdf

Useful websites

American Institute for Conservation (AIC), www.conservation-us.org

Australian Institute for the Conservation of Cultural Material, www.aiccm.org.au

British Library Preservation Advisory Centre (BLPAC, formerly the National Preservation
Office), www.bl.uk/blpac

CALIPR (needs assessment tool), http://sunsite.berkeley.edu/CALIPR/index.html

Canadian Association of Professional Conservators, www.capc-acrp.ca/what_is_capc.asp

Canadian Conservation Institute, www.cci-icc.gc.ca/index-eng.aspx

Collections Link, www.collectionslink.org.uk

Columbia Audio-Visual Survey,
https://www1.columbia.edu/sec/cu/libraries/bts/preservation/projects.html

Conservation DistList, http://cool.conservation-us.org/byform/mailing-lists/cdl

Conservation Online (CoOL), http://cool.conservation-us.org

Conservation Register (UK), www.conservationregister.com

Digital Preservation Coalition, www.dpconline.org

Digital Preservation listserv,
https://www.jiscmail.ac.uk/cgi-bin/webadmin?A0=digital-preservation

Heritage Preservation (USA), www.heritagepreservation.org

Historic Libraries Forum, www.historiclibrariesforum.org.uk

Image Permanence Institute, https://www.imagepermanenceinstitute.org

Institute of Conservation (ICON) (UK), www.icon.org.uk

JISC Beginners' Guide to Digital Preservation, http://blogs.ukoln.ac.uk/jisc-bgdp

JISC Digital Media, www.jiscdigitalmedia.ac.uk

National Digital Information Infrastructure and Preservation Program,
www.digitalpreservation.gov

National Trust Conservation, www.nationaltrust.org.uk/main/w-chl/w-places_collections.htm

New Zealand Conservators of Cultural Materials (NZCCM), www.conservators.org.nz

Northeast Document Conservation Center (NEDCC), www.nedcc.org

2
Emergency planning for Special Collections

Introduction

The threats to Special Collections outlined in Chapter 1 harm collections over a period of years. This chapter discusses threats that can destroy collections or items within them very quickly: the time scale for effective action is much shorter, so planning beforehand is essential. The chapter will cover:

1 Causes and impact of emergencies in Special Collections, with particular emphasis on fire and water damage.
2 How to prevent and prepare for emergencies via the emergency plan.
3 Issues in responding to and recovering from emergencies.
4 Planning for service continuity.
5 Outline security issues and how to manage them.
6 Discuss insurance issues.

A note on terminology

'An **emergency** is an incident that becomes out of control threatening human safety, and damages, or threatens to damage, facilities and resources essential to the running of an organisation' (BLPAC, www.bl.uk/blpac/disaster.html).

The term '**disaster**' is commonly used among librarians to describe such events. However, 'emergency' is a more recognizable term for other colleagues and the emergency services.

Understanding Special Collections emergencies

Special Collections are at risk from emergencies that may harm collections, affect services, and put human life and welfare in danger. Incidents are caused by:

1 **Extreme weather conditions**: heavy rainfall or other precipitation, hurricanes or tornadoes, resulting in floods or destruction/damage of buildings.
2 **Geological phenomena** such as earthquakes, which impact on the building and its infrastructure.

3 Buildings and facilities problems such as electrical fires, leaking roofs and pipes.
4 Accidental damage, for example smoking materials.
5 Arson and other criminal damage.

Accidental and deliberate incidents caused by people are also discussed under security, below. Some **pest infestations** (see Chapter 1) are so quick and so serious as to merit treatment as emergencies. Most incidents feature fire and/or water, so these threats are considered in more detail.

Fire

Fire can kill or seriously injure people and destroy buildings. It is probably the greatest threat to Special Collections: as Artim (2007) says: 'Vandalized or environmentally damaged structures can be repaired and stolen objects recovered. Items destroyed by fire, however, are gone forever. An uncontrolled fire can obliterate an entire room's contents within a few minutes and completely burn out a building in a couple hours.' If not totally destroyed, items in collections may crack and be distorted by heat, and be harmed by smoke and soot. Firefighting adds water to the equation.

Witness the Norwich Central Library fire of 1994. Caused by a fault in old secondary wiring, the fire spread so quickly that although the fire brigade arrived within two minutes, they could not even enter the building. The Local Studies books, the 2nd Air Division Memorial Library, and all the lending books were lost; the County Archives, stored in fireproof vaults, were saved although wetted. Hammond (1996) gives a vivid picture of the impact of this major disaster on collections, on staff, and on users.

The **fire triangle** is a helpful model for understanding how fires start and how to extinguish them: a fire needs fuel, oxygen and heat – remove any one and the fire will stop (you may also encounter the **fire tetrahedron**, which includes combustion that fuels the fire). Stewart (2009) and Artim (2007) are excellent online introductions to fire issues for Special Collections.

Libraries by their nature contain material that will fuel fires. Sources of heat that start fires in libraries include:

1 Electrical problems, for example wiring faults. Both the Norwich fire and the Duchess Anna Amalia Library fire of 2004 (in which 50,000 rare books, sheet music, manuscripts and art works were destroyed) were caused by such faults.
2 Catering facilities, for example stoves.
3 Gas leaks.
4 Smoking: discarded cigarettes or matches.
5 Arson methods, for example Molotov cocktails, lighters. The 1986 Los Angeles Public Library fire, in which half a million books were destroyed, was caused by arson (though a poor building design that allowed tightly packed stack areas to act as a flue resulted in far more damage than would otherwise have been the case). See Various Authors (1986).

6 **'Hot work'**, for example welding, soldering. Times of building work are therefore particularly risky.

7 **Fires from outside sources**, for example bush or grass fires.

Historic buildings are more vulnerable to fire damage by their nature: combustible building materials, older electrical systems and not compartmentalized or otherwise built for safety.

Libraries as public places must follow local laws about fire safety, for example fire extinguishers, fire doors, places of assembly and other key points. Fire safety officers and local fire services may be able to offer advice. Fire detection and suppression systems are key for the safety of people and collections. The sources mentioned above cover the possibilities. In the past, librarians were wary of installing sprinkler systems because of the risk of water into collections storage areas. However, sprinklers introduce far less water than firefighting hoses, and materials can survive wetting as they cannot survive burning (witness the survival of the archives at Norwich). Modern sprinkler systems have become increasingly sophisticated: water-mist methods use smaller quantities of water at higher pressures than traditional sprinkler systems.

Water

Water-based incidents in Special Collections occur at different scales: from common building problems, for example leaks from pipes, toilets, roofs, windows, drainpipes, etc., to major floods of rivers, lakes and seas caused by extreme weather or earthquakes, which crack dams or cause tsunamis.

Like fire, water is an incredibly destructive and deadly force. Depending on its source, it may be contaminated with sewage or other hazardous materials. Floodwaters contain large pieces of debris and move with shocking speed and power. However, water incidents caused by building problems (unlike fire incidents) may have a natural limit because of the amount of water in the system. An example of a relatively small (but still destructive) water incident appears later in this chapter.

Water harms items in collections because, as we noted earlier, they absorb it. This happens at different rates depending on their materials. Figures quoted by Waters (1993): hand-press era manuscripts and books may absorb water to 80–200% of their original weight, most modern books 60%.

Some results of water absorption:

- modern bindings may disintegrate
- pages on coated paper (shiny/glossy), as used in magazines and illustrated books, stick together when wet
- vellum, parchment and paper cockle
- photographic emulsions and water-soluble inks run
- books become larger, heavier and more fragile, distorting their structures. Their weight will buckle shelves, sending volumes tumbling to the ground, where more damage from standing water and debris is likely.

Alongside this mechanical damage, high relative humidity will encourage mould growth.

Detecting water incidents with internal causes is about good maintenance and staff awareness. Various kinds of water alarm are available, which may be helpful particularly for rarely accessed spaces.

Preventing and preparing for emergencies in Special Collections

Prevention begins with identifying and assessing the risks to Special Collections, looking at factors that could cause incidents, as discussed above.

Risks that stem from geological or climate factors are unavoidable and often devastating as they affect whole regions. Prevention may centre around building and refurbishment to appropriate standards and planned action if a warning is received. See Miller and Pellen (2006) and the CoOL database (http://cool.conervation-us.org) for many case studies of libraries coping with such incidents.

More can be done to minimize risk from building and human problems. Risks to consider include:

- **Physical nature of the collections**. Is there hazardous material? How might different collections react to water immersion?
- **Inside the library building**. Locations of sewage and water pipes? Flat roofs? Heating plant on roof? Smoking areas? Catering facilities?
- **Outside the building**. Storage of rubbish? Neighbouring buildings?

Existing preventive measures should also be considered – are they adequate?

Action should be taken to remove or mitigate any risks where this is possible and practical. Risks inherent in the location of the library or the basics of the building will be out of the control of library or organization staff. The impact of these can be reduced by effective planning.

In addition to regular risk assessment, constant awareness by staff of Special Collections spaces and the areas around them is essential. Many incidents begin small, and, if contained, result in little harm, for example a fire or burst pipe may do no damage if caught early. This includes:

- making sure fire exits are kept clear, fire doors shut and fire extinguishers in their proper places
- monitoring known water leak locations
- looking out for poor storage of materials that could fuel fire
- understanding how the building works: what sounds, smells and temperatures are normal?
- looking out for anything unusual.

Staff should be extra vigilant during:

- building works
- vacation times. Risk is increased because buildings are closed, and key staff are away.

Good housekeeping is also vital, for example putting materials away in boxes or on shelves when not in use, for extra protection from water and fire.

Creating the emergency plan

Developing an emergency plan for Special Collections is a major task. If Special Collections is part of a larger library, librarians and conservators can also become involved in emergency planning for the rest of the service.

Fortunately there is an extensive literature in published and online form. Several templates for plans for libraries, archives or museums can be found online, such as Brown (2007) from the NEDCC. Some plans are intended as online resources, for example dPlan™; others are downloadable or printable templates, such as the Generic Disaster Plan Workbook, by the California Preservation Program, the National Network of Libraries of Medicine (NN/LM) Toolkit, the Harwell Document Restoration Services (HDRS) templates and the M25 Consortium of Academic Libraries template.

However, the template is just a starting point. The 'plan must be more than words on paper, it should be a framework for action' (Matthews, Smith and Knowles, 2009). No real-life incident ever fits exactly into a pre-planned structure, but an effective plan gives staff the tools and ideas they need to cope.

The following areas include questions to consider in creating the plan.

Communications

Who might find the incident? Remember cleaning staff and security guards as well as library staff. Who should they contact? Out of hours, who can be called in? How will they travel, where might they be based? Telephone trees and mini-versions of the plan containing contact details are useful ways to manage communications.

Decision making

There are many decisions to be made quickly in emergency situations. Staff need to be trained and empowered to make these decisions, and roles defined. Many libraries will be part of a larger public body that will have its own emergency management structure, including a crisis management team. If this is the case, Special Collections staff need to be part of this structure and form links with the other key people. In the event of a large disaster (loss of a whole building, for example) emergency management teams may be in action for several years.

Set priorities for rescue and salvage

Which Special Collections are central to your mission, irreplaceable or heavily used? A 'grab' list of the most important materials to rescue first may be useful, though be wary of how and where this list is publicized. Note materials that need special care (e.g. glass plate negatives should not be frozen) and remember key Special Collections documentation, for example accessions registers, card catalogues. Remember the time constraints for wet materials before mould grows and that if dealing with general library stock, salvage of the physical items may not be the best option.

Develop procedures for rescue and salvage

Don't let the first time you or colleagues handle wet or damaged materials be the time you have a disaster. Seek practical training and share with colleagues. Small quantities of damaged material can often be salvaged by in-house air-drying (see note below). In general, protecting undamaged stock (by removing it or covering with plastic sheeting) is the first priority.

Identify equipment

Many Special Collections create wheeled boxes or bins containing items for dealing with small incidents (e.g. hazard tape, newsprint or blotting paper, scissors, gloves, absorbent booms, aprons, etc.). The boxes should be stored somewhere accessible but not tempting for casual use, and a member of staff should be responsible for filling, monitoring and replenishing contents. Other useful material to have to hand: plastic sheeting, plastic buckets or bins for catching leaks, plastic crates. Preservation suppliers often sell emergency kits.

In an emergency, it is easy for staff to become confused about which kind of formats need particular care. What can be air-dried? What should be kept wet, or not? What should be frozen, or not? The waterproof salvage wheel, available from preservation suppliers, is a cheap aide-memoire. Items that would need special care can also be marked, for example boxes containing glass-plate negatives could be marked 'Don't freeze' – in waterproof ink.

However, boxes should not be relied on for a major incident. The planning process should identify other sources of useful materials. For larger items such as pumps, dehumidifiers and emergency lighting other sources such as the estates department (if you have one), local hire firms and co-operative networks should be explored. In large incidents affecting whole areas of cities such equipment will be hard to obtain locally, in which case networks of support may be able to help. The rise of 24/7 supermarkets and garages is a boon for acquiring many useful basics in a hurry. Methods of emergency payment for equipment should be agreed in advance with finance staff.

Develop networks

Establish links with relevant colleagues such as health and safety or estates staff, and try to become involved with the wider organization's emergency planning. Document recovery services offer discounts on and help with large-scale transport, freezing and freeze-drying, and access to independent experts with experience of similar events.

Help and support can be found via formal or informal arrangements with other libraries and heritage organizations. A couple of examples are:

1 The Yorkshire Rapid Response Network (Johnstone n.d.) mobilized archivists and conservators during Christmas 2010 to help a small museum whose textile collection was damaged by a burst water pipe (reinforcing the point made about vacations, above).
2 The coordinated statewide emergency preparedness (COSTEP) framework is a planning tool intended to help US regions cope with area-wide disasters by bringing cultural institutions and other agencies together.

Salvaging wet materials
Air-drying
Small numbers of wetted books can be air-dried with excellent results. The following techniques are fine for general library books and certain Special Collections items if carried out by trained staff; but valuable, vulnerable or fragile formats should be assessed by a conservator.

1 **Saturated books**. Handle as little as possible. Stand the book on absorbent paper, propped if necessary. Keep changing the paper until the book is wet rather than sodden.
2 **Partially wet books**. These should be interleaved with absorbent paper and laid flat. The interleavings should extend beyond the edges of the volume; make sure interleaving goes right into the gutter. Interleaving takes staff time (which will be at a premium) and will distort the book's structure if overdone. Every 20 pages or so is recommended.
3 Slightly **damp books** may be dried without interleaving by fanning them open in a current of air.
4 Once books are **almost dry**, they can be pressed back into shape: lay flat, place absorbent paper between covers and text block, and lay a light weight on top. This should only be attempted when the book is almost dry, otherwise mould will grow.

Blotting paper or newsprint are suitable absorbent papers, the latter can sometimes be obtained cheaply as ends of reels from local printers. It is best to keep a stock pre-cut to standard interleaving sizes. Newsprint (as we note elsewhere) is acidic and so should not be left in rare books longer than absolutely necessary to dry them.

Coated papers should be separated from each other while still wet; if allowed to dry it will be impossible to separate them. In this case, interleaves must be put between every page.

The storage area should be well ventilated (by fans if necessary) to encourage evaporation, the temperature kept stable and humidity kept low by dehumidifiers if possible. Results will vary depending on the nature of materials: some cockling and distortion may be inevitable but a usable book should be the result.

Other salvage techniques

In larger incidents, when particular Special Collections are affected, or once mould has started to grow, air-drying is not practical. The safest way is to freeze wet materials using the facilities of a document recovery service. This prevents the growth of mould. Material can be stored in this way indefinitely, allowing time for insurance and other decisions to be made. It can later be dried out using the freeze-vacuum drying technique and conserved.

Planning for service continuity

Service continuity issues often receive less attention in Special Collections than the obviously pressing issue of saving unique collections. However, they should not be ignored: if services are unavailable, the consequences would include:

- **Impact on users** ranging from minor inconvenience and cost of a cancelled visit to serious threats to their career, for example if dependent on particular collections to write a PhD.
- **Loss of income**, for example from reprographics or retail facilities. A prolonged closure goes beyond this to threaten the entire mission.

Planning for service continuity is similar to emergency planning for collections care and should be considered in parallel:

1 **Identify services**. Alongside the obvious visits and enquiries, virtual services, teaching and anything else offered to the public should be considered (see Chapter 7). A similar process should be followed when planning exhibitions, events and other projects.
2 **Identify risks** to those services and activities. Not only the emergencies outlined above, but incidents that affect staff availability, spaces and equipment used for services, but which may not necessarily harm collections, for example impact of staff sickness or resignation, problems with lighting/heating in the reading room, or problems with software or hardware. Major building projects are likely to have a serious impact on services, possibly requiring closure for several months.
3 **Assess risks.** Work out how likely events are to happen and the impact if they did.
4 **Prevent risks** if possible, for example avoid software issues by choosing widely used, well supported, interoperable systems. However, many of these risks are unavoidable, so:
   — **Plan to minimize risks**, for example how can services be made available in different ways? It may be as simple as booking a back-up room for a key event or arranging for training for another member of staff. However, legal and preservation issues should be considered: it may not be safe to relocate the reading room function, so when the room itself is out of action, that service might have to be closed.

— Consider how to communicate with users in these situations, for example informing those with appointments. Useful ideas include using the out of office reply function, social media (see Chapter 8), and publicizing via Special Collections listservs and networks relevant to your collections. Particular care needs to be taken with services that do not require appointments, as it may not occur to regular users to check before their visit.

Sometimes a problem can be turned into something positive, for example the flight home of a Magna Carta manuscript belonging to the Bodleian Library on tour in the US was delayed by the 2010 volcanic ash cloud; it was possible to arrange an exhibition at the Morgan Library in New York during the delay so more people had a chance to see this treasure. The manuscript and the work of the Bodleian also got extra positive publicity.

Responding to Special Collections emergencies

1 **People matter most.** Your health, and that of your colleagues and users, is more important than any materials! Make sure that you and your staff understand this and do not put yourselves at risk. While working, whoever is in charge should be mindful of the personal needs of staff (arranging for refreshments and loo breaks), and counselling should be made available to support them.

2 **Appreciate the scale.** The shape of response will be very different for different scales of incident. For example, it may be possible to air-dry 50 wet books in two days using existing staff, space and materials, with business as usual going on around. 5000 or 50,000 will be a major disruption, and require specialist help with packing, transport and, probably, freezing. The Norwich, Los Angeles and Anna Amalia fires mentioned above show the scale of major incidents: hundreds or thousands of volunteers involved, millions of items affected, conservation and rebuilding efforts lasting years.

3 **Assess and document the damage.**

4 **Protect undamaged stock and materials,** by covering them or removing them from the building.

5 **Categorize damaged stock** and put plan into action.

6 **Think insurance.** See note on insurance, below. When an incident is large enough to consider making a claim, communicate with insurers as soon as possible. They will send a loss adjuster if the claim will be large. Document what is happening, take photographs and videos and record actions taken.

7 **Communicate.** Effective communication with users, staff and other stakeholders and management of press demands are vital. The press office (if you have one) or head of service would deal with the media, but staff will need guidance on how to cope with queries. See Chapter 8 for more on communication and the media.

The Boston Athenaeum had a water leak (caused by a sprinkler pipe) in January 2011, typical of the incidents that most Special Collections face. The staff put their disaster plan into action: 'Many works of art were removed to secure areas of the building. We called in specialist contractors to remove the large volume of standing water; to pack wet books for off-site conservation; to stabilize the building environment; to repair the broken sprinkler system; and to re-set the security systems and fire alarms.' (www. bostonathenaeum.org/node/439). This quick, effective response meant that none of the rare books or other valuable items in the building were damaged (though some rugs and 900 books were wetted). Note from their website also how the disaster response team managed staff (most worked from home) and communicated with stakeholders.

Recovering from Special Collections emergencies

1 **Lessons learned?** After any incident, however small, it is important to review what has been learned. What worked? What didn't work? Did you have the materials you needed? Keeping an incident log is useful as it reveals patterns of small incidents that may suggest a more significant problem. The lessons learned could also help other libraries.
2 **Slow process**. The long-term impact of a disaster on the individuals involved can be huge. The response to large incidents can take years. If an emergency affected the whole region, staff and users will have suffered other losses. Communication remains vital: keep staff, users and the public involved in the ongoing story.

For example, imagine a major fire affecting a historic building containing Special Collections. It may take three months for anyone to be allowed to enter the building if the stonework has been damaged. The team involved in recovery may be huge, consisting of the loss adjustor, many staff including Special Collections representation, and external organizations such as the local council or heritage bodies. It may be three years before restoration work is completed on the building and its contents.

Security and theft in Special Collections
Understanding the problem
Special Collections are vulnerable to theft. Materials such as early printed books, first editions or atlases are portable, may have high market values and other iconic or aesthetic qualities. The theft of individual plates and maps from volumes, to increase the value of a poorer copy of the same work or to sell as individual items, is particularly difficult to prevent and detect.

The nature of Special Collections work means that simply locking material up is not an answer. Use, marketing and outreach are essential for the survival and development of Special Collections. These activities may increase risk by raising the profile of treasures, yet they may also secure further funding that means that cataloguing, awareness and protection can be increased.

Security and emergency planning overlap. A fire may be started to disguise or distract from a theft. Special Collections are also at risk from terrorism, vandalism and other criminal activity.

Developing a security policy

The Association of College and Research Libraries/Rare Books and Manuscripts Section (ACRL/RBMS) guidelines (Association of College and Research Libraries, 2009a) suggest appointing a Library Security Officer or a larger group of staff with responsibility for security. In smaller services, this role may be undertaken by the Special Collections librarian. A service lacking in-house expertise might bring in a security consultant, though they should be carefully vetted first. As with the emergency plan, risks should be identified and assessed, preventive measures taken where possible, and plans for response and recovery created and shared. Key issues are shown below.

Building security

The library building can be protected by measures such as high-quality locks on exterior and interior doors, grilles over windows, security guards, security systems and lighting, and closed-circuit television (CCTV). Entrances/exits should be kept to a minimum. However, such measures work best against out-of-hours intruders, so should not be completely relied upon. Human factors and theft during opening hours pose significant risks.

Collection management

Effective management of Special Collections can help prevent incidents and make sure the damage is known if they do occur. More guidance is available in the ACRL/RBMS recommendations (Association of College and Research Libraries, 2009a) and see Chapters 3–5 for more information about these activities.

1 **Acquisitions and cataloguing**. Good record-keeping and cataloguing mean libraries will know that a theft or damage has occurred and what has been lost/damaged. Material should be accessioned on arrival in the building and its location noted. Copy-specific cataloguing that covers provenance and condition means that the value of a lost book and the damage done to a mutilated one can be seen.
2 **Processing**. Unique and indelible marking of materials should be considered where this is compatible with their preservation needs, for example a discreet embossed book stamp for rare volumes.
3 **Stock-taking** of material against catalogues and lists. Ideally all collections would be checked at least once a year, but in practice most Special Collections do not have the staffing to do so. Ways to make the most of whatever stock-checking is possible include irregular patterns of checking (to deter in-house theft) and concentrating on the collections of highest market value, for example atlases, philatelic materials. Records should be kept of missing materials (which may of course be mis-shelved) and their shelf locations regularly checked.
4 **Internal transfer**. Rare material on open shelves is particularly at risk: see Chapter 4 on internal transfer procedures to Special Collections.

5 **De-accessioning**. This process should be properly documented and guidelines followed in marking de-accessioned works (see also CILIP Rare Books and Special Collections Group, 2009b).

Users

Theft in Special Collections tends to happen during use by readers (unlike say art galleries and museums where break-ins out-of-hours are more of a concern), probably because it would be very difficult to locate a particular item during a break-in, and researchers using Special Collections are allowed to handle them. A balance between access and security should be sought, matching security concerns with the issues discussed in Chapters 7–9. The library needs to decide who is allowed to use material and how they register and prove identity, for example asking users to sign a user agreement, bring photo ID, or arrange a letter of recommendation. Access to uncatalogued material requires extra care; advice can be found in Chapter 5. The key points are:

1 **Browsing**. Users should only interact with materials brought to them by staff and should be supervised during the process. They should never be allowed to browse unsupervised in strong rooms. Where collections and users share space (in historic libraries), measures such as alarmed wires across shelves will be needed. Some collections in a reading room, for example modern bibliographies, could be browsable.
2 **Quantities**. Users should not have too much material at once. How much is too much depends on the service and nature of collections. Center and Lancaster (2004) include examples of typical rules on this subject in US and Canadian research libraries.
3 **Check in and out**. Materials should be checked in and out. One technique to consider is weighing at check in and out with sensitive scales to ensure nothing has been removed (see Wilkie 2006).
4 **Records** of materials accessed should be able to match a person to the exact items they have used. Given that it can take many years for stolen works to emerge on the antiquarian market, these records should be kept for long periods or even indefinitely.
5 **Belongings** can be used to mutilate volumes and conceal thefts, so libraries need restrictions on what can be taken into the reading room, lockers and cloakrooms for personal belongings.

These measures may be impossible for smaller libraries, for example there may be no space for lockers. Such services must rely on personal observation and interaction with users; larger services such as national libraries cannot generally supervise individuals as closely, so need tighter restrictions on access and belongings.

Even where these measures are in place, it is dangerous to assume that these will keep collections safe. Thieves are ingenious. East and Myers (1998) tell the story of a thief who cleverly altered documents after removing philatelic rarities so that it would not have been apparent to staff checking the documents back in that anything had been changed. Librarians need to be aware of the monetary value of their collections and understand what is most likely to appeal to thieves. Different procedures may be needed for the most valuable collections, for example access to medieval manuscripts only with evidence of research.

Staff

Staff who are well managed, motivated, care about the collections and are observant can be a great help in avoiding theft. Rules about access and use need to be clear, and staff empowered to challenge unexpected situations.

Sadly, staff, interns or other trusted persons have been known to steal from Special Collections. The risks of such theft can be minimized by restricting access to storage areas, controlling keys (especially when staff leave) and developing clear procedures for staff use of collections. Staff should keep their personal belongings away from the reading room and strong rooms. Any removal of Special Collections from the building should be for Special Collections purposes such as exhibitions or teaching, and be properly recorded: it should not be normal for staff to remove items from the premises. 'An atmosphere of trust and concern for the collections is probably the best guarantee against theft by staff' (Association of College and Research Libraries 2009a).

High-risk times

Extra vigilance and planning are needed to minimize risks at high-risk times, for example:

1 **Building work**. New people are in and around the building, and new opportunities for theft may arise, for example access via external scaffolding (note how many times building work crops up as a risk factor in these chapters!).
2 **When in transit**, for example for exhibition loan or conservation work. Resource (2003) is full of useful detail on managing couriers.
3 **Emergencies**, even if not directly affecting collections, may open opportunities for theft.

Responding effectively to an incident

1 **Reporting**. Thefts and mutilations should be reported to the organization's security services and the police. External networks may also be able to help: local antiquarian booksellers or those who specialize in the subject, antiquarian booksellers' associations and other librarians. There are several useful resources that list stolen materials, including the Art Loss Register, Missing Materials and the RBMS security site. Booksellers also suffer from theft, whether directly from their premises or by buying stolen goods: it is advisable to work with them (see Chapter 4 for more about booksellers). Booksellers' databases of stolen material include Stolen Book; the Antiquarian Booksellers' Association (ABA) sends e-mail alerts highlighting thefts from their members.

2 **Publicity and prosecuting**. Librarians who are victims of theft are in a difficult position, in not wishing to advertise security weaknesses. However, publicity makes recovery of stolen material more likely. Even if a theft is only discovered some time after it happened, it is still worth reporting and publicizing it: the nature of the antiquarian book trade is such that material may come to light years later.

3 **Recovery**. In addition to the networks listed above, materials stolen from libraries may be listed on eBay and other internet sites. Libraries who have suffered a loss should monitor these, and other libraries may also find them useful to spot thefts that may not have come to light. Larger services may have recovery teams who target fairs and sites selling relevant material.

4 **Lessons learned**. After a theft, access and security arrangements need to be reviewed to avoid a repeat. Subjects or genres that have suffered mutilation or an unexplained rise in interest may be vulnerable to theft. The results can be shared to help other libraries protect their collections, for example the New York State Archives suffered insider theft loss in 2008; they are now sharing lessons learned with other archives in their area.

Case study: the Durham First Folio

A Shakespeare First Folio was stolen from an exhibition at Durham University in 1998, and recovered sadly mutilated ten years later. An individual was convicted not of its theft but of handling stolen goods. After its return, the volume is to be the centrepiece of a new exhibition in a major exhibition space at the University, after which it will be conserved.

Some important points about this story:

1 The timescale: the Folio was recovered thanks to the awareness of experts at the Folger Library, when it was handed in for valuation, many years later.
2 Lessons were learned and security was tightened.
3 The use of publicity by the University, which highlights six other books taken in the same incident that have not so far been recovered, and promotes their other important Special Collections.
4 The book was mutilated to disguise its origins, but the nature of early printed books, discussed in Chapter 3, meant that experts were able to find evidence that confirmed it was Durham's copy.

A note on insurance

Insurance is a tool for managing risk and is an important part of recovering from emergencies and security issues. Organizations pay a premium to insurers to take risks to themselves. Many Special Collections are part of larger organizations and are covered by an overall insurance policy. In other organizations, a specialist insurer may be used.

Despite the complex language of insurance, the key issues are those covered in these first two chapters: the nature of collections, the risks they face and the actions taken to minimize the impact of these risks. Keep your insurer informed of changes such as the arrival of new collections, altered risks (e.g. major building work), exhibitions or loans of collections, or new co-operative or third-party arrangements.

Special Collections librarians find valuation particularly difficult, as frequent pleas to the listservs suggest. They may be overwhelmed by the idea of having to come up with market values for millions of items (not to mention that market values fluctuate constantly). Other material has little or no market value, but immense contextual or research value, for example collections of ephemera, pamphlets, objects, newspapers or local material. Another concern is the growing divergence in practice from general libraries, which nowadays in the event of damage to physical collections might seek to replace the 'knowledge base' with electronic resources rather than try to salvage actual books. Librarians need to ensure they understand that Special Collections are an appreciating asset.

If market values are needed, specialist appraisers such as antiquarian booksellers should be used. It is common practice to list individual items above a certain market value and insure a percentage of the market value of the rest.

Some senior managers in libraries used to argue that as Special Collections are irreplaceable, there was no point in insuring them as replacements could not be bought. This idea seems to be in decline, as Martin's (2002) survey of US and Canadian research libraries revealed. It misses a key point: unless there is total loss through fire or theft, objects will survive in some form: wet, burned or otherwise damaged. Even stolen books may be returned – though as in Durham's case mutilated. Damaged artefacts can be salvaged by freezing, freeze-drying and conservation processes; expensive but quantifiable processes for which an insurance payout is essential.

Communication is key: advance, documented agreement between the library/organization and the insurer about the value of significant items and how value will be established in the event of a loss. It may be reassuring to know that, compared to the risks faced by artworks, Special Collections are considered low risk by specialist insurers: they are kept in one place, by people who care about them, and public access is closely supervised. In addition to the standard insurance, it is worth investigating schemes that help cultural institutions cope with the cost of commercial insurance, for example in the UK, the government indemnity scheme covers loans of objects for exhibition to many organizations including libraries.

Conclusion

Emergencies (especially fire and flood) pose great risks to Special Collections and services. However, good planning makes it possible to prevent emergencies or at least minimize their impact, by assessing risks, training staff and preparing equipment and procedures. Theft and vandalism are also major concerns; a balance has to be found between security and access. Again there are ways to prevent and reduce damage through managing collections, access and buildings. Understanding insurance is an important part of managing such incidents.

In Chapters 1 and 2 we have discussed the basics of care of Special Collections. Many improvements, such as bringing storage to BS 5454:2000 level, are expensive; however, well trained staff who care about the collections and their users, and good housekeeping practices can improve care even in less well resourced libraries.

Further reading

Useful books on emergency planning: Matthews, Smith and Knowles (2009), Miller and Pellen (2006), and Wilkinson (2010).

Security: Association of College and Research Libraries (2009a) ACRL/RBMS guidelines on security and theft; CILIP Rare Books and Special Collections Group (2009b) code of conduct for librarians and booksellers on theft of books and manuscripts. Resource (2003) offers detailed help on fire and security. Kahn (2008) is a detailed guide to building issues.

Examples and case studies

Anna Amalia Library, www.anna-amalia-bibliothek.de/en/index.html

Bodleian Libraries: Travel Disruption keeps Magna Carta in New York,
www.bodleian.ox.ac.uk/news/2010_apr_21

Boston Athenaeum: Frequently Asked Questions about the Water Leak,
www.bostonathenaeum.org/node/439

Durham University Celebrates Return of Shakespeare First Folio,
www.dur.ac.uk/news/newsitem/?itemno=10344

To Preserve and Protect: Security Solutions for New York's Historical Records,
www.nyshrab.org/about/about_projects_security.shtml

Useful websites

Many of the preservation resources listed in Chapter 1 cover security and emergency issues, and see CoOL database for full text articles.

Art Loss Register, www.artloss.com

Australian Library and Information Association disaster recovery pages,
www.alia.org.au/disasterrecovery/

California Preservation Program template,
http://calpreservation.org/disasters/generic/index.html

COSTEP, www.nedcc.org/disaster/costep.php

DPlan™, www.dplan.org/default.asp

Government Indemnity Scheme (UK),
www.mla.gov.uk/what/cultural/objects/government_indemnity

HDRS templates, www.hdrs.co.uk/templateplan.html

Heritage Emergency National Taskforce (US),
    www.heritagepreservation.org/PROGRAMS/TASKFER.HTM
ILAB Stolen-book.org, www.stolen-book.org
M25 Consortium of Academic Libraries template, www.m25lib.ac.uk/m25dcp/prevent.html
Missing Materials database, http://missingmaterials.org
NN/LM Emergency Preparedness & Response Toolkit, http://nlm.gov/ep
RBMS Security Committee, www.rbms.info/committees/security/index.shtml

3
Understanding objects in Special Collections

Introduction

Objects in Special Collections include any format that has ever been used for communication, from papyri to digital files. Librarians need to understand the objects in their collections to manage them effectively. Understanding the materials and construction of objects is essential to make the right choices in preserving Special Collections, while understanding their context and creation helps with acquiring, marketing and sharing them with readers.

This chapter introduces the formats that are the historic basis of Special Collections, as foundation collections or gathered by antiquarians and bibliophiles: manuscripts and early printed books. It also covers the key skills of analytical bibliography and common modern formats with preservation issues.

1 Medieval manuscripts.
2 Early printed books (including typography, paper, illustrations and bindings).
3 Analytical bibliography.
4 Important printed formats: private press, artists' books, ephemera.
5 Key modern materials: photographs and plastics.

Special Collections librarians in national or other large libraries may be responsible for one type or era of material, for example Western manuscripts. Others in smaller libraries may manage all kinds of materials, though such libraries may collect a more limited range of formats.

A note on terminology

Book is nowadays used for published works. However, the term originated to refer to folded sheets sewn into a binding (or, later, cut sheets glued into a case). The book had many advantages over rival formats like rolls, scrolls and tablets: it was portable, compact and made it easy to access any point in the text. To distinguish printed works from manuscripts bound in book form, the term **printed book** is used. **Codex** is another word for the book format, mostly now used for medieval manuscripts.

Bibliography is used for many kinds of lists about books, including the list at the end of this work. The term also means the study of books as physical objects; this chapter introduces analytical bibliography. **Codicology** is the study of manuscripts; **palaeography** the study of handwriting. The term **diplomatics** is also used: the study of documents to establish whether they are authentic.

There are many specialist terms in the study of books, manuscripts and other Special Collections formats. Some are defined as they occur; links to glossaries will help with the others, and see the controlled vocabularies in Chapter 5 and resources in Appendix A. Librarians need to know these terms to understand book historians, bibliographers and the antiquarian book trade and make sense of the materials in Special Collections.

Understanding medieval manuscripts

Until the invention of printing with movable type, knowledge was recorded and communicated in Europe via handwriting. Medieval manuscripts may be the most valuable, iconic and significant objects held by Special Collections. Each is a unique artefact with its own name, story and meaning, as this case study shows.

Case study: long valued, newly found

Two remarkable manuscripts produced within a few years of each other are very different in origins, physical nature and provenance; both offer extraordinary historical insights.

The Macclesfield Psalter. This amazing illuminated manuscript came to light only in 2004 when the Library of the Earl of Macclesfield was dispersed. It was bought by the J. Paul Getty Museum, but an export bar was placed on it, and funds were raised to keep it in the area it was created: it now lives at the Fitzwilliam Museum. Suffering from rough handling and then long neglect, the manuscript has been conserved and is regularly on show to the public. Made circa 1330, possibly for the Earl of Warenne, it is evidence of a rich network of East Anglian artists and patrons, and full of funny, fantastic images: 'an ape-doctor tricks a bear-patient with a mock diagnosis. An enormous skate fish frightens a man out of his wits. Wielding a sword against a giant snail seems pointless' (www.fitzmuseum. cam.ac.uk/gallery/macclesfield/about). The Psalter's story exemplifies the pressures and desirability of such treasures, the huge public interest they arouse, and how surviving manuscripts can be a window into a medieval worldview otherwise lost to us.

In contrast, the **Auchinleck Manuscript** has been known to scholars since the 18th century: it was presented to the Advocates Library in 1744 by Lord Auchinleck (Alexander Boswell, father of James); the Advocates gave it to the new National Library of Scotland in 1925. Dating from the same time as the Psalter (between 1331 and 1340), it is a collection of poetry in English, particularly romances in verse. Burnley and Wiggins (2003) explain its significance, as a vital source of information about language and popular stories. It shows the ideas on which Chaucer drew and is the earliest example of a book commercially produced in English for a lay audience. It also influenced Sir Walter Scott's medieval romances and hence the Gothic revival. The Manuscript's story shows how valuable an individual document can be in encouraging scholarship and creativity, with a long history of scholars exploring its history and codicology.

To make sense of medieval manuscripts, we need to understand why they were created. Many of course were created for religious purposes, showing the importance of religious life and faith and its dominance of written culture. Such manuscripts include Bibles, the lives of saints and theological works. **Psalters**, like the Macclesfield example above, contained the psalms from the Bible and were used for prayer and as aids to literacy. Liturgical works are often encountered, documenting the prayers and other texts needed for church services, for example **missals** or mass-books, containing the service of the Mass for the year, and works containing the texts (**breviaries**) and sung parts (**antiphonals**) of the Divine Office: the daily cycle of prayers, i.e. matins, lauds, etc. **Books of Hours** are prayer books belonging to individuals, containing prayers and psalms for different times of day, and are often very personal documents.

Other works were written to entertain, educate, document or convey information, though of course many of these would include religious elements. Secular medieval manuscripts include histories, letters, classical literature, legal and government documents, handbooks and practical guides for professions or crafts and literary texts such as poetry, sagas and romances (like the Auchinleck Manuscript).

Medieval manuscripts might be written in Latin, Greek, Hebrew or in vernacular languages. Titles and title-pages as we know them did not exist: instead **incipits** or **explicits** (the opening or closing words) are often used to identify manuscripts.

The making of manuscripts

Manuscripts were written on vellum or parchment. These skins took careful preparation: soaking in lime, scraping off hairs, stretching on a frame and rubbing with **pounce** (any of various substances, e.g. pumice or chalk) to whiten and otherwise improve the surface. Before the text was written, lines on the surface were **pricked** with a stylus to act as guides for the scribe.

Scribes were based in monastery scriptoria or attached to courts, and, later, as professionals in university cities. The ink used from the 12th century was iron gall ink, made from oak galls (growths formed around wasp eggs) and copperas or vitriol. Writing was skilled work: the handwriting or **scripts** used had to be uniform and legible as print does now. Well-known styles include insular majuscule (Book of Kells), which developed into the Carolingian minuscule of Alcuin and Bede, the basis of modern lower case letters. This was supplanted by textura, the familiar style of Gothic or blackletter.

To make the most of time and precious materials, scribes developed many abbreviations, particularly for Latin texts. To quote the British Library online glossary (www.bl.uk/catalogues/illuminatedmanuscripts/glossary.asp), there are three main types:

- suspensions, in which the end of a word is abbreviated, signalled by the use of a horizontal bar or another graphic symbol;

- contractions, in which another part of a word is abbreviated with the use of a graphic symbol;
- abbreviation symbols, used for whole words and often derived from the tachygraphic (shorthand) systems of antiquity (that of Tiro, Cicero's secretary, being most influential).

Reading a manuscript is made much easier by knowing the kinds of words to expect in a document of that particular type and the common abbreviations (see 'Further reading' and 'Useful websites' below).

After the writing had been completed, manuscripts would often be decorated:

1 **Illumination** was the 'embellishment of a manuscript with luminous colours (especially gold and silver)' (www.bl.uk/catalogues/illuminatedmanuscripts/glossary.asp), the gilding usually gold leaf.
2 **Miniatures** are the individual images in a manuscript, independent of the text.
3 **Historiated** initials or borders contain images of particular scenes or people, sometimes relating to the text.
4 **Marginalia:** writing or images in the margins of the manuscript. Marginalia may be part of the original work, comment on or translate it, or deal with other matters entirely.
5 **Rubrication**: process of writing, titles and other instructions in the text, usually in red ink, hence the name.

The fates of manuscripts

The study of manuscripts is not limited to the few that have survived whole. Manuscripts in Special Collections have survived in many different states, from tiny fragments to entire rolls or codices. In addition to harm from the threats outlined in Chapters 1 and 2, the expensive and useful vellum and parchment might be scraped and reused for other texts (resulting in **palimpsests**, as we saw in Chapter 1). The skins might also be reused as **pastedowns** in book bindings: manuscript or printed books would be sewn into boards, with the pastedowns being used to cover the attachment of the cords to the boards.

Manuscripts have often been **dismembered**. Collectors (including, famously, John Ruskin) cut out and kept the illuminations, discarding the rest of the book. This was the fate of most of the miniatures in the Auchinleck Manuscript. There remains a financial incentive to dismember manuscripts, both for booksellers who have bought whole works legitimately and for thieves to steal parts of works. The growth in internet selling offers many new opportunities to sell dismembered works. Kidd (2004) quotes de Hamel: 'You buy a manuscript for a thousand dollars (for example). You break it in two and each half is worth $900. You tear it in half again and each quarter is worth $800; you split it again and each eighth is worth $750; and so on'.

Digital technologies make it possible to reunite scattered leaves online so scholars can study them together. Witness the Codex Sinaiticus, a fourth-century manuscript containing the earliest known New Testament text. The complex history of the manuscript has resulted in four libraries holding leaves from it (the British Library, Leipzig University Library, St Catherine's Monastery, Sinai, and the National Library of Russia). The Codex Sinaiticus Project will reunite them in digital form.

Understanding early printed books

Alongside medieval manuscripts, early printed books are core to Special Collections. Printing pre-dates Gutenberg's innovation of movable metal type in the 1450s: printing with wooden blocks was known in China six centuries before (the earliest dated printed book, a copy of the Diamond Sutra held at the British Library, was made in 868 AD). However, movable type was a great advance because it could be set quickly, corrected during the printing and later reused for other works.

The earliest printed books to 1501 are known as **incunables** or **incunabula**: the name comes from the idea of the 'cradle' or birth of printing. Early printed books were naturally similar to the manuscripts they were replacing, both in content and appearance. The earliest typefaces resembled handwriting and the scribal abbreviations mentioned above continued to be used. The modern apparatus of title pages, indexes and half-titles took time to develop; early printed books tended to use the **colophon**: a feature at the end of the book giving details of printing and other information, which appeared in some late medieval manuscripts. In fact, printing technology remained relatively unchanged until the industrial revolution, although the content and appearance of books changed rapidly as printers realized the potential of the new technology.

The making of early printed books

The printing **types**, stored in compartmentalized trays known as **cases** (hence lower and upper case), were assembled for printing by a **compositor**, first in a composing-stick then moved to a larger tray called a galley (more about type below). Lines of type were separated with **leads**.

Books were not printed page by page. Many pages at a time were printed on large sheets of paper and then folded and cut. The terms for formats, **folio**, **quarto**, **octavo**, **duodecimo** (plus some rarer types), are based on how many times a sheet had to be folded, for example quarto format was folded twice creating four leaves. A book made up of such leaves would also be called a quarto. Early books might have the leaves numbered (**foliation**) rather than the pages as with modern books. The right-hand pages were known as recto, the left-hand verso.

Whole sheets were fixed in iron frames known as **formes**, a process called **imposition**. **Proofs** were made from the formes, and checked against the original manuscript. The compositor then re-set the type from the corrected proofs.

The printing process used a machine called a **printing press** (hand-press), which pressed the sheets of paper against the inked type. Generally it was worked by two workmen, one who did the inking, the other placing the paper and working the mechanism that operated the press.

The printed sheets were then folded to the size of the book, in groups of **leaves** called **gatherings** or **quires**, which were then sewn together. Each gathering would have a **signature** on the first page to identify it and enable the binder to put the gatherings together in the right order when the book was bound. These are usually (though not always) letters. The use of a catchword was continued from manuscript practice to provide extra help for the binder: the first word of the next page was printed at the foot of the previous page.

Faulty leaves were replaced by printing a new version on a later sheet. The cancelled leaf is known as a **cancellandum**, and the replacement a **cancellans**. After the sheet was folded, the cancellandum was cut out and the cancellans pasted onto the remaining stub.

Typography

Type was made by punching the shape of the letters into a **matrix** of copper, which was held in a mould while hot **type-metal** was poured in. A whole set of type of one size and design, with all the cases and letters was called a **fount**. The size and design (**face**) of types are of interest to scholars. Body-sizes quickly became standardized – examples of sizes include pica, small pica and long primer.

Type faces are an incredibly varied and interesting subject. The earliest types, naturally, were modelled on the types of handwriting already mentioned: textura type faces called Gothic or **black letter**, which survived as German Fraktur into the 20th century, are still used for particular purposes. Roman types were modelled on Renaissance humanist handwritings (in turn based on the early medieval forms mentioned above); as they were more readable, they tended to replace the Gothic forms. Typographers continued to develop new forms of these Roman faces: Jenson, Aldus (who developed the first italics and effective Greek typefaces), Caslon, Baskerville and many more.

Paper

Although vellum and parchment continued to be used, the growth of printing led to a great increase in the use of paper, made in paper mills. Like printing, the technology remained stable until the 19th century. Paper was made of pounded or minced linen rags. Mixed with water, the resulting **stuff** was stirred in vats. A mould, which resembled a flat wire sieve, was held in a wooden **deckle** and dipped into the vat. The worker then shook the mould in two directions to create a sheet of paper. The papers were laid on felt and squeezed to remove water. These papers then needed to be dipped into hot **size** (a solution of animal gelatine) so they would be less absorbent. Researchers can learn about handmade paper from the patterns of the **chain lines** of the mould and the watermarks, trademarks attached to the mould to show on the finished paper.

Illustrations

The earliest illustrations in printed books were produced from **woodcuts**, a technique older than the use of movable type. Woodcuts are cut along the grain of the wood. They could be printed alongside the type in the forme and were therefore useful for elaborate initials and decorations. They work well for strong, simple shapes.

Copperplate engraving is an **intaglio** technique: an image is engraved onto a copper plate, ink is applied, rubbed off and the print made from the ink left in the lines. Although such printing had to be carried out by separate specialists, it offered finer detail and thus became more popular than woodcuts in the 16th century. Woodcuts continued to be used in books for children and popular printing, and, later, in many private press books (see below). Later, wood engraving, in which the image is cut across the grain, was also used.

To understand the fine detail possible via engravings and how this helped advance science, witness Robert Hooke's *Micrographia* (1665), one of the most famous illustrated books. It contains magnificent plates showing Hooke's depictions of what he saw through the microscope: a flea, a louse, mould, the point of a needle.

Bindings

Early printed books were generally not bound as part of the printing process. Instead, booksellers would bind copies in trade bindings (simpler in design) or sell them unbound for the purchaser to have them bound to their own taste, featuring their armorial emblems or other personal symbols.

The medieval craft techniques used for binding manuscripts continued in the age of printing. Binders collated the sheets, putting them in the correct order, using the signatures and catchwords to help. The book was then sewn onto thongs or cords, onto which the **endleaves** were sewn. These, also known as **endpapers**, would be attached to the boards as pastedowns or left loose as flyleaves to protect the book. The boards (originally wood, later various kinds of paper-based board) were attached using the cords, and the outer edges of the book cut down. The edges might be then be painted or gilded. Until it became common to put books on shelves with spines facing outwards, the title would appear on one of these edges. The **headbands**, which gave extra protection to the book when being taken from the shelf, were also sewn on. Finally the book was covered with leather or other material and decoration applied using heated metal stamps or tools. Decorations could be left **blind** (left ungilded) or further enhanced with gold leaf. Medieval books had often featured clasps, necessary to keep parchment or vellum from cockling, and these continued to be used for paper books.

Materials used for bookbindings have included various kinds of leather: calfskin, goatskin and pigskin. Vellum and parchment, wood, metal, decorated papers, many kinds of cloth and embroidery have also been used.

Introducing analytical bibliography

Analytical bibliography is concerned with the matters discussed above: the study of books as physical objects. Bibliographers look at the relationship between the printing process and texts transmitted to us, for example the spelling and other quirks of the various compositors of Shakespeare's First Folio, as this is the only source for 18 of his plays.

They are interested in the creation of books for their own sake, the trade in books, and their role in society and culture. This wider interest is often known as **book history**.

Analytical bibliography and library cataloguing are in some ways moving closer together. As Chapter 5 explains, Special Collections cataloguing no longer involves short entries on catalogue cards, clearly distinct from bibliographies. Now controlled vocabularies are used to describe the matters that interest bibliographers and other researchers: paper, bindings, provenance, etc. Any librarian working with early printed books needs to know some analytical bibliography, especially these key concepts:

1 **Edition, impression, issue and state**. Vital for any librarian dealing with bibliographers or the book trade. They help describe priority of publication. Collectors tend to desire the earliest form in which a book was published, preferring the uncorrected state of the first issue of the first impression of the first edition to all later ones' (Belanger, 1977).
    — An **edition** is all the copies printed from the same setting of type (the printing may have taken place at several times over a long period).
    — An **impression** is all the copies printed at one time.
    — An **issue** is part of an edition sold or planned at the same time.
    — **State** covers small differences between copies, for example if an error is found during printing and corrected, or if an erratum slip is added after some copies have been sold.
    Note that publishers have often used the term edition loosely, for what might be called an impression or issue. The matter is also complicated by methods used in the machine age, when particular settings of type could be reprinted by relief plates or photographic methods many years later.
2 **The Ideal Copy**. A standard used by bibliographers to represent the best intentions of the printer for a particular edition at the time of printing. This includes such matters as blank leaves, illustrations on plates, and cancels and inserts. Surviving copies are compared to this standard.
3 **Collational formula**. A standardized way of describing the exact structure of an early book, and referring to its individual parts. It lists the gatherings, leaves and cancels, based on the ideal copy. The alphabetical or other signatures assigned to the gatherings are entered with superscript figures to show how they were folded. Bowers (1994) is the definitive account; Gaskell (1995) a very useful introduction. Practical training is essential, for example via Rare Book School or Rare Books and Special Collections Group (RBSCG) events. The Chapter 5 section on fingerprints shows another use for signatures in analytical bibliography.
4 **Quasi-facsimile title page transcription**. This involves copying the text of the title page in full and as printed, i.e. VV for W where present in the original. The rules include using a vertical stroke for a line ending and underlining italics. The process may seem unnecessary when copies of title pages can easily be made, but it

is part of the historic practice of bibliography and helps build understanding of the nature of early books.

Managing provenance in Special Collections

Special Collections librarians need to understand the importance of **provenance**, simply defined as 'previous ownership' (Pearson 1998). Interest in provenance now goes beyond the idea of **association** copies, works valued by booksellers and purchasers because they had been owned by a famous person, to an interest in the whole story of an object. Each manuscript or early printed book is unique, not just because of the way it was created as we discussed above, but because it has been owned and treated by different people in different ways. Witness the two manuscripts above, the Auchinleck Manuscript, with its association with the famous Boswell and its great lists of former owners, and the Macclesfield Psalter with its fascinating early story and hidden later history.

There are two ways to look at provenance:

1 **Who owned a book?** And, more widely, who read or otherwise had access to it?
2 **Which books were owned** by a particular person or organization? For instance, a library may hold some books owned by a collector and wish to know more about his other interests.

Provenance is studied by considering evidence on the physical objects, added by owners, readers or booksellers, for example:

1 **Inscriptions**. These might be as simple as an individual writing their name, a gift or prize inscription, mottoes or verses. Pen-trials, scribbling or writing to test a pen, are often found.
2 **Annotations**. Owners and readers might have underlined or commented on the text or added notes unrelated to it.
3 **Insertions**. Letters, bookmarks or other ephemera.
4 **Book-plates, labels and stamps** show ownership by individuals or libraries.
5 **Bindings** might contain the arms or another symbol used by an individual or library, or otherwise reflect their tastes and interests.

These methods are as old as the techniques of printing and book production: owners naturally wished to personalize their books and to list them.

Much evidence of previous history has been lost to insensitive rebinding, dismemberment and other mutilation and of course many books have themselves been lost. However, provenance study is not limited to surviving books but can take into account what once existed. This is thanks to **external evidence**, such as catalogues of libraries, printers' lists, inventories, lists of forbidden books, and sales catalogues produced by booksellers and auctioneers.

Special Collections policies and procedures need to take the importance of provenance into account:

1 **Preservation**. Conservation treatments should not remove evidence of previous ownership (registered conservators will of course be aware of this). Special Collections processing (Chapter 5) should not obscure earlier evidence, for example by putting a bookplate on top of an existing one. Provenance will also be a factor in planning conservation work and setting salvage priorities.
2 **Metadata**. Ideally any evidence of provenance should be recorded in an item's metadata (see Chapter 5 for details) and researched further to identify the person or organization concerned. How far librarians can take this research depends on resources. There are fortunately many experts and sources of help available (see Appendix A and note that help can also be sought on listservs, e.g. lis-rarebooks and Ex Libris).
3 **Marketing**. Past owners of books offer stories and, sometimes, the thrill of ownership by famous people, invaluable for marketing and outreach.

Introducing modern formats
Printed books and the industrial revolution

Book production methods changed rapidly during the 19th century, enabling printers and other book industries to meet and build demand from growing mass markets created by increased education. Machine-powered printing presses were developed and hand composition replaced by typesetting machines (e.g. Monotype and Linotype). The supply of rags for paper could not meet the demand: it was largely replaced by **wood pulp**. The cheapest kind, mechanical wood pulp, made from ground-up logs, enabled newspapers and books to be produced and sold in great quantities, but as noted earlier, it is chemically unstable.

The new methods transformed the look and feel of printed books. Heavy, absorbent handmade paper, deeply indented by the hand-press, was replaced by thinner, smoother paper with little or no indentation, which was sometimes very brittle.

Binding was also mechanized and made cheaper: for example the use of ready-made cases and cloth instead of leather. It became the norm for books to be sold in trade or edition bindings. Cloth lent itself to elaborate decoration: witness the beautiful pictorial bindings of the 1880s and 1890s.

The post-1850 book poses different challenges to the librarian from its hand-press forerunners. It needs more care, as its components are often chemically or mechanically weaker. Its printing history can be as complex and it can tell us a great deal about society and culture. Hence many Special Collections are carrying out exciting work on these materials, for example the Cambridge University Library Tower Project, which is cataloguing 19th and 20th century popular books received via legal deposit, many otherwise unknown.

Private press and artists' books

Hand-press and other craft techniques of book production did not, however, disappear. Private presses use these methods to create beautiful books or otherwise explore the text used and the nature of the book format. Many Special Collections collect the books made by private presses, because of their aesthetic qualities and interesting and instructive use of printing techniques.

The private press movement began with William Morris, who rejected what he saw as the shoddiness and alienation inherent in industrial methods of production. He founded the Kelmscott Press in 1891, using incunabula as a model: he developed 15th century style types, used handmade paper and bindings, and integrated text and images in a medieval decorative style. The finest achievement of the Press is the magnificent *Works of Chaucer* (1896).

Morris's ideas were taken up by printing schools, art colleges and other presses, including the Doves Press, founded by T. J. Cobden-Sanderson, who wished to create 'The book beautiful', with a simpler aesthetic than Morris's, and the the Vale, Eragny and Essex House presses. In the 20th century, private presses were set53

up by individual enthusiasts or groups. Their limited edition works often feature careful choice of type, woodcuts or other interesting illustrative techniques, and creative use of high-quality paper in the bindings. Well-known firms include the Golden Cockerel Press and the Rampant Lions Press; current firms include Gwasg Gregynog (which revived the Gregynog Press), the Old Stile Press and the Whittington Press.

Private press ideas are taken further by **artists' books**: 'books, unique or multiple, that have been made or conceived by artists' (Victoria and Albert Museum, www.vam.ac.uk/page/a/artists-books). Such books are usually issued in limited editions, self-published or via small presses, and are a late 20th century artform, generally held to begin in the 1950s with the works of Ruscha and Dieter Roth. **Book arts** and **bookworks** are also used to describe them, along with **livres d'artiste**. Special Collections specializing in art and design often build collections of these fascinating works. Pushing the boundaries of the book form and using unusual methods and techniques, they need special care, but, as we will see in Chapter 9, they can inspire and delight Special Collections users.

Ephemera

Ephemera is defined by the Ephemera Society as 'the minor transient documents of everyday life', such as 'leaflets, handbills, tickets, trade cards, programmes and playbills, printed tins and packaging, advertising inserts, posters' (www.ephemera-society.org.uk). One of the best known ephemera collections is the John Johnson Collection at the Bodleian Library, which contains over a million items. Johnson's definition, quoted in Bodleian Library (1971), was 'Everything which would ordinarily go into the waste paper basket after use, everything printed which is not actually a book …'

Ephemera interests Special Collections users because it was produced to meet the needs of the moment. It is primary source material for those interested in local, social, political history, not to mention the history of printing and design. As the CILIP Working

Party on Ephemera (2003) noted, it can be difficult to acquire, catalogue and manage in conventional ways. However, its format and strong visual appeal means it is perfect for digitization and marketing activities.

Audio and visual media

Alongside printed and manuscript material, Special Collections care for all kinds of audio, visual and audiovisual media, particularly photographs, sound recordings and film. These are often among the most interesting and popular materials held by a service, but they are also among the most vulnerable. As with the other materials in this chapter, librarians need to know the basics of production of these media in order to manage them effectively.

In all cases, the story is one of rapid innovation, seeking easier processes, longer-lasting results, improved reproduction and accessible technologies. For example, in photography, the daguerreotype produced on a silvered copper plate exposed in the camera lasted longer than previous formats but only one copy could be made of an image. Fox Talbot's invention of the negative allowed many prints to be made; the dry negative process and the arrival of film allowed many more people to take up the activity.

However, the rapid pace of change left a complex legacy of multiple formats with varying preservation needs. Artefacts are made of various substances, often hard to identify, and various layers. Photographs and film comprise the support (e.g. paper, glass or film), binder (albumen, collodion or gelatin) and the chemical sensitive to light (often silver). Audio recording tape is made of a polyester backing with a polyurethane binder on top that holds the oxides onto the tape. Plastics, the basis of most modern media, raise many issues. Shellac (used for 78 rpm records) is prone to physical damage. Lambert (2008) cites three 'problem plastics' with inherent vice often found in Special Collections:

- cellulose nitrate and cellulose acetate: films, photographs, architectural drawings and other archival materials
- polyvinyl chloride: gramophone records.

There are no easy answers to the inherent vice of such materials and no such thing as benign neglect: some plastics will harm other items in collections as they decay. Conservation techniques can do little to help these modern media, other than replacing poor quality mounts and other associated materials. However, appropriate storage (low temperature, low humidity, low oxygen) slows the rate of decay. Special Collections holding the most problematic modern media should be aware of these issues and consider surrogacy and discard of original materials or storage with specialist museums.

Conclusion

This chapter offers just a taste of the amazing objects held by Special Collections services and the issues involved in managing them. As we have seen, manuscripts and early printed books require knowledge of their manufacture and meaning to unlock them, along with understanding of the ways in which they can help scholars bring their period to life. While generally more chemically stable than more modern materials, they have suffered damage and dismemberment, and are vulnerable to theft. New manufacturing methods in the 19th and 20th centuries brought books, newspapers, photographs, film and sound to millions. Here the difficulties lie in making sense of the multitude of different processes and formats used and coping with the chemical instability of the materials.

Further reading
Manuscripts
Many medieval manuscripts can be seen online, for example via the Digital Scriptorium, a database of 27,000 images from 30 US research libraries, and the Catalogue of Digitized Medieval Manuscripts, which indexes digitized manuscripts. The following published works are recommended for librarians: overviews in Clemens and Graham (2007), De Hamel (1994) and Parkes (1991), creation of manuscripts De Hamel (1992) and Brown (1990, 1994 and 1998), illumination Watson (2003) and Alexander (1992), and gilding Whitley (2010).

Early printed books
Classic texts on the history of printing: Chappell (1999), Eisenstein (2005), Febvre (2010) and Steinberg (1996). See also Appendix A, which includes details of digitized early printed books. Blogs on incunabula cataloguing projects (e.g. at Cambridge University Library) offer insight into the management of these complex resources.

On particular topics, see Carter and Mosley (2002), Dowding (1998) and Lawson (1990) on type and Hunter (1978) on paper. Recommended overviews of illustration history: Hults (1996) and Harthan (1997); Gascoigne (2004) is a practical guide to identifying techniques.

Key texts on the history and techniques of bookbinding: Pearson (2005), Foot (2006), Lindsay (2009), Miller, Spitzmueller and Jones (2010) and Randeria and Foot (2004). Pearson, Munford and Walker (2010) is a useful guide to caring for bookbindings. Of the many bookbindings on show online, try 'Plain and Simple to Grand and Glorious', an online exhibit introducing many binding topics from Princeton University's Firestone Library, and the British Library's comprehensive Database of Bookbindings.

Bibliography
McKerrow (1994) and Bowers (1994) are the classics; Gaskell (1995) an essential introduction. See also Harris (2004) and Tanselle (2009); Carter and Barker (2004) is a highly readable glossary of bibliographic terms.

Provenance
Pearson (1998, 2011) and Myers, Harris and Mandelbrote (2005) for case studies. Enjoyable online exhibits of provenance include Glasgow University's 'Provenance – the ownership history of books' and the 'Private lives of books', from the National Library of Scotland.

Modern printed works

Gaskell (1995) covers production of modern books; Association of College and Research Libraries (2000a) discusses issues in managing 19th century collections. Histories of artists' books: Bury (1995) and Drucker (2004); Farman (2008) introduces management issues. On ephemera, see by Rickards and Twyman's encyclopedia (2001), and Hudson (2008) for a historical overview. Private presses: Cave (1983, 2001).

Modern formats

Photographs: Clark and Frey (2003) and Clark (2009), which includes a table to help identify the processes used to create images. Audiovisual: Association of Moving Image Archivists (n.d.) storage standards; International Association of Sound and Audiovisual Archives (2005) preservation strategy and ethics. Lee (2009) is a best practice guide for film and sound archives. Plastics: Lambert (2008), Shashoua (2008) and the website of the Plastics Historical Society.

For more detail

See detailed bibliographies and lists of links on the subjects of this chapter:

- CILIP RBSCG links, www.cilip.org.uk/get-involved/special-interest-groups/rare-books/pages/links.aspx
- RBMS Bibliographic Standards Subcommittee web resources for the rare books cataloger, http:// lib.nmsu.edu/rarecat
- reading lists from the Rare Book School, www.rarebookschool.org/reading, and London Rare Books School, http://ies.sas.ac.uk/cmps/events/courses/LRBS/index.htm (of course it's best to attend courses too if possible!).

Examples and case studies

Artists' Book Collection at the University of Wisconsin,
  http://digicoll.library.wisc.edu/ArtistsBks
Artists' Books Online 'a repository of facsimiles, metadata and criticism',
  www.artistsbooksonline.org
Auchinleck Manuscript, http://auchinleck.nls.uk
British Library Database of Bookbindings, www.bl.uk/catalogues/bookbindings/Default.aspx
British Library Diamond Sutra, www.bl.uk/onlinegallery/sacredtexts/diamondsutra.html
British Library Kelmscott Chaucer,
  www.bl.uk/onlinegallery/onlineex/landprint/kelmscott/index.html
Cambridge University Library Incunabula Project,
  www.lib.cam.ac.uk/deptserv/rarebooks/incblog
Cambridge University Library Tower Project, www.lib.cam.ac.uk/deptserv/towerproject
Codex Sinaiticus, www.codexsinaiticus.com/en
John Johnson Collection of Printed Ephemera, www.bodley.ox.ac.uk/johnson
Macclesfield Psalter, www.fitzmuseum.cam.ac.uk/gallery/macclesfield/about

National Art Library at the Victoria and Albert Museum,
    www.vam.ac.uk/collections/prints_books/features/artists_books/index.html
National Library of Medicine copy of Hooke's Micrographia,
    http://archive.nlm.nih.gov/proj/ttp/flash/hooke/hooke.html
Plain and Simple to Grand and Glorious,
    http://libweb5.princeton.edu/visual_materials/hb/hb.html
Private lives of books, http://digital.nls.uk/privatelivesofbooks/index.html
Provenance exhibition at Glasgow,
    www.gla.ac.uk/services/specialcollections/virtualexhibitions/provenance
Unregulated Printing (private presses),
    www.lib.cam.ac.uk/exhibitions/unregulatedprinting/index.html

Useful websites

ARLIS (visual arts and design librarians), www.arlis.org.uk/index.php
Association for Manuscripts and Archives in Research Collections, www.amarc.org.uk
Association for Recorded Sound Collections, www.arsc-audio.org
Association of Moving Image Archivists, www.amianet.org/index.php
Bibliographical Society, www.bibsoc.org.uk; other societies listed here:
    www.bibsoc.org.uk/links.htm
Book-arts L listserv, www.philobiblon.com/book_arts-l.shtml
Bookplate Society, www.bookplatesociety.org
British Library Illuminated Manuscripts Glossary (revised text of Brown 1994),
    www.bl.uk/catalogues/illuminatedmanuscripts/glossary.asp
Catalogue of Digitized Medieval Manuscripts, http://manuscripts.cmrs.ucla.edu/index.php
Centre for Ephemera Studies, www.reading.ac.uk/typography/research/typ-researchcentres.aspx
Consortium of European Research Libraries (CERL), www.cerl.org/web
Digital Scriptorium, http://scriptorium.columbia.edu
Early Book Society, www.nyu.edu/projects/EBS
Ephemera Societies (UK), www.ephemera-society.org.uk and (US) www.ephemerasociety.org
HoBo, History of the Book events, www.english.ox.ac.uk/hobo
International Association of Sound and Audiovisual Archives, www.iasa-web.org
Le Manuscrit Médiéval, http:// blog.pecia.fr
LIBER Manuscript Librarians Group, http://liber-manuscripts.kb.nl/index.html
Plastics Historical Society, www.plastiquarian.com
Society for History of Authorship, Reading and Printing, www.sharpweb.org
Subject Guide to Audio Preservation/Restoration,
    http://guides.lib.washington.edu/content.php?pid=57767&sid=423018
Victoria and Albert Museum, www.vam.ac.uk

4
Acquiring and developing Special Collections

Introduction

In this chapter, we consider:

1 The ways in which libraries acquire Special Collections: foundation collections, donation and deposit, purchase, internal transfer and proactive collecting.
2 How librarians can use these methods to ensure Special Collections are assets, not problems.
3 Record-keeping issues in the acquisitions process.
4 Special Collections disposals.
5 Remote storage of Special Collections.
6 Bringing all these issues together in the Special Collections development policy.

Special Collections may arrive as entire collections put together by an individual or organization, be created from different sources, or a mixture of the two.

Managing foundation collections

These are the libraries that were established or grew along with the organization that holds them. At one time they would have been working books, general collections; time has made them rare and precious. Such collections are typically found in libraries in historic foundations, such as cathedrals or ancient public libraries.

Managing foundation collections is about ensuring their historical importance to their library is recognized and that they are not dispersed. They should be a high priority for preservation and for salvage. The sale or other breaking up of such collections is a great loss and strongly discouraged by professional bodies such as CILIP Rare Books and Special Collections Group (2009a) – more on disposals later.

If foundation collections have already been dispersed, libraries may consider projects to reunite them physically or intellectually. For example, the Sloane Printed Books Project is creating a database of the books once owned by the scientist Sir Hans Sloane, which he bequeathed to the nation and which formed one of the foundation collections of the British Museum Library, now the British Library. Many of Sloane's books were dispersed in different British Library collections, or were sold in the British Museum's 18th and 19th century duplicate sales and are now held by the Wellcome Library and other Special Collections.

Working with donors and depositors

Special Collections and their users everywhere owe a debt to the individuals and organizations that donated to or deposited material with them. Many great Special Collections libraries bear the names of donors: the Huntington Library, the John Rylands Library, the Lilly Library, the Brotherton. ... For convenience, the following refers to 'donors' and 'donations', but 'depositors' and 'deposits' should be understood.

Special Collections donors and donations take many forms:

1 **Level of connection**. Donors may know Special Collections well, or have some other connection, for example a member of academic staff in a university. However, some donors are complete strangers. The donor may be the original creator or collector of the material or an heir seeking a home for inherited material.
2 **People or bodies**. Donors are not always private individuals. Special Collections receive material from political parties, pressure groups, businesses, theatres and many other organizations.
3 **Collections or items**. Material may arrive as entire collections or in small quantities over many years, while the donor is alive, or as a bequest in their will.
4 **Wanted or not**. Donations may fit the Special Collections well, or be completely unsuitable.

Given all these possibilities, managing donations can be one of the most challenging aspects of Special Collections work. This section should be read alongside the section in Chapter 10 on fundraising through 'Individual giving', as motivations and issues are similar. Donors of materials may become financial donors, and vice versa.

Issues in working with donors and donations
Ownership

The most important question: will the material be owned by the library or the donor? If the donor is to retain ownership, it is essential to draw up effective agreements that protect the investment the library will make in the material (storage, cataloguing, preservation).

Sensitive times

Donations often happen at emotional times, for example downsizing to a smaller home or after the illness or death of the original creator or collector. It is important to handle any offer with respect for the feelings of those involved, while making a decision that is right for the library and its users. A written collection development policy, as discussed below, helps make rejections less personal, and understanding the collecting policies of other libraries will help the librarian suggest suitable alternatives. To avoid these difficulties, wherever possible, build relationships with potential donors to encourage donation while they are alive and active in their field. This can be satisfying for both parties, and result in a better resource for users.

Time pressure

Following on from the above, often Special Collections are donated because the place they are housed is to be sold, demolished or otherwise no longer available, for example after the death of the creator. It is important not to let this pressure the library into taking material it would not otherwise have accepted.

The donor visit

It is often helpful to visit a donor's home to see the collection *in situ* and assess its relevance. This can be a fascinating experience, offering insight into the material and the personality of its creator/collector. Many Special Collections librarians have anecdotes about such experiences. Witness the visit of the British Library's Jamie Andrews to writer John Berger's French Alpine home in 2010: the papers were stored in the stables, and the visitor helped with the hay harvest.

Again, be wary of visiting a donor if you already know you are unlikely to accept their material. It is harder to say no when you are in their space and accepting their hospitality. There are also health and safety issues, for example damp, dust and mould in attics, garages and other storage places.

Importance of documentation

Any librarian who has inherited significant collections without any paperwork to indicate their source or ownership will understand how important it is to have proper documentation for donations and deposits.

The donation or deposit agreement must clarify any points that could cause problems later and reassure the donor that the library will take proper care of their material. The documentation must:

1 **Transfer ownership** to the library, or, if the donor is retaining ownership, outline when the arrangement will be reviewed and the notice period for either party to end the arrangement.
2 **Record details of the donor**: name and address (see Chapter 6 for managing this personal data). The donor should be asked to inform the library if these details change.
3 **Identify the material**: type, quantity, provenance, reference. If the material is to be a separate named collection, the name chosen should be agreed: donors may have strong feelings about this issue.
4 **Outline what the library will do with the material**: access, storage, cataloguing, preservation, exhibitions, copying. To avoid future misunderstandings, it is

important to ensure that donors realize that material will be made available to the public unless there is a legal restriction, and that funding for cataloguing and preservation is limited.

5 **Address issues of weeding, disposals and sales**, for example that the material may be weeded in accordance with professional practice, but that it will not be discarded or sold without the donor's permission.

6 **Address copyright issues** (see Chapter 6). If the donor has rights in the material, they should be encouraged to assign them to the library or licence the library to use the material for educational and promotional purposes.

7 **Cover the worst case**: what if the library ceased to exist? Generally the material would be offered to other Special Collections on the same terms.

Clearly the level of documentation and discussion required will vary depending on the kind of material being donated. The donation of a single piece of ephemera that has little or no market value and no emotional value to the donor may be quickly decided and require little paperwork. The donation of large collections of rare books or archives with a high market value may take years of negotiation. However, even the most insignificant donation should be recorded in writing to avoid future problems, and all donors should be properly thanked.

Be wary of taking material on terms that restrict what the library can do with it. Collections taken under difficult terms use up scarce space and other resources and will not fulfil their potential. Occasionally it may be worth accepting such material because of the importance of the collection or donor. This must be clearly agreed and the difficulties must be proportionate to the perceived value of the connection.

A note on 'permanent loan'

The term 'permanent loan' is often encountered in older loan agreements. As the National Archives (2006) guidance on loan agreements notes, the idea is a contradiction in terms, and therefore subject to varying interpretations that cause problems when depositors decide to sell the material. The term should be avoided in new agreements and should be renegotiated, if possible, in existing ones.

Problems with existing deposits

One common problem, especially in libraries that have lacked professional staff, is Special Collections with poor documentation. Historic agreements with donors and depositors may be ambiguous or disadvantage the library.

For example, the papers of landed estates are deposited with many record offices and university Special Collections in Britain. These are immensely valuable for historical research, but are vulnerable if the owners need to realize the market value of these assets. A recent case with a happy ending exemplifies the problems. The Broadlands Archives are huge collections of papers of the Temple (Palmerston), Ashley, Cassel and Mountbatten families, who have played major parts in the history of Britain, India and

Pakistan. The Archives have been on deposit with the University of Southampton, where they have been key resources for social, political and international history. In 2009, the Trustees of the Archives wished to sell them; a successful appeal was launched that raised the £2.8 million needed to buy the Archives for the University.

Ideally, historic deposits should be renegotiated on more favourable terms for the library. However, as with copyright issues (see Chapter 6), these matters can be time-consuming and even impossible to investigate and solve, so it is important to set priorities. If it proves impossible to trace the original source of material, all staff can do is document their actions, and ensure that everything they do with the collection is appropriate.

Even if depositors are known, it will not always be possible to renegotiate. If depositors do not wish to give the material to the library, it could be at risk of removal and sale. Where such collections have high market value and would be a serious loss to the library's work (as with the Broadlands Archives), it is advisable to assess the risks and plan ahead, so that if a sale is announced, the library will be ready to raise funds or take other action.

A note on tax and donations

Librarians can encourage and manage Special Collections donations of materials or funding by being aware of government schemes that offer tax incentives to donate (more in Chapter 10). In the UK, the **Acceptance in Lieu** scheme 'allows people to offer items of cultural and historical importance to the State in full or part payment of their inheritance tax, capital transfer tax or estate duty'. Items are allocated to appropriate heritage organizations, enabling the organizations to acquire an important item at no cost (sometimes one already held on long-term loan). Recent examples relevant to Special Collections include the Archive of Sir Joseph Rotblat, allocated to Churchill College, and private press books produced by Essex House Press, allocated to the Guild of Handicraft Trust.

What about digital donations?

The digital age will see great changes in donation and deposit. If digital files are housed on physical storage in the donor's possession, such as their hard drive or floppy disks, these may reach Special Collections in the same way as paper-based materials. Most collections of papers created nowadays will be **hybrid**: part paper, part electronic.

However, the use of physical digital media like disks is in decline: people do not necessarily hold their digital files in any physical sense. They may read e-books, communicate via e-mail and social media, upload their photographs to Flickr and store their files in the 'cloud'. This means there may be no physical objects for them or their heirs to need to re-home. Files may be hidden behind passwords unknown to others, and licensing may mean that material cannot be used. Individuals may also not see that such material has any historical value, and not consider offering it to a library, whereas printed books, papers, photographs, maps and so on are seen as having historical and financial worth.

This means that libraries wishing to develop their Special Collections with digital material must be proactive, raising the awareness of potential donors and working with them to ensure collections will be received and usable. The work of the futureArch project at the Bodleian offers useful insights for other libraries working with hybrid and born-digital collections. We discuss proactive forms of collecting later.

Purchasing Special Collections

Some Special Collections librarians have acquisitions budgets to spend on enhancing their collections. Many, however, do not, as budgets are squeezed by pressures and cuts elsewhere. They need to build collections via the other methods discussed in this chapter. In either case, fund-raising for a particularly desirable purchase may be required, see Chapter 10 for advice.

Working with antiquarian booksellers

Many purchases for Special Collections will be made from the antiquarian book trade: booksellers who deal in hand-press era printed books, manuscripts, papers and archives, modern first editions, private press books, ephemera and other material that appeals to collectors. Some advice on working with booksellers:

1 **Make links**. Libraries purchasing from booksellers are competing with collectors who can decide to buy instantly. It is therefore worth building effective relationships with book dealers who specialize in the relevant subjects or formats, so they know your collecting interests and inform you when material is available.
2 **Associations**. If possible, deal with members of the International League of Antiquarian Booksellers (ILAB) and the national associations of booksellers, whose members sign up to codes of ethics. These associations also offer databases to help find booksellers with the relevant specialism.
3 **Book fairs** bring booksellers and collectors together en masse. They offer the chance to see a wide range of materials, get a feel for pricing and meet many booksellers. Major fairs include London, New York, San Francisco and York. Find out about fairs via ILAB, the national associations and the Provincial Booksellers Fairs Association. Fairs may specialize in particular types of material, for example ephemera.
4 **Auctions** are a potentially rich source of material for Special Collections. However, they can be tricky for the inexperienced, so it is advisable to use a purchasing agent who will bid on your behalf.

Booksellers can offer other services such as:

1 **Purchase** of unwanted materials from libraries (see disposals discussion below).
2 **Security**. Booksellers, like libraries, suffer from book thefts – whether directly from their premises or by being offered stolen goods. Chapter 2 offers advice on working with them on these issues.

3 **Valuations** for insurance or other purposes.
4 **Knowledge**. Booksellers are often immensely knowledgeable and enthusiastic about historic materials, and their catalogues are full of useful information. Several can be found on listservs such as Ex Libris. In turn, librarians can help with research relating to books in Special Collections.

The trade online

Physical bookshops are becoming rarer, thanks to pressure from internet selling (and, in the UK, charity shops), except for locations such as capital cities, university towns, and 'book towns' like Hay-on-Wye. Increasingly interactions with the antiquarian trade are online. Many antiquarian booksellers have their own websites, through which books can be purchased. Some specialist booksellers now work only online.

There are many websites that offer databases of rare books for sale, from booksellers or, in some cases, from individuals. These are useful to librarians: for finding a book anywhere and for getting an idea of rarity and market value. However, it is important to understand how these databases work and the differences between them.

1 **Cross-searching tools** cover many sales sites, for example Via Libri, which specializes in rare books. These are useful to get a basic idea about what is available, but may not offer the sophisticated searching of individual sites.
2 **Independents** are groups of booksellers, which may have less coverage, but require higher quality standards for descriptions and booksellers. They have strong ethical codes and wish to promote trust between sellers and buyers. These include Booksatpbfa, iBookNet, Independent Online Booksellers Association, TomFolio and UKBookWorld.
3 **Corporate sites** (Abebooks, Alibris, Amazon) offer wide coverage but should be used with caution. Listers may not be experienced booksellers and so may not produce helpful descriptions. False hits and print-on-demand photocopies are a particular problem. Some sites require a high commission; it might be cheaper to deal with the bookseller directly or through an independent site.

Other sources

Depending on the nature of your Special Collections, the material you wish to collect may not be valuable enough to interest the antiquarian trade. Try charity shops and their websites: they tend now to appreciate and price accordingly historic material, which is often transferred to specialist bookshops or advertised on the web. EBay can be useful for acquiring ephemera and local material; however, *caveat emptor*: read feedback, look at descriptions, and ask for pictures if not supplied.

More about tax

As with donations, there may be favourable tax arrangements to support the sale of heritage materials to public institutions. For example, in the UK, items which have been granted conditional exemption from capital taxation can be purchased by **private treaty sale** by a body listed in Schedule 3 of the Inheritance Tax Act 1984 (this could include certain Special Collections); the buyer would pay only 70% or so of the market value and the seller pays less tax.

Managing purchasing

1 **Systems**. A general library will buy new materials regularly from one or two suppliers, whereas Special Collections may buy expensive items occasionally or less expensive items from many different suppliers. They need to work with their financial colleagues to make sure that this is understood and purchases progress smoothly through the library and finance systems.

2 **Prices**. There may be options for negotiations, for example if a library has cared for particular material on deposit that is now for sale, their investment in cataloguing and preservation will have increased its value, which could be recognized by a discount.

3 **Legal**. There may be legal restrictions on what can be sold. For example, in the UK, there are laws concerning the sale of public records such as manorial documents, and the export of archives and manuscripts is subject to restrictions, see National Archives (n.d.).

4 **Ethics**. Purchasing for Special Collections is often a matter of personal connections and knowledge. Librarians must be mindful of their ethical responsibilities (discussed in Chapter 6) and ensure that they do not personally profit (or appear to do so) from transactions undertaken on behalf of the library. If buying directly from an individual, the involvement of third parties to value material is essential. Association of College and Research Libraries (1992) offers detailed guidance.

Purchasing digital archives

It will be interesting to see whether a trade develops around digital materials. These appear to lack the drivers behind collectability that increase market value: uniqueness, provenance, physical presence. Digital archives purchased at present seem to be mainly part of hybrid collections also containing paper, such as the recent purchase by the British Library of the hybrid archive of poet Wendy Cope, which includes 40,000 e-mails 'retrieved from the cloud'.

Organizing internal transfer

Many Special Collections are part of a wider library service. They need policies and procedures for the review and transfer of materials in the main stock that would benefit from transfer to Special Collections. Special Collections staff may systematically seek out items in the main stock, or colleagues may suggest relevant material encountered when shelving, weeding, etc. The ultimate decision about transfer should rest with the Special Collections staff as they will understand the nuances of collecting, though of course in consultation with colleagues. Association of College and Research Libraries (2008) includes detailed guidelines. Barnes, Kelly and Kerwin (2010) reflect on these issues in a case study of a project at Eastern Michigan University to identify material for transfer systematically.

Candidates for internal transfer should include material that is unique, rare, valuable financially or historically, or fragile, for example:

1 **Unpublished material** such as manuscripts, photographs, archives.
2 **Hand-press era books**. Usually a cut-off publication date between 1800 and 1850 is applied, before which everything is automatically transferred to Special Collections.
3 **Later 19th century books** are becoming rare and worth automatic inclusion: a cut-off date of 1900 is now applied by some libraries in their internal transfer policy.
4 **Limited edition formats** such as private presses and artists' books.
5 **Other modern material** may be transferred because of its provenance, fragility, size (very large or very small), market value, rarity or the presence of maps or plates that could be attractive to thieves.

It should be made clear to library colleagues that a move to Special Collections is not the same as storage in a closed stack: the latter essentially relegates material and makes it less likely to be used. A move to Special Collections results in different kinds of use and value.

If Special Collections contain the archives of their own organization, they will need to establish procedures for the transfer of non-current records to the archive service. However, this is part of the records management system and beyond the scope of this Handbook.

Collecting proactively

The above methods concern materials that have already been identified as collectable in some way by individuals, libraries or booksellers. Other sources of Special Collections may create materials from scratch or form collections from objects not otherwise valued. These routes are particularly useful for building collections around popular culture, protest and hidden histories and offer opportunities for involving online and physical communities. They are discussed separately, but will overlap in many collections. See also Chapter 6 on collecting to promote equality and diversity.

Collecting ephemera

Special Collections staff may collect ephemera from the place it was distributed, or encourage others to do so on their behalf. Such material might be of great research value, but without Special Collections intervention, would probably have been discarded. It is particularly helpful for the study of alternative culture, protest, music and illegal activities. The Grateful Dead Archive, based at University of California Santa Cruz, includes 'show files, programs, newsletters, posters, cover art, photographs, tickets and stickers ... stage props, tour exhibit material, and, of course, tee-shirts', vital for understanding the band's touring career and role in the lives of its enthusiasts. Such an archive is a partnership between curators, the band and the fans.

Managing oral history

Oral history records memories of the past. It captures aspects of the history of working class people, migrants or others whose stories may not have appeared in mainstream sources. It may also be useful for aspects of the parent organization's history. See for example the University History Project at Westminster University, which is gathering 'spoken testimony, stories and experience' from alumni from the 1940s onwards. The stories are being added to the University Archive and will appear in a history to be published in 2013, the 175th anniversary of the institution.

The results of such work are invaluable for researchers and learners, and gathering oral history recordings can be an ideal project for volunteers. However, it can be difficult to devise the right questions, manage the technology and, above all, deal with the legal and ethical issues that arise (of which more in Chapter 6).

Digital collections

Unlike paper-based materials that may survive for many years before they become part of a library, preservation and management of digital formats are inextricably entwined, as we noted in Chapter 1. Digital collections are formed in two ways:

1 **Digitizing existing materials** in Special Collections or elsewhere. This brings huge benefits, for example surrogacy, new forms of access, educational use and multiple access points and added value (see Rare Books and Manuscripts Section 2009).
2 **Curating born-digital materials**. As noted in Chapter 1, this term covers many types of material. These are the materials of future history, which merit the attention of specialists to ensure they survive in usable form.

Existing materials may be digitized in-house, on demand for users, as needed for marketing or as part of a project. Erway (2011) includes case studies on speeding up this process and see Birrell et al. (2011) for work on user-driven digitization. They may also be digitized by external commercial firms, as an individual collection or as part of a large-scale digitization initiative (LDSI). Many firms offer digitization services: it is vital to choose the right company and arrangement. See Association of Research Libraries (2010a) guidance on working with firms and further comments in Chapter 1.

'Further reading' offers excellent advice on the details of digital curation beyond the scope of this book. Note, however, key points:

1   Librarians need to understand the life cycle of digital objects: creation, use, management and delivery. Each stage needs careful planning to ensure digital assets continue to be useful and retrievable into the next stage.
2   Collaboration between libraries can offer economies of scale in digitization and digital curation. Smaller libraries may benefit from working with larger organizations that already have the infrastructure for mass digitization. Witness the Life-Share Project in which three 'White Rose' Yorkshire (UK) universities developed collaborative strategies to share digitization skills and equipment and, on a larger scale, the Hathi Trust, a worldwide digital collaboration involving over 50 partners.
3   Choice of software platforms for managing and delivering digital material is critical. Possibilities include digital collection management software, for example Content-DM (from OCLC) and Digitool (from Ex Libris), social and open-source media such as Omeka or WordPress, or the use of an institutional repository (common in universities).

Digital collections appear throughout this book; see in particular Chapter 5 on metadata, Chapter 7 on virtual services and the service side of digitization, Chapter 8 on social media and Chapter 9 on outreach with digital material.

Empowering community collections

Digital materials don't have to belong to, or be housed by, Special Collections to benefit from links to them. They can be created by communities uploading their own content or by enhancing existing material. Community collections can offer cheap, innovative ways of enhancing collections and involving people. To be successful, however, they need to relate to existing online communities or issues that many people find interesting. The Great War Archive, for example, drew on enthusiasm for family and military history, scanning photographs belonging to members of the public and adding the digital images to the online archive. The project is now encouraging German people to share their Great War materials.

Community collections can take advantage of the scale of online communities to carry out work that would be beyond the resources of staff or physical volunteers (**crowdsourcing**), for example transcription of large quantities of handwriting. See for example the Old Weather project, in which online communities are transcribing early 20th century ships' logs to find out more about climate change.

Keeping acquisitions records

As already mentioned when discussing donations, it is essential to keep good records concerning all the matters discussed in this chapter, for transparency and to assist future staff.

Accessioning is the formal acceptance of materials into Special Collections. It should include creating and keeping:

1 **Evidence of transfer of title**, for example a legal copy of the relevant section of a will, a letter from a donor, a formal agreement or paperwork for a purchase.

2 **The accessions record**. In mainstream library practice, the accessions register is obsolete: new materials arrive ready-catalogued so the catalogue is the record, and in any case collections are not kept indefinitely. However, in Special Collections, material is intended to be kept indefinitely and there may be a considerable gap between material arriving in the building and actually being catalogued. So the accessions register is vital to document uncatalogued material. Depending on the nature of the library, paper registers, spreadsheets, databases or the accessioning features of museum or archive software may be used for the purpose. The register is an essential document whose back-up needs to be considered as part of emergency planning.

Managing Special Collections disposals

De-accessioning is the opposite of accessioning: the formal removal of material from Special Collections. This should be a rare activity. Material is added to Special Collections because it is believed to be worth preserving indefinitely. Unlike the general libraries of which they may be part, weeding and disposal of outdated stock is not a natural part of Special Collections work.

However, it may sometimes be appropriate to de-accession Special Collections material. Unsuitable material may have been added, especially if the service has lacked professional management, or collections accepted that would be better suited to other libraries.

There is also the weeding of duplicates and extraneous matter undertaken by librarians and archivists as part of accessioning and cataloguing, and which would not be considered problematic (though donors need to know that it happens). As much effort as is practical should be made to find new home for duplicates and other unwanted material, for example via networks of similar libraries or the listservs.

This issue is complicated by the market value of many Special Collections, which puts them at risk of being sold to raise funds. Collections (especially in public libraries) are particularly vulnerable in the present climate of public sector cuts. The threat is not just that a collection will no longer be associated with the original organization that gathered it, or even that the wishes of the original donor are ignored. Sale often means splitting up collections, which are sold to many different purchasers, and thus can never be reunited. The items will have lost their context, their original meaning and their links with local experts. This was the risk with Broadlands, mentioned above.

Sometimes a solution can be found that results in a collection being kept and given new life. Recently a collection of 14,000 rare books at Cardiff Central Library was threatened with sale, but found a new home with Special Collections at Cardiff University, where a project to catalogue and make it available is now in hand (see Peters 2010). However, universities and other major libraries are under similar pressures to public libraries and are less able to rescue collections than in the past.

Professional associations CILIP Rare Books and Special Collections Group (2009a) and Association of College and Research Libraries (1992) offer guidance on this complex issue; for more on advocacy to prevent inappropriate sales of special collections, see Chapter 10.

Case study: to sell or not to sell?

Dr Williams's Library, an independent library that forms 'the pre-eminent research library of English Protestant nonconformity' (www.dwlib.co.uk), in 2006 took the difficult decision to sell a copy of Shakespeare's First Folio. The care and insurance of the volume was a disproportionately heavy burden, and the volume was not central to the library's mission. The sale fetched £2.8 million. The sale money would be invested in the library's endowment fund to keep it running in the future. Find out more in Ford-Smith (2010). What are the arguments for and against the sale of the First Folio at Dr Williams's? What would you have done?

Managing remote storage of Special Collections

Storing Special Collections outside the main library premises is a useful option. However, it requires careful assessment of risks and ongoing management to ensure that the collections are safely stored and not 'out of sight, out of mind'.

Secondary storage

In Dooley and Luce (2010), a recent survey of US and Canadian research libraries, two thirds of the libraries surveyed had collections in secondary storage. Often known as **out-housing**, this is the removal of stock from prime space in the main building to cheaper alternatives elsewhere. Out-housing keeps collections out of the way of disruption, possible damage and loss during times of major moves and refurbishments. If there is sufficient warning, it may be an option during serious emergencies.

The alternative space may be elsewhere on the premises. If such space is not possible, it is best to use experienced companies, for example in art or records storage. The recent trend for deep storage in salt mines can offer security and an appropriate climate. Collaboration with other libraries may help.

The everyday monitoring and awareness of Special Collections staff will not be available when material is out-housed. Material is most at risk when it is stored in this way indefinitely; during a building project, the material will be expected to return, and its well-being will be part of managing the project. It is vital in all secondary storage to have effective agreements in place with the relevant organization. These should include preservation, security, emergency planning, insurance and access (by the library and by out-house workers).

Specialist repositories

Have you formats that you cannot store safely but which you do not wish to de-accession and, if so, could another library take better care of them for you? Film is a classic example: difficult to preserve, requires specialist skills, for example in identifying deterioration, has different storage requirements and needs equipment to access it. Hence many libraries deposit their historic films with specialist film archives, who can offer these facilities. Find out more about the work of UK film archives on the Film Archives UK's website (http://filmarchives.org.uk)..

Introducing the Special Collections development policy

As the above shows, acquiring and disposing of Special Collections are complex matters, involving financial risks and long-term consequences. Poor collecting decisions commit indefinitely scarce and expensive resources to inappropriate materials that could have been used for more worthwhile collections.

A Special Collections development policy helps prevent this, offering many benefits:

1 **Strategic thinking**. It is impossible for libraries to take or buy everything that they might consider or be offered. Even national libraries face constraints and decisions. Policies to manage these processes and decisions help to align day to day decision-making processes with the long-term purposes of Special Collections.
2 **Directing resources** of the parent organization by allowing staff to accept appropriate material, and empowering them to refuse unsuitable collections.
3 **Dealing with offers**. Even libraries with a static Special Collection and no plans for growth need a policy to help staff respond to offers of material.
4 **Better collections for users** as policies try to direct material to the most appropriate homes, to libraries that can care for them, and where there are clusters of related materials and expertise.
5 **Public accountability and transparency**, enabling the library to explain the rationale for its spending choices.

Special Collections development policies vary in size and complexity, depending on the nature of the Special Collections, and policies may be needed for individual collections or groups of collections, subject areas and formats. Where Special Collections are part of a main library, their policy may form part of the overall library collection development policy. However, the complexity of Special Collections issues may overwhelm the wider policy, in which case separate documents work better.

A development policy should be a public document, made freely available on the library's website and shared with libraries collecting in similar areas and national or other bodies who have an interest in collection policies (e.g. the UK's National Archives). This will help others direct relevant donations or materials for sale to your service.

A template suited to Special Collections can be found in Smyth (1999) and many Special Collections development policies are published online. Darbey and Hayden (2008) write about developing such policies for the first time for an organization and Potter and Holley (2010) review current collecting trends in Special Collections. Smyth's article also looks at the purposes of creating such a policy, exploring arguments against it. As we emphasized when considering the emergency plan, such documents are frameworks for action, not ends in themselves.

Writing the Special Collections development policy

However simple or complex the final document, the following should be considered in creating the development policy.

1 **Mission**. As noted in Chapter 1, a library needs to be clear about its mission: why does it exist, and why does it have, and add to, Special Collections? Mission is perhaps most important in collection development, because if a library has not considered its purpose, its resources may be wasted on material that is not relevant, and that material never find its audience.
2 **History**. Special Collections have much to do with the story of the organization to which they belong. For example, the library may seek to recover physically or virtually foundation collections lost, stolen or sold in the past.
3 **Audiences**. Who uses Special Collections? What material would help them? Is the library interested in attracting different audiences? Audience issues are discussed in Chapters 7–10.
4 **Existing collections**. Strengths and weaknesses? Gaps? Which collections are open or closed? This should consider past surveys of collections and note whether more surveys are needed.
5 **Scope of collecting**. This can be defined by geography, timescales, languages, formats or subjects. Collection strengths and any gaps should be taken into account, along with practical issues, for example audiovisual formats need particular equipment and care.

For book collections, policies on editions (firsts, impressions, dust jackets, reprints, paperbacks, translations) and duplicates are needed. It could be argued that there is no such thing as a 'duplicate' copy of an early printed book, or even many modern books. Once books have been owned, annotated, handled, re-bound, given book plates and so on, two volumes from the same impression become distinct artefacts.

Don't forget to include material to support work on collections by users and staff: e.g. databases, directories, textbooks, professional literature (see Appendix A for some suggestions).

The policy may also consider issues of diversity and hidden histories, for example more collections and work around local communities: discussed further in Grob (2003). Mass digitization of early books, as discussed in Chapter 1, may encourage Special Collections services to collect in new areas where they can add value.

6 **Legal issues**. See Chapter 6. Key areas to cover in the policy include: ownership and title, copyright, and data protection/freedom of information, which may limit access.

7 **Preservation issues**. The condition of material is a factor. Will you take items in poor condition and if so under what circumstances? What about conditions that might harm other collections, for example active mould? Collections in poor condition have health and safety implications and higher costs in making available.

8 **Methods of collecting**. The materials acquired by purchase may need to be more closely defined than those that would be accepted as donations. It is also usual to mention the use of an agent for bidding at auction.

9 **Collecting policies of other libraries**. How does the collecting policy fit in to the bigger picture? Who else collects in your subjects and region? Can you work together for mutual benefit? Existing formal or informal collecting agreements should be included in the policy.

10 **Decision making**. The policy should outline who makes decisions about what to accept for Special Collections. This depends on the governance of the parent organization. For most accessions, the decision should rest with the Special Collections librarian, in discussion with other staff and stakeholders as appropriate. The librarian should have the veto, as they will know more about the legal and preservation issues involved and the relevance to other libraries' collecting policies. However, when major new collections are added, particularly ones that are large or likely to be expensive to care for, the buy-in of senior management or governing body is vital to ensure resources will be made available.

11 **De-accessioning**. The library's position on de-accessioning Special Collections and the standards followed when so doing, for example CILIP Rare Books and Special Collections Group (2009a).

12 **Review**. The policy should be reviewed regularly, to cover issues that have caused problems, the impact of new collections and changes in technologies and practices.

Case study: collecting half the world

The Women's Library collects library, archive and museum objects 'to preserve, document and explore women's lives in the United Kingdom of Great Britain and Northern Ireland (UK) in the past, present and future, to inspire learning and debate through the collections and related programmes, and to act as an international resource for women's history research' (www.londonmet.ac.uk/thewomenslibrary/aboutthecollections/collectiondevelopment). Given the overwhelming collecting possibilities this mission offers, the Library copes by setting priorities, for example actively collecting second wave feminism and young women's experience in the early 21st century for the next five years. Collecting scope is precisely defined, chronologically, geographically and by format; for example the policy states exactly what kind of press cuttings are collected. Different priorities are set for different collections: on the archive side, the Library will collect biographical and campaign-related material as part of their responsibilities to the future, whereas museum collecting will focus on current audience development and exhibitions. Their precise but inspiring policy enables the Library tactfully to refuse unwanted donations without causing offence.

A note on desiderata

A collection development policy is not intended to accommodate the operational fine detail of individual titles unless they are exceptionally important to the mission, or very expensive to acquire. Instead, **desiderata** lists can be maintained, recording the particular books required. Such lists enable librarians to respond quickly to offers of material for sale or donation, can be shared with book dealers, partner organizations and donors, and used to create wants lists on the online sites discussed above.

Conclusion

Special Collections grow by donation and deposit, purchase, internal transfer from a general library, and a range of proactive, community-based methods. All these methods have their pitfalls; this chapter has outlined some ways to manage them based on best professional practice. We have also reflected on what to do when collections outgrow their space and how to cope with the complex issues relating to disposal of Special Collections material. By creating effective policies and collaborating with other libraries, Special Collections librarians are better placed to help their service develop as part of a network of collecting organizations making resources available in the most appropriate home.

Further reading

Digital collections: useful guidance on digitization in Bülow and Ahmon (2011), in Harvey (2010) on digital curation and in Terras (2008) on digital images. See also the JISC Digital Media help sheets and the Life-Share digital toolkit.

Community collections: Bastian and Alexander (2009) and the RunCoCo website.

Examples and case studies

Bodleian Electronic Manuscripts and Archives (FutureArch), www.bodleian.ox.ac.uk/beam
British Library: acquisition of Wendy Cope archive, http://pressandpolicy.bl.uk/Press-
    Releases/-Some-sort-of-record-seemed-vital-British-Library-acquires-the-archive-of-Wendy-
    Cope-4e6.aspx, and John Berger visit, www.bl.uk/johnberger/index.html
Broadlands Archive, www.southampton.ac.uk/archives/Broadlands/index.html
Cardiff rare books,
    www.cardiff.ac.uk/news/articles/investment-secures-rare-book-collection-5676.html
Grateful Dead Archive, http://library.ucsc.edu/gratefuldeadarchive/gda-home
Great War Archive, www.oucs.ox.ac.uk/ww1lit/gwa
Old Weather, www.oldweather.org
Sloane Printed Books Project,
    www.bl.uk/reshelp/findhelprestype/prbooks/sloaneprintedbooksproject/sloaneprinted.html

University History Project Westminster,
>   www.westminster.ac.uk/about/archive-services/university-history-project

Women's Library Collection Development Policy,
>   www.londonmet.ac.uk/thewomenslibrary/aboutthecollections/collectiondevelopment

Useful websites

Acceptance in Lieu scheme, www.mla.gov.uk/what/cultural/tax/acceptance_in_lieu (moving from MLA in 2011)

Antiquarian Booksellers' Association, www.aba.org.uk

Antiquarian Booksellers' Association of America, www.abaa.org

Antiquarian Booksellers' Association of Canada, www.abac.org/english.html

Australian and New Zealand Association of Antiquarian Booksellers, www.anzaab.com/Anzaab

Digital Curation Centre, www.dcc.ac.uk

Film Archives UK, http://filmarchives.org.uk

FutureArch, www.bodleian.ox.ac.uk/beam/projects/futurearch

Hathi Trust, www.hathitrust.org

International League of Antiquarian Booksellers, www.ilab.org

JISC Digital Media, www.jiscdigitalmedia.ac.uk

Life-Share, www.leeds.ac.uk/library/projects/lifeshare/casestudy.html

London International Antiquarian Book Fair, www.olympiabookfair.com

Look here!, www.vads.ac.uk/lookhere

Private treaty sales, www.mla.gov.uk/what/cultural/tax/private_treaty

Provincial Booksellers Fairs Association, www.pbfa.org

RunCoCo projects, http://projects.oucs.ox.ac.uk/runcoco

UKOLN, www.ukoln.ac.uk

5
Cataloguing, description and metadata in Special Collections

Introduction

In this chapter we discuss the essential first step in bringing Special Collections to users: creating metadata, which makes public detailed information about collections. This chapter will:

1 Introduce Special Collections metadata.
2 Outline the most important codes, standards and controlled vocabularies for Special Collections metadata.
3 Discuss key developments: linked data, Functional Requirements for Bibliographic Records/Resource Description and Access (FRBR/RDA) and the future of Machine Readable Cataloguing (MARC).
4 Discuss issues in managing Special Collections metadata creation, including the massive problem of 'hidden collections'.
5 Discuss classification of Special Collections.
6 Discuss processing of Special Collections materials.

Many Special Collections librarians have cataloguing responsibilities. All need to understand how the collections in their care have been catalogued, in order to help users and make effective decisions. Librarians new to cataloguing are advised to learn the basics before engaging with the complexities of Special Collections material.

A note on terminology and some key concepts

Here we consider established ideas and methods; new developments are outlined later.

Cataloguing of books, manuscripts and other Special Collections material is based on the idea of **descriptive cataloguing**: describing a copy of a particular edition to enable it to be distinguished from other items (author, title, publication details and details of pagination), following a set of rules. The end product is known as a catalogue record. Users find the record via indexes known as **access points** (names, titles, subjects and other key elements). These are created using **authorities** or **controlled vocabularies**, which bring possible index terms into a system of headings, again constructed according to rules.

As Chapter 3 explained, materials in Special Collections are usually more complex than those in general libraries. Each book in Special Collections is a unique artefact, and for user service, marketing, preservation and security it is essential to have **copy-specific** information (i.e. unique to that copy, e.g. bindings, provenance). Traditional library cataloguing did not consider such matters, as they were not relevant to most librarians or users, hence, as we will see, the development of additional standards for Special Collections materials.

The cataloguing of archives is often known as **description**. It differs from the descriptive cataloguing of books in the concepts of hierarchy, and in the fields included. Description of archives centres on levels: Collection (or **fonds**), Series, File, Item. Collection-level descriptions can also be useful for collections of books. Methods of cataloguing archives in the USA and Canada are more closely linked to the descriptive cataloguing of books than in the UK. Archive catalogues are often known as **finding aids**.

Metadata can be simply defined as 'data about data'. Library catalogues and archival descriptions are metadata, though the term is most commonly encountered when dealing with digital materials. Metadata for such material tends to be embedded within it, whereas catalogue records and descriptions for non-digital material may exist separately from the material they describe. **Crosswalks** map similar elements in different metadata standards onto each other. The match is unlikely to be perfect because different standards record and code information in different ways, but they enable resources to be created from many sources using different metadata.

Note that the term **processing** is often used, especially in the US, to cover cataloguing and other activities required to make materials accessible. Here it is taken in the UK sense: marking up physical materials.

Standards and codes for cataloguing printed books
All metadata creation is based around the use of standards and codes, which produces searchable and predictable results and allows metadata to be shared and reused.

The most important standard in cataloguing library materials is the **Anglo-American Cataloguing Rules** (2nd edition, AACR2; Gorman and Winkler, 1978, and revised several times since). Most Special Collections parent libraries use AACR2. The Rules advise cataloguers how to create a catalogue record, how to select and record information about an item's title, author, publisher, edition and so on, and which headings to use and how to create them.

MARC (Machine Readable Cataloging) formats are used to make records available on computer systems. At first different countries developed their own version of MARC. MARC21, the current version, united the US and Canadian formats. Librarians may still encounter UKMARC or the other MARC formats. MARC has developed fields to meet the needs of Special Collections for copy-specific information in catalogue records, for example 563 for binding information, 561 for ownership history and 026 for 'fingerprints' (explained below).

Special Collections librarians may also see references to **ISBD (A)**. This is an International Standard Bibliographic Description (ISBD) for 'antiquarian' books, or 'older monographic publications'. ISBDs were created by the International Federation of Library Associations (IFLA) to create standard form and content for bibliographic descriptions, so they could be exchanged internationally; the consolidated version (2007) supersedes ISBD (A).

Useful catalogues for rare books and other Special Collections can be created using AACR2 and MARC21, as AACR2 includes sections on the cataloguing of early printed monographs and other rare materials. However, these sections have limitations in dealing with the complexities we have already mentioned, hence the development of the following specialized codes for these resources.

DCRM (B), Descriptive Cataloging of Rare Materials (Books) was published in 2007 by ACRL (Association of College and Research Libraries and Library of Congress 2007). Like its predecessors, Bibliographic Description of Rare Books (BDRB), created by the Library of Congress for its cataloguers, and the second edition, Descriptive Cataloging of Rare Books (DCRB), it interprets and enlarges AACR2's section on early printed books. Unlike its predecessors, designed for cataloguing hand-press era books, DCRM (B) is suitable for cataloguing rare books of any age, reflecting the growing variety of materials in Special Collections. 'DCRM (B) emphasises transcription where AACR2 allows interpretations, requires fuller description or transcription of certain elements, and provides more detailed guidelines for supplying copy-specific detail than AACR2' (CILIP RBSCG Bibliographic Standards website).

These enhancements enable DCRM (B) cataloguers to create metadata that is more relevant to the needs of Special Collections users. The website includes lists of specific differences between the two codes and the changes between DCRB and DCRM (B).

Special Collections librarians may also find the other manuals in the Descriptive Cataloging of Rare Materials suite useful. Serials (Association of College and Research Libraries and Library of Congress 2008) is published, Graphics, Manuscripts, Cartographic and Music in progress; keep in touch with developments via the RBMS Bibliographic Standards Committee and the DCRM-L listserv.

Standards and codes for cataloguing manuscripts and archives

Manuscripts and archives require different approaches to metadata to unlock their complexities for users. Examples of the two extremes from Procter and Cook (2000):

1 **The historical manuscripts library**, for example manuscripts in the British Library: collections of medieval or early modern manuscripts (like those we met in Chapter 3), best catalogued in detail as individual items with distinct structures and provenance.
2 **The public records service**, for example the Public Records Office (now part of the UK National Archives): modern archival collections, where the context of items and how they relate to others matters more.

Most large Special Collections contain elements of both, for example organizational archives and early manuscripts.

AACR2 includes a chapter on cataloguing manuscripts. However, as with early printed books, experts identified a need for more detailed guidance if pre-modern manuscripts were to have entries on library catalogues (many would already be covered in printed or card catalogues). This was supplied by the **Descriptive Cataloging of Ancient, Medieval, Renaissance, and Early Modern Manuscripts** (AMREMM) by Pass (2003) published by the ACRL. AMREMM expands on AACR2, using insights from the creators of printed catalogues such as historians and art curators as well as cataloguers.

The cataloguing of archive collections is a distinct discipline, part of the training of professional archivists. Two principles are at the heart of archival description:

1 **Respect des fonds**: the archivist's take on provenance. Records with different origins or provenance are kept separately to maintain this distinction.
2 **Original order**: the archivist maintains the original order of the material, if it can be ascertained, so that the way the records were used by their creator can be understood.

Archival collections also differ from other Special Collections because of the concept of **hierarchy**. The **fonds** or collection breaks down into series, then files and finally items, for example a particular letter to an author might be in the file 'Letters to keep 1951', in the Correspondence series within the author's collection of papers. Materials might be catalogued at collection, series or file level, not necessarily item. This approach is encapsulated in the **Manual of Archival Description (MAD3)** by Procter and Cook (2000), widely used in the UK and a useful introduction to archival cataloguing theory. MAD3 uses AACR2 where appropriate but argues that archival description is based upon different principles.

Archival cataloguing standards used in the US and Canada have tended to build more closely on AACR2 and to integrate with library catalogues. **Describing Archives: a Content Standard (DACS)** was produced by the Society of American Archivists (2004). It superseded a similar standard called Archives Personal Papers and Manuscripts (APPM), which may still be encountered. **The Rules for Archival Description (RAD)** is produced by the Bureau of Canadian Archivists (2008).

Whichever standard is used, archivists need to be aware of **ISAD (G) 2**, the 2nd edition of the **International Standard Archival Description**, developed by the International Council on Archives (2000). Like the ISBDs, it is intended for general guidance to be supplemented with more detailed rules. It includes 26 elements, though only 6 are compulsory, and can be used for collection or multi-level cataloguing.

Encoded Archival Description (EAD) was developed to encode archival descriptions. It maps to ISAD (G) fields and is designed to work with multi-level descriptions. It is based on Extensible Mark-up Language (XML), an open-source set of rules for structuring online information. The Archives Hub data creation pages offer a helpful, non-technical introduction to EAD. **Encoded Archival Context (EAC)** is another XML standard, for information about the creators of archives.

More metadata standards

Dublin Core is probably the best-known metadata standard (as distinct from cataloguing codes), containing 15 basic elements, all optional, with possibilities for extension and use of controlled vocabularies. Dublin Core is invaluable to Special Collections as a straightforward way of providing metadata for digital materials, because it is designed for **aggregators**, websites or software that gather and bring together in one place information from across the web.

Cataloging Cultural Objects (CCO) (Baca et al. 2006) is a set of guidelines for cataloguing art, architecture, paintings, photographs, sculpture, prints, performance art and other cultural objects, published by the American Library Association. Complementing AACR2, it is intended for use in libraries and archives as well as museums and art galleries, and will be invaluable for the many Special Collections services that care for cultural materials. It can be encoded using MARC or Dublin Core as well as specialist visual arts coding. Other standards for arts materials include Visual Resources Association (VRA) Core Categories for the Descriptions of Works of Art (CDWA).

Controlled vocabularies for Special Collections metadata

Cataloguers index authors, subjects and other matters that might interest users, with the help of **controlled vocabularies**. These prescribe words, phrases or headings to be used in indexes, eliminating spelling varieties and synonyms. **Thesauri** are vocabularies for particular subjects, **authority headings** organize people's names, titles of books and so on, and **subject indexes** bring order to the subjects of books.

General libraries use vocabularies such as **Library of Congress Subject Headings (LCSH)** and **Library of Congress name and title authority headings**. These are also suitable for Special Collections, offering scope for the needs of rare materials (of which the Library of Congress (LoC) has many!).

Other controlled vocabularies were created for Special Collections and other heritage materials. These vocabularies help librarians to create catalogues to meet the growing needs of researchers who are interested in collections as artefacts (as discussed in Chapter 3) and are looking for examples of a book format, binding, paper or typeface rather than a particular topic or author. All are freely available online unless otherwise stated.

The RBMS Controlled Vocabularies for the cataloguing of rare books and other Special Collections are maintained by the Bibliographic Standards Sub-Committee of the RBMS. They are used with MARC field 655. A couple of examples show the level of detail covered by these essential sources:

- **binding terms**, for example Moiré doublures, Middle Hill boards, Mottled calf bindings
- **genre terms**, for example Abedecaria to Zines

- **paper terms**, for example Lace-papers, Leatherette, Lumps
- **printing and publishing evidence**, for example Dittography, Dummies, Duodecimo
- **provenance evidence**, for example False association copies, Fists, Sammelbands
- **type evidence**, for example Grotesque Types, Ascenders, Tail-pieces.

The **CERL Thesaurus** is managed by the Consortium of European Research Libraries (CERL). It unites authority files created by CERL members and other libraries for names of places, people and organizations in Europe during the hand-press era. The thesaurus brings together variant forms of headings as a useful research tool, but unlike other thesauri does not impose its decision about which form a library should use. The thesaurus can be used to enhance local databases using remote software.

The **Getty Vocabularies**, maintained by the Getty Research Institute, are compiled by Getty-funded projects and other libraries, archives and museums. They contain 'structured terminology for art, architecture, decorative arts and other material culture, archival materials, visual surrogates, and bibliographic materials' (www.getty.edu/research/tools/vocabularies/index.html).

- the **Art and Architecture Thesaurus** (AAT)TM
- the **Getty Thesaurus of Geographic Names** (TGN)TM
- the **Union List of Artist Names** (ULAN) TM
- the **Cultural Objects Name Authority** (CONA) TM, due for release in 2012.

The vocabularies are available online for limited use, with licensing available for more frequent users. Obviously invaluable to collections specializing in art and architecture, the range of subjects covered means the Getty Vocabularies are also helpful to other Special Collections. Many terms relating to printed books, manuscripts, archives and other Special Collections materials are included, for example a search for 'book' in AAT produces types of book such as **coffee-table books** and **chapbooks**, and many kinds of book furniture.

Thesaurus for Graphic Materials (TGM), produced by the Prints and Photographs Division of the Library of Congress, offers subject headings and genre/format terms for 'photographs, prints, design drawings, ephemera, and other pictures' (www.loc.gov/pictures/collection/tgm). The thesaurus links to Library of Congress images containing that index term.

Archivists have also developed thesauri and rules for authority headings to meet the needs on archival collections and users. These include the National Council on Archives **(NCA) rules** (National Council on Archives 1997), which are based on AACR2, and the International Standard Archival Authority Record For Corporate Bodies, Persons and Families **(ISAAR (CPF))** (International Council on Archives 2004), which complements ISAD (G) 2. The **UNESCO** (1995) thesaurus is used by some archive services for subject terms and names of countries.

There are many other possibilities that Special Collections with particular subject or format strengths might consider. Libraries may have developed in-house vocabularies for specialized areas in the past. It is advisable now though to explore the potential of external vocabularies, as these offer more options for sharing and cross-searching.

A note on fingerprints

The **bibliographical fingerprint** is an important tool in the study of early printed books. It is a sequence of characters taken from particular places in the text that acts as a unique identifier for the book. Here are two ways to create a fingerprint:

1 The **LOC project**, a London–Oxford–Cambridge collaboration on a proposed union catalogue, developed a method consisting of 16 characters: 'four groups of two pairs of symbols taken from the last and penultimate lines of four specified pages, one pair of symbols per line' (see Institut de recherche et d'histoire des textes 1984).
2 The **Short Title Catalogue Netherlands** (STCN) fingerprint, 'made by entering the signature of certain pages, followed by the piece of text in the bottom line that is directly above the signature. The chosen pages are the first and last of the preliminaries, main text and appendices' (www.kb.nl/stcn/vingerafdruk-en.html).

In library catalogue records, fingerprints are entered in MARC field 026. The fingerprint is invaluable for cataloguers and bibliographers 'to detect variant settings of type in otherwise matching editions and to identify the reuse of the same setting in ostensibly different editions. It can also act as an identifier for any printed work, assisting identification of partial texts' (McKnight (n.d.)). Harris (2009) offers more detail on fingerprints.

Introducing RDA and the future of MARC

The world of cataloguing is changing. A new code, **Resource Description and Access (RDA)**, has been developed by the Joint Steering Committee for Development of RDA (2010) to replace AACR2. RDA is based on the **Functional Requirements for Bibliographic Records (FRBR)** model, produced by an IFLA Study Group (1998).

The model moves away from the idea of reproducing a traditional catalogue record. Instead it considers relationships between three groups of objects, known as entities:

1 Work, Expression, Manifestation, Item. A Work is abstract, an artistic or intellectual creation that is seen in the realizations or Expressions of the work. A Manifestation is the physical embodiment of an Expression, and an Item is a particular copy of a Manifestation.
2 Person, Corporate Body. People creating, revising, distributing, or curating the physical group 1 entities.

3 Concept, Object, Event, Place. The subjects of the group 1 entities, for example abstract ideas, material objects, occurrences, geographical locations.

FRBR is expanded with **Functional Requirements for Authority Data** (FRAD), which takes a similar approach to the creation of authorities.

By adopting a functional approach, RDA avoids the main difficulty with using AACR2 in the digital age. The latter splits materials by format, with different rules for, say, cartographic materials and electronic formats. In the RDA approach, the Work is central and format changes are dealt with at a lower level. FRBR and RDA offer great potential for Special Collections where works, people, subjects and the relationships between them are more complex than could be expressed on catalogue records, physical or digital.

RDA is still being tested; not all libraries using AACR2 will necessarily decide to change. RDA records are compatible with AACR2 records and MARC21, though several differences are immediately obvious, for example RDA avoids the use of abbreviations, so the Latinisms used to express unknown publishers and places of publication (s.n. and s.l.) will no longer be used.

Special Collections cataloguers have of course joined in the RDA consultations, via RBSCG, RBMS and other groups. As we saw above, DCRM (B) and other guidelines used in Special Collections are based on AACR2. Those responsible for these guidelines and librarian and user communities will therefore need to review them in light of RDA and decide whether to adapt them to the new guidelines or to take a different route.

The future of the MARC formats is also being debated. MARC formats served libraries and their users well in moving library functions onto electronic and online media from the 1960s onwards. However, as the potential of the web has developed, the necessity of creating digital catalogue records is being questioned. In May 2011, the Library of Congress announced a consultation on the future of the MARC formats, to end in 2013. To keep in touch with and contribute to these developments, follow the Library of Congress consultation website, RBMS, RBSCG and the listservs.

Introducing linked data and the semantic web

The **semantic web** goes beyond the internet we know, the 'web of documents' linked together by hypertext links. It aims to create a 'web of data' by using standards that create **linked data**, enabling users to find related data easily (quotes from the World Wide Web Consortium (W3C) website).

These ideas have great potential for bringing users and Special Collections data together. Of course, linking metadata from many organizations is nothing new, witness the catalogues listed in Appendix A. However, linked data transforms these beginnings. Like FRBR and the RDA, linked data means metadata need no longer be about rendering catalogue records digitally, but can instead focus on particular 'things' that may interest users (things being authors, owners, creators, places, titles, volumes …) and the relationships between the things. This may help to get Special Collections metadata and content out of data silos and into places where users will find it.

Two JISC-funded projects are exploring the potential of transforming Special Collections metadata into linked data. The Sussex Archive Linked Data Application (SALDA) project at Sussex University is converting Mass Observation Archive metadata held on Calm archival software to linked data that will then be made publicly available. Linked Open Copac Archives Hub (LOCAH) is converting metadata on the Archives Hub and Copac (see Appendix A) into linked data. The project blogs reflect on wider issues in linked data and discuss the technical issues involved.

Working with community metadata

As well as creating collections (see Chapter 4), communities can help supply metadata. A technique based on work with groups of users, Revisiting Archive Collections, Reed (2009), is a toolkit for 'capturing and sharing multiple perspectives on archive collections' from communities or individual experts. It outlines how to run sessions with communities, and what to do with the resulting information. This methodology works best with visually interesting material created within living memory, for which enthusiastic communities can be traced. It is unlikely to work well for all Special Collections and facilitating such sessions involves considerable staff time and effort. More on working with communities in Chapter 9.

Understanding hidden Special Collections

Most Special Collections services have large quantities of uncatalogued materials. These are often called **backlogs**, but the term **hidden collections** is more accurate: 'First, it's not a backlog because a backlog implies that there's a flow, and what we have here is an unexcavated well. Nothing is flowing; that's the point' Mandel (2004). 'Hidden collections' implies material that is unknown and inaccessible, a long-term problem. Other hidden collections may be poorly catalogued or catalogued only on cards or other paper formats. Collections in small libraries, for example in historic houses, may be hidden because there is no automation; larger libraries may have the technology but not the staff to do the work.

So why do we have what Tabb (2004) calls libraries' (and archives') 'dirty little secret'? The problem has been long in the making: past practice of accepting gifts without any prospect of cataloguing them and long-term lack of resources available for this complex work. Many writers also blame 'our insistence on high-level catalogue records and finding aids' (Clement 2004), which demands considerable resources. New acquisitions, collected under rigorous modern collecting policies as outlined in Chapter 4, tend to jump the queue and become high priority, because they were acquired with use and value in mind, pushing the hidden collections further out of sight.

Hidden collections take up precious resources (especially scarce space) but offer no benefits. Instead they pose many problems for librarians:

1 **Accessibility**. They cannot easily be made available to users or exploited in other ways.

2 **Preservation**. Unrequested and ignored, they are more likely to suffer neglect.

3 **Security**. If uncatalogued materials are stolen, how can anyone know, or prove that theft has taken place? Recovery of stolen material would be very difficult.

4 **Stress and frustration** for staff, prospective users and donors of collections, who may become angry that their collection has not been made available.

5 **Reliance on staff knowledge** rather than catalogues: when staff leave, that information is lost.

Further concerns are listed in the White Paper produced by the Association of Research Libraries (ARL) (Jones 2003): a key text for understanding hidden collections in the USA.

The scale of the problem is immense, as shown in recent surveys. A recent Research Libraries UK survey reported by García-Ontiveros (2010) mentioned 11 million items awaiting cataloguing in the libraries covered, most in Special Collections. An OCLC survey (Dooley and Luce (2010), which covered 275 US and Canadian libraries, found that while coverage of books had improved since the 1998 ARL (Panitch 2000) survey (85% were catalogued), cataloguing of other formats, especially visual, was still very limited.

Librarians have made concerted efforts to tackle the problem. **Retrospective cataloguing** is the process of cataloguing material that is not new to the library but which has not yet been catalogued, or which is covered only by non-automated catalogues, for example card catalogues (the latter is also known as **retrospective conversion**). The latter was sometimes well funded in the earlier days of library automation, for example in the UK using funding made available as a result of the Follett Report. However, the quality of records produced by retrospective conversion varies. Some was done book-in-hand by expert cataloguers, others by less skilled staff matching card catalogues or basic facts about author and title to union catalogues, with misleading results.

More recently in the US and Canada a huge effort has been made to admit to and discuss the problem, following on from the shocking results of the ARL 1998 Survey (Panitch 2000). The White Paper mentioned above is at the heart of this. The 2004 issue of *RBM: a Journal of Rare Books, Manuscripts and Cultural Heritage* is a useful online introduction to the discussion at the time (including several articles already cited); catch up on later developments in Hubbard and Myers (2010).

Managing hidden collections

Managing hidden collections has much in common with the preservation management techniques covered in Chapter 1. In both situations librarians need to set priorities and develop plans to manage vast quantities of problem materials. They should also avoid adding to the problem by considering support for cataloguing and other management when acquiring new material (see Chapter 4).

The first step in dealing with uncatalogued material is to survey it, to understand its origin, nature, format and possible significance and use. In larger libraries this is in itself a massive task. It may include looking at the material itself, checking old paperwork and finding out what colleagues already know about it. Yakel (2005) outlines several methodologies used to assess hidden collections. Some material may not be relevant to the library and can be rehomed or discarded. Priorities then need to be set for the remaining material, based on the mission of Special Collections, demand from users and strategies such as teaching requirements or interest in enhancing diversity.

Libraries new to automated cataloguing are strongly advised to select widely used standards and systems, creating structured metadata with the potential for future sharing and other innovations. This also enables them to acquire catalogue records from other libraries.

New or hidden Special Collections should not automatically be catalogued to the highest level. For many Special Collections materials a 'quick and dirty' approach, for example cataloguing at collection level, will suffice to make the material accessible, saving a great deal of staff time and making it possible to use existing people or interns. Lundy and Hollis (2004) discuss an interesting pilot project that redeployed existing staff to work on a mountaineering collection in the University of Colorado at Boulder libraries. Libraries whose hidden collections include archives are advised to explore the concept of 'minimal processing', as explained in Greene and Meissner (2005), which involves letting go of certain standard archivist activities in order to bring material and people together more quickly.

However, the 'quick and dirty' approach has risks:

1 If copy-specific details of rare books are not recorded, it may not be possible to know if or prove whether theft or mutilation have occurred. Loose single-sheet items like ephemera or photographs could be lost without trace.
2 Modern materials may have data protection or confidentiality issues that require detailed examination.
3 It can increse demand for information about collections that cannot be satisfied.

It therefore requires more careful management than simply trying to catalogue everything to the highest standard. Quantifying the problem as suggested may help to convince senior management that it is not caused by mismanagement but is a historic concern, possibly resulting in more support. Wider initiatives can help, for example thanks to the US efforts mentioned earlier, the Council on Library and Information Resources (CLIR) Hidden Collections funding programme was created (www.clir.org/hiddencollections). In the UK, the National Cataloguing Grants Scheme has helped catalogue many archives (www.nationalarchives.gov.uk/information-management/our-services/cataloguing-grants-programme).

A note on access to uncatalogued Special Collections

Librarians need to decide whether to allow users to access hidden collections and, if so, to what extent. It is natural to wish to help users by allowing access. However, in so doing librarians need to consider the security and legal risks outlined above for basic cataloguing.

There are also practical problems. Procedures that are simple when handling catalogued material become much more difficult with uncatalogued collections, for example how can users request material if it has no reference? How can they reorder what they have seen before, cite it or request copies of it? With a large, complex collection, such issues become unmanageable.

If users are frequently seeking access to a particular uncatalogued collection, it should be moved up the priority order for cataloguing and fund-raising. Such requests are evidence of interest that will appeal to funders.

A note on historic catalogues

In many libraries, Special Collections are catalogued, but in multiple catalogues and **legacy formats**, for example guardbooks, card catalogues, published lists and bibliographies; the Old Catalogues web page at Cambridge University Library shows how complex the situation can become. Librarians need to understand historic cataloguing practice in order to help readers. Catalogues may have quirks well known to long-established colleagues, whose knowledge may be lost when they leave.

Catalogues that exist only in one form, in one place are vulnerable. The card catalogue of the Norfolk Local Studies collection was lost in the fire mentioned in Chapter 2 (Hammond, 1996): not only was the collection lost but the knowledge of what had once existed was also destroyed.

Material covered only by historic catalogues should be considered as part of the hidden collections to be catalogued online to modern standards. However, historic catalogues, even when no longer relevant as tools to access the collections, remain valuable as part of the history and fabric of the library, and as a source of evidence about the Special Collections.

Working with volunteers in Special Collections

As the discussion above suggests, helping librarians to tackle hidden collections is perhaps the most compelling use of voluntary staff in Special Collections. Preservation, digitization and transcription are other activities on a scale where such extra help is needed (this can be remote, as we saw in Chapter 4). Volunteers can also help with market research, stewarding at events and oral history recording.

Like other Special Collections users, volunteers come from many backgrounds and have various motives for becoming involved:

1 Aspiring librarians or other professionals, often known as interns, gaining paid or unpaid experience before, during or after professional study.
2 People building other skills, for example practical conservation skills, possibly for re-employment. This is often an area in which libraries can find grant support from heritage preservation bodies (see Chapter 10).

3 People seeking personal enjoyment or who have some link or commitment to the service, for example family historians with an interest in the sharing of particular resources, former colleagues, trustees, retired librarians.

Using volunteers is not always an easy or cheap option. Issues include:

1 **Ethics**: see Chapter 6.
2 **Preservation and security**: see Chapters 1 and 2. Volunteers should handle fragile material only when trained and security issues must be considered when planning work.
3 **Time**. The use of volunteers requires staff time to organize and train them, and puts pressure on space and facilities. Depending on the nature of the services and the collections, the benefits may not always justify this.

Managing volunteers in Special Collections is as challenging as managing paid staff. They may have different expectations and priorities from the rest of the service and are under less obligation, so may miss time, be late or leave without notice. Structure and policies are helpful to both sides, for example whether expenses are paid or not. Volunteers should be offered training and induction, and made aware of what is offered and expected.

New professionals often find it difficult to manage older, established volunteers who may know the library far better than they do. This is a matter of confidence and experience, of valuing and learning from the volunteers' abilities while being secure in one's own professional and managerial skills. In some libraries, volunteers organize and train each other, notably family historians working on transcripts. However, librarians still need to be aware of what is being done and offer support and guidance as appropriate.

Becoming involved with university programmes that help students find paid or voluntary work can be an excellent way to find good workers and show commitment to university strategies (boosting student employability for example). The National Association of Decorative & Fine Arts Societies (NADFAS) offers trained Heritage Volunteers, best known for cleaning books but also able to assist with preservation, cataloguing and stewarding routines. Friends' groups (discussed in Chapter 10) can also help channel volunteers.

Working with the library management system

Special Collections in a general library will have access to its library management system (LMS), sometimes known as an integrated library system (ILS). These systems are used to manage library functions, usually split up into modules for each function. Well-known systems include Aleph (ExLibris), Millennium (Innovative Interfaces), Horizon and its successor Symphony (SirsiDynix) and Talis.

Special Collections are probably most likely to be interested in the Cataloguing and Online Public Access Catalogue (OPAC) aspects of the LMS, though Acquisitions may be used for purchases and Circulation for checking books in and out of the reading room. Systems are being developed to take advantage of the possibilities of social media and new technology that may help Special Collections users, for example adding tagging facilities, mobile services and digitization or electronic records management packages.

Special Collections staff should take an active part in the choice of a new LMS, considering, for example, the display of the MARC fields for rare material, diacritics for foreign languages, working with records without ISBNs and authority control for names and other controlled vocabularies. They also need to work closely with systems staff to ensure that the catalogue display works for Special Collections material.

The LMS may meet all Special Collections systems needs. However, they do not work well with archival description below collection level, and may not be suitable for circulation and acquisitions in Special Collections, so separate databases and systems may be necessary. Special Collections in archive or museum settings may use systems designed for these services, for example CALM or Adlib.

Classifying special collections

Physical Special Collections need to be effectively organized on shelves and given **shelfmarks** that enable staff to locate them and users to request and cite them easily. Shelfmarks are also known as **call numbers** or **classmarks**.

Some Special Collections of printed books use a subject classification scheme, such as Dewey Decimal or the Library of Congress, especially if books have been transferred from the general library. However, Special Collections do not necessarily have to be physically organized by subject schemes. Closed access material does not need to be browsable and many collections cover such specific subject areas that a subject scheme would be meaningless, i.e. every book would be at the same number.

The order in which physical Special Collections are placed on shelves may derive from the historic organization of a collection or its preservation needs. In particular, a system based on size may be necessary, for example large volumes, rolled items or very small books need to be shelved separately to avoid damage. Author or title order may be appropriate for some collections, for example books by an individual author.

The standard subject classification schemes are also not suitable for medieval manuscripts, whose subject matter is so different from modern published works. Traditionally, manuscript library shelfmarks have been based on the name of the last private owner, with extra designations for donations or other additional material. For example, the Auchinleck Manuscript mentioned in Chapter 3 has shelfmark NLS Adv MS 19.2.1, which shows its current home to be the National Library of Scotland (NLS) and its donor the Advocates Library. The language is also sometimes part of the shelfmark.

Collections catalogued following archival methods are usually arranged in hierarchical systems based on their context rather than by subject, with files numbered in a logical way reflecting the shape of the system.

Processing special collections

As mentioned earlier, **processing** (as used in the UK) means marking library materials in order to:

- identify them as the property of the library
- identify a particular copy
- enable a copy to be shelved in its proper place.

When processing printed books in Special Collections, a balance between these aims and Special Collections issues is needed:

1 **Preservation**. Staff processing Special Collections need to be fully trained in careful handling. As discussed in Chapter 1, materials used with Special Collections should be of archival quality: paper, glue, ink. If the library management system uses barcodes or Radio Frequency Identification (RFID) tags, these can be associated with a book without having to be stuck into it, for example by being attached to a Mylar wrap or archival quality slip inside the book. It is often at this stage that material is put into better containers for preservation reasons (e.g. archival envelopes, file folders, Mylar dustjackets) or otherwise conserved or treated. It makes sense to do this before it is further damaged by being made available to the public. Even if funding is not available at the time, the preservation needs of new material should be recorded so that they can be tackled later.
2 **Provenance**. Processing should respect and avoid damaging provenance evidence, for example old shelfmarks, booksellers' notes, binders' labels. If book plates are used, they should not cover text or images.
3 **Security**. As mentioned in Chapter 2, at least one marking in a book should be irreversible. A discreet stamp, embossed or using archival quality ink, means that the book is more likely to be returned if stolen, and removing it will result in mutilation that reduces the value of the book. For more technical detail and advice (see Association of College and Research Libraries 2009a). Note the advice that material be marked up on accession rather than waiting for cataloguing, for security reasons.

Other materials in Special Collections are likely to be processed more lightly than printed books. This is partly for preservation reasons (it would be hard to find somewhere to put a bookplate on a single sheet item) and partly because of time factors (archives contain thousands of individual items). Archive materials may simply receive a pencilled number on the item.

A note on printed books vs archives

The cataloguing and processing of material that does not fit neatly into the categories of printed books or archives can cause problems. Many Special Collections have different storage, access, cataloguing/processing and staff for their printed book collections and their archival collections, so a decision that seems minor can make a difference to future accessibility. Such material includes heavily annotated printed books, material inserted in books, ephemera and published material in archives. Nicholson (2010) discusses the issues around personal libraries (e.g. of writers, often heavily annotated); and these matters regularly crop up on the listservs. Falk and Hunker (2009) share their experience of cataloguing other tricky formats, for example zines, popular fiction and film scripts, at Bowling Green State University.

There cannot be hard and fast rules for issues with so many permutations; libraries need to develop policies and procedures to fit their situation and users. Initiatives such as ephemera collections, copy-specific book cataloguing and using crosswalks may help. In a wider sense, managing printed books and archives with a vision of their overall value as Special Collections will be useful, especially as the use of printed books becomes more about their physical nature and story and less about the text, increasingly available online.

Conclusion

Creating effective metadata is one of the most important aspects of Special Collections work. It is not an end in itself but the first step in marketing materials to potential users. There are several standards and vocabularies to help capture the richness of detail in Special Collections and changes in thinking and coding may make it possible to share more information than ever before, in new ways, moving from the library automation idea of reproducing catalogue cards digitally. However, librarians face great challenges in managing the vast hidden collections gathered by their libraries. As so often in this book, these can be managed if not eliminated by effective planning, collaboration, exploring new ideas and technologies, and facing up to the situation.

Further reading

Many textbooks cover the above topics, including other works published by Facet. In addition to the sources cited, the CILIP Rare Books and Special Collections Group (2007a) guidelines on cataloguing rare books are essential.

Volunteers: Lindsay (2011) is a practical guide to working with volunteers in archives, Ray (2009) a report, also from an archives perspective, that includes many case studies. Driggers and Dumas (2011) is a comprehensive toolkit for US libraries employing volunteers.

Examples and case studies

LOCAH linked data from the Archives Hub and COPAC, http://blogs.ukoln.ac.uk/locah
SALDA linked data project for the Mass Observation Archive, http://blogs.sussex.ac.uk/salda
The Old Catalogues at Cambridge University,
    www.lib.cam.ac.uk/catalogueguides/oldcatalogues.html

Useful websites
Codes and standards
CCO, http://cco.vrafoundation.org

CDWA, www.getty.edu/research/publications/electronic_publications/cdwa/index.html

Dublin Core, http://dublincore.org

Encoded Archival Description, www.loc.gov/ead

Getty Vocabularies, www.getty.edu/research/tools/vocabularies/index.html

Key differences between AACR2 and DCRM (B),
www.cilip.org.uk/get-involved/special-interest-groups/rare-books/
bibliographic-standards/pages/key-differences-between-aacr2-and-dcrmb.aspx

Key differences between DCRB and DCRM (B), www.cilip.org.uk/get-involved/special-interest-groups/rare-books/bibliographic-standards/pages/dcrmb.aspx

Library of Congress authorities, http://authorities.loc.gov

Library of Congress consultation on the future of MARC,
www.loc.gov/marc/transition/news/framework-051311.html

MARC21, www.loc.gov/marc/bibliographic

RBMS Controlled Vocabularies for Use in Rare Book and Special Collections Cataloging,
www.rbms.info/committees/bibliographic_standards/controlled_vocabularies/index.shtml

Thesaurus for Graphic Materials, www.loc.gov/pictures/collection/tgm

VRA Core, www.vraweb.org/projects/vracore4/index.html

Groups, blogs, listservs
Autocat (US) listserv, www.cwu.edu/~dcc/Autocat-ToC-2007.html

Cataloguing Futures blog, www.catalogingfutures.com/catalogingfutures

CILIP Cataloguing and Indexing Group, www.cilip.org.uk/get-involved/special-interest-groups/cataloguing-indexing/pages/default.aspx

CILIP Rare Books and Special Collections Group Bibliographic Sub-Committee,
www.cilip.org.uk/get-involved/special-interest-groups/rare-books/bibliographic-standards/pages/catguide.aspx

DCRM-L listserv, https://listserver.lib.byu.edu/mailman/listinfo/dcrm-l

High Visibility Cataloguing blog, http://highvisibilitycataloguing.wordpress.com

Lis-ukbibs listserv, https://www.jiscmail.ac.uk/cgi-bin/webadmin?A0=lis-ukbibs

Planet Cataloging blog aggregator, http://planetcataloging.org

RBMS Bibliographic Standards Committee,
www.rbms.info/committees/bibliographic_standards/index.shtml

Other useful sites
Archives Hub, http://archiveshub.ac.uk

CERL thesaurus, http://thesaurus.cerl.org/cgi-bin/search.pl

NADFAS, www.nadfas.org.uk

Revisiting Collections, www.collectionslink.org.uk/programmes/revisiting-collections

STCN-fingerprint, www.kb.nl/stcn/vingerafdruk-en.html

World Wide Web Consortium, www.w3.org/

6
Legal and ethical issues in Special Collections

Introduction

This chapter will cover:

1 Basics of legal and ethical issues in Special Collections.
2 Intellectual property, particularly copyright.
3 Data protection and freedom of information.
4 Cultural property.
5 Personal integrity.
6 Ethics in fund-raising.
7 Equality, health and safety, and working with children.

Coping with legal and ethical matters is one of the most important and difficult aspects of managing Special Collections. These matters are important because they crop up throughout Special Collections work and, if not managed properly, can have serious consequences for the organization. Furthermore, Special Collections librarians have 'extraordinary responsibilities and opportunities associated with the care of cultural property, the preservation of original artefacts, and the support of scholarship based on primary research materials' (Association of College and Research Libraries 2003).

The following factors make legal and ethical issues difficult to manage:

1 **Complex legal situations** (especially, as we will see, copyright law). It can be hard to be sure whether an action is legal or not. Legislation is frequently amended, and understanding of the law is further refined via interpretations in court decisions.
2 **Grey areas**: often there is no 'right' answer and a balance between conflicting values has to be found. 'When values come into conflict, librarians must bring their experience and judgment to bear on each case in order to arrive at the best solution, always bearing in mind that the constituency for special collections includes future generations' (Association of College and Research Libraries 2003).

Readers are reminded of the note in the Introduction: the author is not a lawyer, and offers these suggestions to assist in practical management. Libraries are advised to seek expert advice before taking any particular action that may have legal consequences.

The laws relevant to Special Collections vary between countries. This chapter highlights general points; space prevents dealing with the complexities of each law in each country: 'Further reading' and 'Useful websites' (below) offer more detail on individual countries.

Understanding copyright in Special Collections

Intellectual property (IP) rights are a group of rights relating to 'creations of the mind: inventions, literary and artistic works, and symbols, names, images, and designs used in commerce' (from the World Intellectual Property Organization (WIPO) website). They include laws relating to **copyright, moral rights, trademarks, patents** and **designs**.

Copyright is probably the IP right that is most relevant to the work of Special Collections librarians. Copyright law, like the other IP rights, is created by individual countries, though there are international treaties and arrangements, notably the Berne Convention, which sets out minimum copyright durations and protects authors' rights in other countries.

Special Collections librarians managing modern materials deal with a mixture of third-party copyrights, organizational copyrights and unknown copyrights. They need to balance the rights of copyright holders with the desire to help users, and consider the risk of litigation for infringement. Copyright affects all aspects of Special Collections work (especially preservation, user services and marketing) and should be considered in all policies and procedures.

Copyright is becoming harder to manage in the digital age. Copyright law evolved when copying was not easy or universally possible (the English copyright law tradition began with the Statute of Anne in 1710). It is struggling to keep pace with innovations. The ease of digital reproduction methods and the ease of access to material on the internet mean that users have different expectations about availability.

What is copyright?

In the English common law tradition, followed in the USA and other English-speaking countries, copyright is an **economic property right**: the author or creator of a work is the **copyright holder** and has the right to benefit from the economic results of their work for a certain period of time; this right can be sold or bequeathed by the author as with any item of property. Others cannot make copies, publish or perform a work without the permission of the copyright holder: known as **infringement**, this can result in court action. When contacted, the copyright holder may refuse permission, or waive or charge a fee.

Which materials does copyright cover?

Copyright applies to many kinds of material in Special Collections: **literary** (text-based) works, **artistic** productions such as photographs, maps and artworks, software, databases and typographic layout. Works covered by copyright have to be **original** in some way; quality is irrelevant. Copyright does not apply to ideas, facts or trivia such as book titles.

Who are copyright holders and how long do their rights last?

Copyright becomes very complex once we consider holders and durations of copyright. A single Special Collections object may have several copyrights and other IP rights, held by different people or firms and lasting for different periods. For example, the layers of rights in a film will include the images in the film, music, design and screenplay.

Copyright may be held by the author or creator of the work, joint authors, their employer, governments or companies. The holder can **assign** (transfer) copyright, or license other people or bodies to do certain activities. Ownership of copyright is independent of ownership of a physical object containing the work: Special Collections may own a manuscript but not necessarily the copyright of the work it contains.

The Berne Convention requires copyright to be automatic: it comes into existence as soon as a work is recorded. If their country has a copyright office, copyright holders (including Special Collections) may find registering with them helpful, for example to act against infringements.

Copyright lasts for a fixed period of time. How long it lasts varies between countries, types of material and with dates of creation or publication. This variety causes many difficulties for Special Collections librarians. Usually the fixed period is dated from the date of death of the author or from the date of publication/creation for an anonymous work. The Berne Convention has a minimum of life of author plus 50 years for most kinds of published material, but countries can allow longer, for example plus 70 for the UK. Australia is now plus 70, Canada and New Zealand are plus 50.

Duration of US copyright law is particularly complicated, as the American Library Association (ALA) website explains, 'any work published before 1923 is in the public domain, but the copyright status for copyrighted works after 1923 can be difficult to determine because of varying copyright registration requirements over the years and because the term of copyright has changed a number of times'. Useful tools for working out duration can be found on the ALA's copyright web page, including the Public Domain Slider; Hirtle (2011) is a useful chart.

Special Collections holding musical or artistic works, photographs or films should note that the law in these areas is complex and does not necessarily follow the standard patterns for literary works. Take UK copyright law relating to photographs. The first copyright holder for photographs created before 1 July 1912 and after 1 August 1989 is the creator of the photograph (usually, the photographer); between those dates, the holder is the person who owned the material on which the photo was taken (possibly the photographer's employer).

Librarians should be wary of making assumptions about age and copyright. Until 2011, the oldest published work still in copyright in the UK and still protected was a poem published in 1859, 'The Sea Girt Home', by Jessie Saxby, who died in 1940 (Minow and Hirtle 2010). In the UK, all unpublished literary works are in copyright: the former perpetual copyright was removed in the 1988 Act, replaced by a further 50 year term: many materials will come out of copyright in 2039.

Exceptions to copyright

Special Collections services are restricted in what they can do with materials in copyright whose rights have not been assigned to them. However, copyright legislation allows for some exceptions to copyright for educational and cultural purposes. These exceptions vary considerably between countries, may not apply to all types of library and may exclude certain types of material.

Fair use and fair dealing

This relates to uses of copyright material that the law considers fair and may apply to particular activities by individual users. In the US, Section 107 of the Copyright Code allows 'fair use' of a copyrighted work, for purposes that include teaching, scholarship or research, i.e. many Special Collections purposes. Factors to consider include the purpose of the use, the nature of the work, the amount used and the effect of the use on the market. The ALA website includes a Fair Use Evaluator to help librarians assess whether what they intend to do is legal.

In the UK, the law around fair use is more restrictive: it is unlikely to apply to any activity carried out by librarians; however, it may cover digital photography by users.

Australian law includes a variant: **flexible dealing**. The Copyright Amendment Act 2006 includes section 200 AB, a flexible exception that can be used by libraries and archives for 'certain socially useful purposes'. Simes (2008) discusses the possibilities, which include format-shifting, use of orphan works (discussed later) and digitization.

Copying by libraries and archives

Where fair use is not relevant, legislation permits libraries and archives to carry out certain activities without permission, for example copying for preservation or on behalf of users. The former may seem to be an obvious public benefit, but legislation restricts materials, methods and number of copies allowed, and which organizations may copy for preservation.

In the US, Section 108 of the US Copyright Code allows libraries and archives to make copies for certain purposes without permission, subject to certain criteria. Crucially for Special Collections, these purposes include preservation (three copies, certain criteria, e.g. non-commercial use only) and copying literary texts for users (including whole copies if a new or used copy is not available at a 'fair price'). The Section 108 Spinner on the ALA website is a useful introduction.

In the UK, The Copyright (Librarians and Archivists) (Copying of Copyright Material) Regulations 1989 and subsequent amendments apply to copying. Libraries/archives in non-profit organizations may supply whole copies of unpublished or small parts of published literary, dramatic and musical (not artistic!) works for non-commercial research, subject to various stipulations. Preservation copies for reference only may be made by any libraries/archives of literary, dramatic or musical works in their permanent collections.

In Australia, preservation copying is permitted: 'key cultural institutions' (i.e. state libraries and national archives; other libraries can apply for this status) can make up to three copies from the work for the purpose of preserving against loss or deterioration. For more guidance, see Australian Libraries Copyright Committee and Australian Digital Alliance (n.d.). For New Zealand's exceptions, see Millett (2011).

Licensing

If no exceptions apply, then any copying in Special Collections needs a licence:

1 **Blanket**, for example with societies or licensing agencies such as the Newspaper Licensing Agency (UK) or the Copyright Clearance Center (USA). While these may not be helpful for the rare or unique materials held in Special Collections, it is worth finding out what is available, particularly for collections with modern holdings.
2 **Open**, for example Creative Commons licences, which allow the holder to keep copyright while allowing certain uses of the work (or to place it in the public domain).
3 **Case by case (transactional)**: the copyright holder grants permission for a particular use of a particular item.

Tracing copyright holders

To obtain a transactional licence, the library must trace the copyright holder to ask permission. This can be difficult and time-consuming. Exhibitions, digitization and other projects dependent on third-party permissions need to allow time for research and to bear in mind that, when located, the copyright holder may refuse permission or charge higher fees than the library can afford. It is therefore good practice to build strong relationships with key copyright holders, to assure them that Special Collections staff understand their rights and points of view.

Information about copyright holders may be found on the object itself or in paperwork relating to it. If these yield no results or cannot be followed up, other useful sources include:

- Writers, Artists and Their Copyright Holders (WATCH) and Firms Out of Business (FOB) databases at the Harry Ransom Center: copyright contacts for writers, artists and vanished firms
- copyright offices (USA and Canada)
- publishers
- 'collecting societies' and other rights holders, for example Design and Artists Copyright Society (DACS), who manage visual arts rights
- professional associations, for example of photographers

- libraries, archives, museums holding relevant collections. Art galleries such as the National Portrait Gallery can be particularly useful
- trade journals
- wills of former copyright holders.

Attempts made to trace copyright holders should be recorded, so the library can prove **due diligence** should there be a query later.

Managing orphan works

What if a copyright holder cannot be found? Their name may not be associated with the work or, if their name is known, they may be impossible to trace. Works in this situation are known as **orphan works** and are in a kind of legal limbo. Being unable to identify or contact a copyright holder is not a legal defence against infringement, but librarians may not be able to find anyone to give them permission. As Korn (2009) says, 'Works of little commercial value but high academic and cultural significance are languishing unused, access to an immense amount of this material essential for education and scholarship is badly constrained and scarce public sector resources are being used up on complex and unreliable compliance.' This quotation is from a survey that estimated that 50 million orphan works are held in the UK public sector, many in Special Collections.

Attempts are being made in many countries to alter legislation to unlock this material: in the UK, the Hargreaves (2011) report recently made recommendations to enable digitization and use of orphan works.

Meanwhile, libraries may decide to take a risk-managed approach to using orphan works, as publishers do, asking, is the library likely to be sued for this? Factors to consider include whether the work was created for commercial purposes (which means the holder is more likely to sue) and what the library intends to do with the work. These risks can be quantified, for example the online risk management calculator produced by web2rights is useful for UK librarians. Risk can be reduced by a prominent disclaimer on the website and effective procedures for taking down material that has been queried. Projects may budget for contingency funding to pay copyright holders if they come to light so that items can remain online and insurance for higher risk uses could also be considered. The Strategic Content Alliance website contains useful advice on managing orphan works in the UK.

Case study: peace protest photos

The PaxCat Project at Special Collections, University of Bradford, UK (funded by the National Cataloguing Grants Scheme), catalogued archives of material relating to peace protest since the 1950s. Staff wished to digitize items from the collections for marketing, but most of the material is third-party copyright, including many orphans. A risk-managed approach was used in order to get these long-hidden collections the attention they deserve, but avoid the University ending up in court. What do you think would be the risk of using the following?

1 A flyer for a 1960s peace march, created for a defunct pressure group whose archives are held at the University, creator unknown.
2 An amateur photograph of the march, by an unknown photographer.
3 A professional photograph of the same march, by a named professional photographer who cannot be traced, despite due diligence.
4 A professional photograph of the same march, rights now held by an easily traced picture library.

Special Collections staff used their judgment in making these decisions; here we run these examples through the web2rights calculator, which agrees with the assessments of these experienced staff. Item 1 and Photo 2 are very low risk (6 and 7). Photo 3 is higher risk (560). Photo 4 is much higher risk (5600). The PaxCat Project would digitize and place online 1 and 2, but not use 3 and 4: the project's funding was too limited to take such risks. Procedures are in place in case there are queries about the digitized material that has been used.

Copyright and Special Collections users

Librarians should take care in dealing with requests to publish or otherwise use orphan works or other copyright material. It is the users' responsibility to ensure they comply with the law, and librarians should avoid appearing to authorize infringements. Ensure that the proper signs about fair dealing appear at any self-service copiers and that declaration forms are used as appropriate, for example for copying under library/archive exceptions. In addition, librarians can try to educate users in copyright issues relating to Special Collections, for example via web pages or teaching.

Organizational copyrights and Special Collections

Special Collections may manage organizational copyrights (e.g. in a university's historic material) and copyrights that have been assigned or licensed. While this is easier than dealing with third-party copyright, there are still decisions to make, for example who will be allowed to use these materials and under what circumstances? What will be done if infringements are found? The answers will depend on whether income can be or should be raised from the material, for example licensing publishers to use it. In many libraries, the benefits of making material freely available will outweigh the possibilities of income generation. It is of course possible to have both sets of benefits, for example putting low resolution versions of images online to enable people to see them and decide whether they wish to purchase better quality images for publication. For example, the Wellcome Images picture library allows free download 'for personal, academic teaching or study use, under one of two Creative Commons licences', but charges for prints, larger files, new photography and publication (more on income generation in Chapter 10).

Copyright and other IP rights of course apply to the material staff produce in the course of their work in Special Collections, for example metadata, academic articles or web pages. Copyright in these would usually be held by the employer. Most are written to explain or publicize Special Collections or to contribute to scholarly debate, so the copyrights have little financial value. However, some Special Collections staff work on innovative digitization software or other products with financial value. In these situations, and when working with external partners, freelancers and people not employed by the same organization, it is essential to define who holds the rights.

Other IP rights and Special Collections

Special Collections librarians need to be aware of the other IP rights, which also vary between countries. In particular, **moral rights** give the authors the right to be identified as such and to object to 'derogatory treatment' of the work. These rights have to be asserted, and, unlike other rights, are not economic. They cannot be sold or transferred though they can be waived. Those holding sound and audiovisual material need to be aware of **performers' rights**: actors, dancers, musicians and other performers have rights in their performances. Other IP rights relate to databases and trademarks.

Introducing data protection and freedom of information

These areas of law are about access to information. Data protection (DP) law aims to keep personal information gathered by government bodies private and to allow individuals to know what information is held about them by government. Freedom of information (FOI) legislation aims to give people access to information held by government and other public sector bodies. Special Collections librarians need to understand them because:

1 Collections may include personal data about individuals, for example survey answers, oral history.
2 Records gathered for managing Special Collections contain personal data, for example contact details of collection donors.
3 Their organization may be subject to FOI legislation.
4 If Special Collections includes the organizational archives/records management function, it may be responsible for managing these issues.

Again, legislation varies considerably between countries. In the UK, DP and FOI apply to many Special Collections. This is often not the case elsewhere. However, even if these areas are not covered by law, the principles of openness and respect for data about people should be considered in managing Special Collections.

DP and FOI in Special Collections

Any service holding modern records needs to be aware of its responsibilities. Where many collections are held, it may be impossible to go through all in search of personal data, in which case the riskiest collections should be highest priority. It is often impossible for libraries to know or ascertain the dates of death of the many individuals named in their collections or records: assuming a lifespan of 100 years is suggested.

Good practice is essential in acquisitions and cataloguing to minimize problems with user access. Oral history is a particularly tricky area. As Ward (2003) emphasizes, without **informed consent** the laws of copyright and data protection make it difficult to share these recordings. More advice can be found on the Oral History Society website. Caution in the wording of metadata is advisable, to avoid inadvertently sharing information that is closed. For guidance and examples, see National Archives et al. (2007).

Good practice for FOI is good practice for access. Materials should be made available unless there is a good reason not to do so. It is difficult to defend blanket bans on access. Donors and depositors need to be made aware that collections will be used. Note that the situation relating to deposited archives and FOI in the UK is complex: see National Archives (2005).

DP and Special Collections records

Special Collections services need to collect and keep personal data about individuals: collection and financial donors, copyright holders, enquirers, visitors. The data may be needed indefinitely, as relationships with donors, copyright holders and many enquirers are lifelong. Association of College and Research Libraries (2009a) advises that checkout records such as call slips 'should ... be retained indefinitely in order to be available to law enforcement authorities if thefts or vandalism later come to light'. Librarians need to:

1 Act as an intermediary rather than giving out personal data, for example forward an e-mail with a copyright enquiry to the copyright holder.
2 Keep correspondence and other paperwork about donation/deposit/purchase with Special Collections records rather than in the collection it concerns.
3 Use mailing lists responsibly (see Chapter 8).
4 Ensure visitors cannot see personal data, for example on a staff computer in the reading room.
5 Create a retention schedule for Special Collections records so that data is not kept by default.
6 Be careful about what is said in e-mails, social media and other public spaces about identifiable individuals. This may lead to complaints, even legal action.

Further advice on DP and FOI in the UK can be found on the websites of the Information Commissioner and the National Archives.

Case study: call slip commotion

A major public library in the US created a small online exhibit on their blog about surviving call slips of famous individuals who had used the library in the 20th century. In comments on the site and on listservs, librarians came to different conclusions about this use of call slips. Some librarians believed the exhibition should not have been created, arguing that these records should not have been kept in the first place, and it was not appropriate to display them: a librarian should keep a user's reading activity confidential. Others observed that laws about privacy did not apply to the dead and the books on the call slips were not in any way scandalous or surprising. Some observed that records of reading were an invaluable resource for researching writers: perhaps serious research was acceptable but not blogging about them? When do records cease to be records and become historical evidence? The use of records of reading is perhaps a particularly sensitive issue in the US because of the Patriot Act, which enabled the authorities to access library records of reading.

Introducing cultural property issues

This is one of the most difficult issues in Special Collections management. Millennia of conflict and trade mean Special Collections have received items from all over the world, sometimes via illegal or ethically doubtful activities by someone in the long chain of transfers. Should materials acquired by such methods be returned, and if so how? Or should they remain in the institution that has taken care of them and made them available? More generally, considering the worldwide nature of Special Collections, does cultural property belong to the region or nation which created it, or to the world? Museums and art galleries encounter these issues because of the high market value and desirability of the items they collect. Rare books, medieval manuscripts and archives also have immense market and symbolic value: witness calls to move the Lindisfarne Gospels from the British Library to the North-East where they were created; the British Library would argue that it is obliged to provide access for all to material whose importance reached far beyond its original region. In most cases there are powerful arguments on both sides and no easy answers.

However, there are situations in which the moral rights of the original owners are so strong that legal mechanisms have been created to enable libraries and other organizations to return material easily. For example, the Spoliation advisory panel in the UK 'resolves claims from people, or their heirs, who lost property during the Nazi era, which is now held in UK national collections' (www.culture.gov.uk/what_we_do/cultural_property/ 3296.aspx), and return is made possible via the Holocaust (Return of Cultural Objects) Act 2009. The work of the panel led to the return of the Beneventan Missal to Benevento in 2010. The manuscript, thought lost, was bought by a British soldier from a bookseller in Naples in 1944, acquired at auction for the British Museum in 1947, and later transferred to the British Library (which cannot de-accession British Museum material without special arrangements).

These issues should be considered when acquiring material for Special Collections. It is essential to ensure that whoever is giving or selling material has title to it and to be sensitive to issues around sacred books and other materials. If problematic material is already in Special Collections, the library needs to take a position on what will be done. Where conflict arises, it may be possible to find compromises that satisfy all parties: loan arrangements or technological innovations.

Managing personal integrity

The privilege of working with the historic and valuable objects in Special Collections requires extra attention to personal ethics. As Association of College and Research Libraries (2003) states, 'Special collections often have great monetary as well as documentary and aesthetic value. Special collections librarians must exercise extreme caution in situations that have the potential to allow them to profit personally from library-related activities'. The document goes on to outline possible problem areas, for example valuations, discussed in Chapter 7. Personal collecting is another: where a librarian collects for their own interest in areas in which the library also collects. The librarian may as a result have better understanding of their work, but they must be open about the situation with their employer and agree protocols. Above all, materials and funds used for library and personal collecting must be clearly distinguished.

Difficulties also arise in the use of companies such as conservators or booksellers for conservation, acquisitions and disposals. Librarians should not profit personally from disposals or other activities, and should be wary of accepting gifts or other incentives. Many parent organizations will have their own policies on such matters.

Considering ethics in fund-raising

As we will see in Chapter 10, funding from individuals or businesses is a major source of income for Special Collections. Given cuts in public spending mentioned elsewhere, the pressure on libraries to seek such funding can only increase.

However, there are risks. Individuals, businesses or governments seeking to fund Special Collections or their parent organizations may not be as ethical in their behaviour as could be wished. Their motives may include corporate 'greenwash' or seeking to use an organization's good name and values to improve their own standing. There have been several high-profile cases recently where universities and arts organizations (not actually Special Collections services) have suffered as a result of accepting funds from polluting businesses or dictatorships. Large, well-known libraries, particularly those with an international reputation, are probably most at risk of offers of funding from unacceptable sources. Special Collections librarians may not be able to influence high-level decisions to take such money, particularly if it is not for their service, but they should do what they can.

Defining what is unacceptable is difficult, and changes with time. Examples might include businesses concerned with alcohol, tobacco, arms, pharmaceuticals, mining or use of fossil fuels, animal testing, child labour, sweatshops, or oppressive regimes. It will also depend on the nature of the library, for example there may be religious objections to alcohol or gambling sources (which would exclude Heritage Lottery, a major UK funder). These issues need to be defined as part of fund-raising programmes.

Equality and diversity in Special Collections

Equality and diversity are frequently mentioned together: diversity is about celebrating different backgrounds and ideas, while equality is concerned with fairness and access for all. As a public service, Special Collections may be covered by legislation concerning equality, which might cover disabilities (physical and mental), sex/gender, age, race and sexual orientation, for example the Equality Act 2010 in the UK.

Access is the most obvious aspect of Special Collections management in which equality should be considered. This includes considering access to buildings and spaces, for example for wheelchair users and other people with walking difficulties. It also includes making sure that websites and other online services can be used on various browsers and by software used to help disabled people, for example screen readers for the visually impaired. The use of other languages (e.g. in bilingual countries) and the way language is used are also important. The British Library web page on diversity policy raises issues to be considered by a large library used by many people from all over the world. Recruitment/selection of staff is another area in which equality is enforced by legislation, for example asking only for qualifications that are actually needed to do the job and ensuring all candidates are asked the same questions.

However, diversity and equality are about more than the letter of the law. There are wider issues involved: access is not just about ramps, and diversity in staffing is about more than removing obvious barriers. Organizational culture and wider social issues also need to be considered. Grob (2003) discusses diversity issues in the rare books profession in the USA and Dewey and Parham (2006) includes case studies on Special Collections and diversity. See also the Association of College and Research Libraries statements (2003) on ethics and (2009b) access.

With its flexible programmes and active outreach, Special Collections can take positive action to help parent organizations become more representative and fair. For example, the collecting policy (see Chapter 4) could aim to enhance holdings about local minority groups wherever possible, for example as Northeastern University did with communities in Boston (Krizack 2007). Marketing can re-examine collections to bring them to new audiences, for example via the opportunities offered by the History Months (see Chapter 8). Witness too the Re-framing Disability exhibition at the Royal College of Physicians. An example of remixing existing collections, this exhibition explores, 'historical portraits of disabled people held within our collections ... includes the voices of 27 disabled participants from across the UK, who came together to discuss the historical portraits and their own identities and lives'.

Health and safety in Special Collections

Special Collections spaces are public areas used by readers and other members of the public and workplaces for staff and volunteers. Librarians need to be aware of relevant health and safety legislation to protect people, and to reduce the risk of litigation. Compared to many industries, Special Collections work is not high risk. However, here are areas to consider:

- **manual handling**, for example shelving, fetching and transporting materials and use of mobile shelving
- **working at height**, for example using ladders and steps to reach material
- **lone working**, for example in smaller libraries or out of hours
- **exposure to dust and moulds**
- **conservation and preservation** activities, for example use of machinery, chemicals, knives and scalpels
- **use of screens**. Special Collections staff often do close work using personal computers, for example cataloguing and digitization; they need screen breaks and an appropriate set-up
- **other workplaces**. Setting up exhibitions elsewhere, acting as couriers, visiting donors' homes or otherwise collecting or assessing material. In the latter, dust and mould can be a serious problem, and staff need to be careful around their personal safety.

These issues can be tackled by identifying and assessing risks and setting priorities for improvements. It is preferable for the librarian to carry these out proactively or at least be involved rather than leaving to a rep who may not understand the nuances of collections care or services. Large organization such as universities will have health and safety policies and other guidance. Training of staff and volunteers in manual handling and the use of equipment is vital, as is storing protective equipment somewhere convenient.

Working with volunteers in Special Collections

Chapter 5 considered the practicalities of using volunteers in Special Collections. The legal and ethical issues discussed in this chapter with regard to staff also arise when using volunteers, for example ensuring health and safety in the workplace. In addition, librarians need to be mindful of the long-term future of the profession and those it serves by considering these particular points:

1 Use of interns in the UK in government, media and arts/heritage is controversial: keen to find a niche in competitive professions, they can easily be exploited, expected to work for months or years without pay. This excludes many from those professions. These excesses appear to be rare in Special Collections at present but rising demand for such work may change this. Libraries using interns are advised to develop policies that protect them and to structure posts to avoid excluding less well-off candidates.

2   Use of volunteers is complicated by political pressures that downgrade the role of professional librarians, archivists and other trained experts, seeking to replace them with volunteers (more on this in Chapter 10). Librarians should try to affirm the value of their professional skills and use volunteers only for appropriate tasks.

Working with children in Special Collections

Some Special Collections are part of organizations for young people, for example schools; many students in colleges or universities may be under 18. Other Special Collections librarians may work with children and young people in outreach, for example if the library is part of a family-oriented attraction such as a historic house, or offers visits for groups of schoolchildren. Legal and ethical issues mean this work has to be carefully planned. Related issues crop up in work with vulnerable adults, such as people with learning disabilities. The wider organization may already have policies and procedures; however, a separate version may be required if Special Collections does distinct work. Where working with children and young people is an integral part of a Special Collections role, staff and volunteers will need Criminal Records Bureau checks (UK). The procedures are under review at the time of writing. This process may slow down recruitment, a concern where there will be a gap in staffing or a funded project. Generally for occasional work with children, it is easier for librarians to work with teachers and external experts. There is more on outreach to schools in Chapter 9.

Conclusion

Legal and ethical issues crop up in all aspects of Special Collections work and can be the most challenging matters librarians have to manage. There are few easy answers and many decisions to make. Of course, not all librarians will face all these issues all the time. A service holding mainly modern unpublished material of little market value will have copyright and data protection concerns, but fewer worries relating to cultural property or financial matters than one holding valuable early published material. In all these situations, librarians need to understand the law or other situation, assess the risks, and take planned and effective action. Fortunately, there is plenty of help available from other Special Collections staff, archives, libraries and professional organizations.

Further reading

Behrnd-Klodt (2008) on legal issues for archives in the USA. For UK copyright law: Pedley (2007, 2008), Padfield (2010) (vital for unpublished material) and Cornish (2009), and, for the US, Hirtle, Hudson and Kenyon (2009).

Examples and case studies

British Library diversity web page, www.bl.uk/aboutus/stratpolprog/diversity
PaxCat Project, www.bradford.ac.uk/library/special/paxcat.php

Re-framing Disability exhibition,
  www.rcplondon.ac.uk/museum-and-garden/whats/re-framing-disability
Spoliation Advisory Panel, www.culture.gov.uk/what_we_do/cultural_property/3296.aspx
Wellcome Images, http://images.wellcome.ac.uk/

Useful websites

ALIA copyright advisor, www.alia.org.au/advocacy/copyright
American Library Association Copyright pages,
  www.ala.org/ala/issuesadvocacy/copyright/index.cfm
Australian Copyright Council, www.copyright.org.au
Australian Digital Alliance, www.digital.org.au
Australian Libraries Copyright Committee, www.digital.org.au/alcc
Canadian Intellectual Property Office – Copyrights,
  www.ic.gc.ca/eic/site/cipointernet-internetopic.nsf/eng/h_wr00003.html
Canadian Library Association Copyright Information Centre,
  www.cla.ca/AM/Template.cfm?Section=Copyright_Information
Copyright Clearance Center (US), www.copyright.com
Copyright Council of New Zealand, www.copyright.org.nz
Creative Commons, http://creativecommons.org
Design and Artists Copyright Society (UK), www.dacs.org.uk
FOB: Firms Out of Business, http://tyler.hrc.utexas.edu/fob.cfm
Information Commissioner's Office (UK), www.ico.gov.uk
Intellectual Property Office (UK), www.ipo.gov.uk
JISC Legal (UK), www.jisclegal.ac.uk
Library Law blog (US), http://blog.librarylaw.com/librarylaw
National Archives (UK) on DP, FOI, etc., www.nationalarchives.gov.uk/information-
  management/legislation-and-regulations.htm
Newspaper Licensing Agency (UK), www.nla.co.uk
Oral History Society, www.oralhistory.org.uk/index.php
Strategic Content Alliance IPR and licensing module,
  www.web2rights.com/SCAIPRModule/index.html
United States Copyright Office, www.copyright.gov
WATCH File: Writers, Artists and Their Copyright Holders, http://tyler.hrc.utexas.edu/watch
Web2rights calculator, www.web2rights.com/OERIPRSupport/risk-management-calculator
World Intellectual Property Organization, www.wipo.int/portal/index.html.en

7
User services in Special Collections

Introduction

This chapter will cover individual services to users. It will:

1 Discuss the nature of Special Collections users.
2 Discuss managing typical services: enquiries, physical visits, virtual and mobile visits, reprographics and inter-library loans.
3 Examine ways of improving services to users.

It should be read alongside the marketing advice in Chapter 8, which can be used to improve these services.

A note on Special Collections staff

This book considers management of collections in more detail than management of staff, because much of the former is unique to Special Collections; the latter is good practice in any service environment. However, Special Collections people are as important an asset as the collections themselves. People make the difference between neglected hidden collections and dynamic resources fulfilling their potential. They are also as important as the services they deliver, as their attitude and helpfulness can make all the difference to the experience of the user.

Managing staff to deliver effective services with minimal resources is a great challenge, complicated by the variety of audiences and demands found in Special Collections. In difficult times, front-line staff often bear the brunt of user frustration, having to explain policies and procedures that they did not create, and they may in turn become frustrated. Most people who work in Special Collections care about the collections and helping their users. Good management is about supporting and empowering them to do these things, and trying to offer hope and vision in difficult times.

Understanding Special Collections users

In order to manage and improve user services, it is essential to understand who users are and why they might wish to use Special Collections. In Chapter 8, we consider ways of analysing users and how to develop new audiences in more detail. Here are some basics to consider.

Internal and external users of Special Collections

A crucial question is the relationship of a user to the library or parent organization:

1 **Internal**, for example members, staff or students of a university, trustees, or other employees. A finite and known population.
2 **External**, i.e. general public. Much more scope for growth, but also harder to analyse. External users are more likely to want remote or virtual services, but when they do visit will need opening hours that allow them plenty of contact with collections.

(Of course, an individual interested in particular Special Collections might be internal or external at different times of their life!)

The balance between internal and external users that is right for a library will vary. Heavy internal use demonstrates value to the organization and helps maintain resources, but funding bodies will need evidence of use by external readers. In some libraries, for example subscription libraries or learned societies, internal users may be (perhaps should be) dominant. However, if Special Collections contain unique and appealing material, and are marketed as discussed in this book, external people will want to use them.

Special Collections user groups

Some common types of user:

- **academic staff** studying bibliographic history, literature, humanities, geography, archaeology, theology, philosophy, politics, history of science …
- **postgraduate students** (research or taught courses)
- **undergraduate students**. There is a growing interest in using primary sources for third-year dissertations in history and other humanities subjects
- **marketing staff** or others in the organization needing help with its business history
- **creative people** looking for inspiration for art and writing
- **family historians**. People researching their personal history are a variant on this idea
- **local historians**
- **other libraries**, archives, museums
- **media**, for example publishers seeking images or journalists needing research help
- **tourists** and other people wanting an enjoyable day out.

As with the internal/external divide, the same individual may have different needs at different times.

These groups will vary in:

- **motivation** for using Special Collections
- **experience** of using this or similar services
- **value of the research process** as opposed to need for an answer
- **timescale**. How quickly they need an answer
- **relationship** they will have with the service, from a single encounter to lifelong engagement
- **emotional involvement** with the collections
- **level of skills needed to access collections**, including research techniques, IT skills, languages and palaeography.

For example, academic researchers wish to study Special Collections in person, and are willing to spend time on this because it is their job and usually their passion. They could be expected to understand how such services work (pencils only!) and what to expect. Media users know what they want, need it now, have no wish to visit and ideally want you to solve their problem. Be wary, however, of stereotyping people too much: these are trends and may not apply to individuals.

Not all Special Collections attract all kinds of users. Librarians need to consider which groups are core to their service and which they wish to attract, to ensure services are targeted appropriately and that marketing is effective (see Chapter 8).

Managing Special Collections users

Bringing Special Collections and people together can be incredibly rewarding. However, as with any role involving working with the public, there can be difficulties. Some typical problems and suggestions about how to manage them:

1 **Conflicting demands**. Different individuals and types of users have different needs, which cannot always be reconciled, leading to conflict and stress for staff. The service needs to focus on the needs of core or majority users, while accommodating others as much as possible.
2 **Mismatch of expectations**. Users may have unrealistic expectations of a service. This may be because they have never used Special Collections services, or they may have experienced a different kind of service, for example moving from a large service with continuous staffing and long opening hours to a small Special Collection with one member of staff: appointments may be needed, copying may take longer. All you can do is be honest about what you can deliver, managing expectations in publicity, correspondence and conversation.
3 **Rules and regulations** restricting behaviour, for example handling restrictions, rules about food or mobile phones, legal restrictions about access and copying, costs and charges. Further problems arise when staff members apply rules in different ways. A service needs clear, fair rules that all staff can explain, based on

principles of preservation, legal requirements and consideration for others. A style of management that empowers staff to enforce rules sensibly is essential, along with consistent messages from managers about what is or is not acceptable. Expectations of users should be made clear via the induction process.

4 **People issues**. Special Collections attract all kinds of people, often with enthusiasms, even eccentricities, or lonely people who wish to talk. Others may find the experience daunting and be unable to get the best from their visit (more about barriers to access in Chapter 9). It is helpful if staff are tolerant of different kinds of people, and accept that it is not possible to change people's personalities, though they can adapt their behaviour. Staff training on dealing with difficult people and on mental health issues may be useful, as can any training or reading that helps staff to reflect on what makes people 'tick'.

Managing Special Collections enquiries
Introduction to enquiries

Many (but not all) visits to Special Collections begin with an enquiry, but many enquirers will not need to visit. Enquiries may arrive via e-mail, phone, letter or in person. A fax enquiry is now probably rare! If you or your library is active in social networks, enquiries may also arrive via social media. Many libraries have explored instant messenger (IM) services to users, although the author has not discovered any Special Collections case studies. Enquiries in Special Collections may take a few moments to answer, or involve a relationship between user, collections and staff over many years.

The reference encounter

Also known as the **reference interview**, this is an interaction in which a librarian tries to establish exactly what a user needs. Users may not ask for this, but ask a question they think the librarian can answer. The experienced librarian does not take this at face value but asks more questions to elicit more information. The nuances of body language and intonation help, which is why enquiries received by e-mail and other written methods need extra thought. Not all Special Collections users require such interpretation: experienced researchers will have checked the catalogues and know exactly which resources they need. Inexperienced users may have no idea how to frame a question in Special Collections and may need a great deal of help from staff.

As outlined in an ARL survey, Turcotte and Nemmers (2006), many Special Collections use a 'triage' approach to enquiries, in which the enquirer first encounters a paraprofessional staff member or student worker, who then refers them to the appropriate specialist. Others have a more random approach in which whoever is on duty deals with the enquirer, while in others all reference encounters are managed by a professional librarian. The most suitable method depends on the nature of staffing, but all require investment in staff skills and support.

Having found out what the user needs, staff can check whether Special Collections can help. This requires skills in using the catalogues, and understanding of issues relating to access, preservation, data protection restrictions and so on. Staff should be familiar with the key reference sources in Appendix A, works relevant to individual Special Collections, such as biographies and bibliographies of significant authors, and know how to find out about related collections elsewhere.

Research services

Special Collections need to develop policies on doing research on behalf of users. For some users, for example academics, the research process is part of what they are trying to achieve by engaging with Special Collections. Others may be unable or unwilling to visit to do their own research. It is easy for helpful staff to turn answering an enquiry into detailed research, which will take up scarce time. This should only be done as a matter of policy. It is difficult to say how much research for users is too much. It depends on the nature of the collections and staffing, who is asking and why they need it. Sometimes it is as quick to look something up for someone as to deal with the practicalities of a reader visit.

Some services (notably UK record offices) find that the best way to manage demand for research from family historians in particular is to offer a paid research service. The Borthwick Institute's service is a typical example of costs and services offered. Usually some time is offered free and a certain quantity of photocopies included in the price.

However, paid research may not be appropriate for all libraries. If staff time is short, it becomes irrelevant whether funding is raised – unless sufficient income can be raised to employ more staff. Much depends on how skilled the research needed is, whether it requires the specialist skills of library staff or could be carried out by volunteers or students. The act of paying also raises user expectations. Maintaining a list of local researchers who will research on behalf of enquirers can be helpful, particularly if the library has access to a large pool of ex-staff or local students.

Whether the library charges for research or not, it is important that staff understand what is possible and where to look. If skilled staff haven't found an answer within a certain time (depending on the nature and storage of collections), it becomes less likely that the answer will be found.

Managing Special Collections visitors

There are many kinds of visitors to Special Collections: individuals using the collections, groups, casual visitors and, now, virtual visitors.

The traditional way in which researchers engage with Special Collections is in a dedicated space, known as the **reading room** or **search room**, in which staff:

- supervise use of the material and ensure rules are followed
- offer help to users as required.

For preservation and security reasons, as discussed in Chapters 1 and 2, ideally the physical collections are housed elsewhere and brought to readers via a fetching service.

Some reading rooms also contain collections: for instance, in historic buildings, there may be no scope for separating readers and stock. Larger services may have several reading rooms for different formats or subjects; consolidation might in certain circumstances enable a better service with longer hours to be offered.

Opening hours

All Special Collections services need to decide reading room opening hours. The pattern that works best will depend on the needs of users and on the resources available to staff and support the service. Opening hours should be shorter than the hours staff are paid to work, to allow for opening and closing and for visitors who are slow to finish, without expecting staff to work unpaid overtime. They should take account of staff needs for lunch/breaks, and allow for disruption by annual leave, sickness and travel problems, plus staff meetings and training sessions. It may be better to provide a good service during limited hours than a stretched and unreliable service during longer hours.

It helps users if opening hours are kept simple, and services should avoid closing for lunch if they possibly can, as this seriously breaks up the day for travelling visitors.

Advertise opening hours on the web and everywhere else possible. Special Collections visitors, for example travelling academics, often plan trips well ahead, so try to sort and publicize Christmas, Easter and summer opening in advance.

Opening hours should be reviewed regularly to ensure they work. Users should be consulted about changes, especially if cuts are being made. It will be impossible to satisfy all users, so opening hours should be built around the needs of the majority and of core/internal users. Virtual and remote services (see below) make it possible to help visitors who cannot travel or visit during opening hours.

Appointments

Services also need to decide whether visits should be by appointment only. In smaller libraries, this will be essential. Even in larger services where the reading room is continuously staffed, appointments enable staff to predict user needs, have material ready and plan effectively. Many large services do not require them, though they may encourage out-of-town visitors to pre-book, to avoid wasted journeys and expenditure. Some services operate a drop-in service during core times with extra times available by appointment.

If appointments are needed, visitors need to know how to book them, for example by telephone or e-mail. An effective system for managing appointments is required, particularly if several staff are involved in taking bookings. An appointment book (if bookings are only taken in one place) may be workable; electronic online calendars and schedules offer more flexibility.

Reader places

Services also need to decide how many reader places to offer. This is not a question of how many chairs and tables can be squeezed into the reading room. It is about how many readers staff can properly support at any one time: taking requests for materials, fetching, issuing, returning and shelving materials, supervising and offering help. As with opening hours, sickness, annual leave and other staffing issues should be considered.

Staffing

While staff on duty in the reading room may be able to do other work, their priority should be supervising and helping readers. The work done should not relate to confidential matters, should be compatible with supervision and not require the use of hazardous materials.

Design and facilities of the reading room

The reading room should have:

1 **Natural light, or lighting** that enables readers to see well without strain. Note that natural light, as discussed in Chapter 1, will harm stock and that direct sunlight is not pleasant to work in.
2 **Seating and tables** of appropriate size and shape for the collections being consulted.
3 **Laptop** facilities.
4 **Reference material** to help visitors use the Special Collections, such as bibliographies, printed catalogues and directories. If these are electronic or microform-based, the appropriate equipment is needed.
5 **Audiovisual equipment** if needed.
6 **Equipment to promote good handling**, as discussed in Chapter 1: book supports, snakes, weights, pencils.

The desk or counter used by staff needs to be angled so that staff can see what readers are doing, but readers do not feel oppressed by their gaze. The staff area needs room to store forms, trolleys and other equipment.

A note on Special Collections spaces

We have covered collections care and spaces for users. It can be helpful to look at these and other Special Collections functions holistically. Figure 7.1 (overleaf), a simplified version of one in Kitching (2007) for archives services, shows the key functions and flows in Special Collections. For security reasons, the flows of collections and visitors are kept separate except in designated areas: the reading room, learning spaces and exhibition areas.

Many libraries struggle to offer spaces that manage these functions and flows effectively and provide appealing and ergonomic workspaces for users and staff. A survey of US and Canadian Special Collections librarians reported in Dooley and Luce (2010) found that space was by far the most frequently cited 'most challenging issue'.

Special Collections services can acquire more and/or better spaces by:

- building a new building, relocating functions from an existing building, for example a new university library, or bringing together different services
- extending an existing building

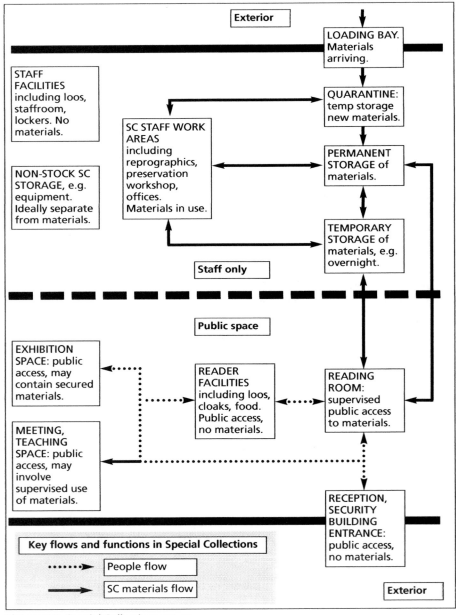

Figure 7.1 *Special Collections spaces*

- refurbishing an existing building
- converting another building.

We will encounter some space projects later on, for example the Aberdeen University library in Chapter 10 and the Hull History Centre later in this chapter. Both illustrate the scale of such projects.

In addition to collections care and user needs concerns, problems arise with:

1 Historic buildings: legal and aesthetic issues.
2 Shared buildings. The main library service and others in the building have different space needs and priorities. If Special Collections spaces are scattered, lack of clarity about ownership can result.

Any major building project involves many people and priorities; much will be out of the control of Special Collections librarians. Librarians whose space is being rebuilt or refurbished need to understand good design for Special Collections and how major projects work, so they can influence the outcomes. The most successful projects for archives and Special Collections buildings include genuine consultation and involvement of librarians and other experts in collections care, along with users. This ensures that the functions and their relationships are understood, and that trends in user and staff needs are considered. Otherwise, the new space may not offer the level of collections, customer or staff care that could have been possible.

Librarians in poor spaces without current hope of major works may still be able to improve the ways in which those spaces are used by thinking creatively. Tools like the diagram above may help them to think more strategically about the spaces they have. Likewise, external experts or users may bring a fresh perspective. It also helps to visit other services to see how they use space and find inspiration. The use of benchmarks (see Chapter 1) will give a sense of progress towards desired aims, however slow.

Planning the fetching service

Users request items, which are fetched by staff from the storage areas, handed to the reader, used by them, returned and re-shelved. This process may be managed via paper call slips or an electronic system.

The fetching service is crucial to the user experience and how they spend their time: in particular, how long they have to wait to receive the items requested.

1 **Fetch on demand or at set times?** A small service with strongroom in or adjacent to the reading area might be able to operate on demand. Larger reading rooms may need a more regulated system.
2 **Set times? How often?** This is regulated by staffing levels and the physical relationship between the reading and storage spaces. Collection from remote or off-site storage will take much longer between request and receipt. The set times need

to bear a logical relationship to the opening hours of the service. It is usual, for instance, to restrict fetching in the run-up to closing time, so that readers do not accumulate unused material.

If a long wait is unavoidable, then manage expectations: publicize likely waits in correspondence, on web pages and other public places. Setting up mechanisms by which readers can request material prior to their visit means their time is spent using materials rather than waiting.

Security and preservation

These must be central to planning services to visitors. See Chapter 1 for guidelines on handling by users, Chapter 1 and below for reprographics, and Chapter 2 for security.

Legal issues

These are discussed in detail in Chapter 6 with useful references listed in 'Further reading'.

Equality and access

These issues are discussed in detail in Chapter 6 and elsewhere.

The visitor experience

Planning for visitors should also consider:

1 **Transport**. Public transport, for example nearest station/tube/metro, bus numbers, taxi advice. What parking is available for visitors? Do they need permits and, if so, how are they obtained? Is there a charge? Barriers?
2 **Arrival**. Where should they report? For example porter's lodge, library reception, direct to Special Collections? It may help to inform other staff in advance of expected visitors. Signs are important!
3 **Personal belongings**. For security reasons, most Special Collections require users to leave belongings in cloakroom or lockers rather than bringing them into the reading room. Locker size and restrictions should be publicized (e.g. no suitcases). Many libraries also impose restrictions on what can be brought into the reading room, for example no sharp implements (to prevent mutilation of materials).
4 **Induction/orientation**. Explain rules, fire exits, toilets.
5 **Loos and refreshments**. Visitors will appreciate advice on where to buy food or consume their own. If there are particular issues in your location, for example no shops nearby, publicize these.

Visitors need guidance before the visit, during, and afterwards. This could be offered via video guidance online and virtual campus tours as well as detailed information on web pages.

Managing group visits

Special Collections can be very appealing for groups such as schools to visit and community outreach often involves visits by groups. These work very differently from individual research visits. Ideally a service should have access to separate spaces suitable for group work. There is more on outreach and groups in Chapter 9.

Many Special Collections are familiar with the short notice visit by a visiting dignitary or group: they are part of the tour of the organization's points of interest. This is positive: it shows the parent organization values the service enough to show it to visitors. However, it can be difficult to manage. It is good practice to have standard 'treasures' that can be quickly fetched and a basic presentation that any member of Special Collections staff can deliver.

Managing casual visits

Not all visitors have to enter the reading room to encounter Special Collections. Many collections are part of buildings that are visitor attractions or offer public exhibitions, such as historic houses or museums. Such visitors need less motivation and less individual attention. Huge numbers can be handled in this way. Witness the Hull History Centre, which combines the City Archives and Local Studies services with the University's archive collections in a new building with plenty of scope for unsupervised visits: 40,000 visitors in the first year since opening.

Note that people will visit Special Collections for other reasons, for example business meetings and maintenance work, and donors and supporters will also visit. Security and access issues need to be considered to help these visitors and protect collections.

Managing virtual visitors

Many Special Collections services, especially if their spaces are not purpose-built, are constrained in the numbers they can accommodate and what they can offer them. Physical location and transport issues may prevent interested people from visiting in person.

However, one of the most exciting aspects of Special Collections management in the 21st century is the scope for worldwide outreach via online services, unconstrained by poor quality spaces or geography. A virtual encounter with collections may lead to a physical visit, but it may be a valid, enjoyable, useful interaction on its own terms. Virtual services relieve pressure on physical services and on the Special Collections and have a key role in marketing, because of their visibility outside the organization.

Virtual Special Collections services may include:

- website, see Chapter 8
- digital collections, see Chapters 1 and 4
- reflective blogs and social media, see Chapter 8
- online exhibitions, see Chapter 8
- online learning objects, see Chapter 9

- mobile services, see below.

Virtual visitors need relatively little management compared to physical ones. However, the service needs to decide how to attract and manage feedback, and to offer ways in which virtual visitors can contact the service if they wish to explore services further.

Developing mobile services

Virtual visits no longer require fixed-location personal computers. Many individuals now own smartphones, which offer possibilities for mobile services:

Mobile apps are pieces of software that carry out specific tasks on smartphones and other mobile devices. They offer great potential for bringing collections and services to users in an exhibition, building or on the move. Apps can include zoomable high resolution images or film of collections and audio or video narrations that introduce and explain them. Ideas include:

- To highlight 'treasures' of Special Collections, for example the British Library's Treasures Gallery app.
- To enhance tours of library, campus or town, for example North Carolina State University's 'WolfWalk': a mobile app that tells the history of the University's campus using historic images from its Special Collections.
- To draw attention to a particularly appealing collection, for example the app for National Library of Scotland's John Murray Archive, an amazing publishing history.

Augmented reality (AR) places a layer of computer-generated information over whatever the camera on a mobile device is showing, assuming the device has a mechanism for registering its location. This offers many possibilities for Special Collections: imagine, for example, an exhibition in which a visitor can point their device at an item and thereby see much more information and images, a richer experience. An interesting example is Quadmented, by Stanford University: a layer that 'assembles representative moments from the Main Quad's (and Stanford's) history through pictures, videos, audio files, text and hyperlinks' (http://lib.stanford.edu/special-collections-university-archives-blog). See Chapter 9 for the SCARLET (Special Collections using Augmented Reality to Enhance Learning and Teaching) project, which takes AR into work with students.

QR (quick response) codes are a kind of barcode that can be scanned by smartphones using a free code reader, linking to further information, usually online. QR codes are becoming increasingly familiar through commercial advertising, for example in newspapers and billboards, and can be printed or shown on almost any surface. Again, there are endless possibilities for improving Special Collections services:

- if they are used on the library catalogue, full details of a title can be saved to a user's phone without them having to write them down
- add extra information (e.g. a narrative) to floor plans to help readers find their way

- use in exhibitions to unlock further details.

None of this software is difficult to create, for example apps can be created by anyone with Java skills. The difficulty lies more in coming up with ways of using these ideas that really work for users and libraries. Creating such software might make excellent projects for students or skilled colleagues.

Managing reprographic services

Reprographics means reproduction of materials via various mechanical and electronic means. Until the last five years or so, these services were limited to photocopying, microfilming and photography. Now digital technologies have revolutionized what is possible and enabled users to access high quality reproductions of Special Collections materials.

In setting up services to supply copies of Special Collections to users, librarians have to balance:

- copyright law, see Chapter 6
- preservation of the originals, see Chapter 1
- equipment and staffing available.

Services carried out by staff

This balance has meant that most Special Collections have allowed only copying by trained staff for users. As explained in Chapter 1, contact methods such as photocopying or scanning can do great damage to collections. These services (usually photocopying, scanning or digital photography) may be carried out by Special Collections staff; some services have separate photographic departments.

When providing such services, librarians must comply with the copyright law of their country. For example, in the UK, fair dealing does not apply to this activity and librarians must base their service on the library/archive exceptions, which allow some copying of literary works in copyright for users.

This service can bring in income, but can also use a great deal of staff time. Workflows and processes need to be carefully considered to ensure they are efficient. Schaffner, Snyder and Supple (2011) give pragmatic advice on running an effective scanning service and integrating its outputs into other digitization programmes.

Self-service reprographics

These days it is common for users to have their own digital cameras, smartphones and other portable devices. Such devices do not need to touch an original to produce a high quality image. As the process is relatively safe preservation-wise, Special Collections services are increasingly allowing users to take images with their own devices. Miller, Galbraith and the RLG Partnership Working Group on Streamlining Photography and Scanning (2010) survey the benefits and issues to consider.

Key benefits:

1 Much more convenient for readers than copying by staff.
2 'Gentler on collection materials' (Miller, Galbraith and the RLG Partnership Working Group on Streamlining Photography and Scanning 2010).
3 Frees up staff resources.

Key issues:

1 Financial. Some libraries charge users to use their own devices, annually, per visit or per image. Others, however, find this not to be cost-effective, justifiable or practical.
2 Reprographics income will drop (this could be significant in many services).
3 Preservation. Contact methods such as digital pens that touch the material they are copying should not be allowed.
4 Services. Use should not disturb other readers, for example no extra lighting, tripods, flash or climbing on chairs to get a better shot.
5 Legal. Appropriate forms and signs should be created to suit local circumstances.

This service is evolving fast; monitor listservs and surveys to see how it becomes standard practice.

Some services offer self-service machines in the reading room to photocopy modern reference texts or obtain prints from microform readers. Copyright notices concerning fair dealing and use should be displayed near the machines.

Commercial research and image supply

The above relates to non-commercial services offered to researchers: they may generate income but exist to meet user needs. Some Special Collections hold materials suited to commercial research or image supply. As these services are created for income generation rather than to serve users, they are discussed in Chapter 10.

Managing inter-library loans

If Special Collections appear on union catalogues, the service is likely to be asked to loan items for the use of individual readers elsewhere under **inter-library loan** schemes. The issues have much in common with those relating to loans for exhibitions (see Chapter 8). The Association of College and Research Libraries (2004) guidelines are currently being revised and merged with those for exhibition loan.

Policies need to be established in advance of a request. These should balance preservation and access, and consider the risks of transit, of possible insecure storage and unsupervised handling by readers. Key points:

1 Many Special Collections items would not be suitable, for example anything unique, rare or fragile.

2 Modern printed books or duplicates might be suitable.
3 The decision to lend should be taken by the Special Collections librarian or other expert member of staff. It should not be automatic, but decided case by case.
4 Setting conditions on the loan helps safeguard the item, for example for reference in the host library only, no renewals of the loan.
5 If copyright and preservation permit, creating a surrogate for loan may be a better solution.

Valuations and care of books

It is not unusual for Special Collections staff to be asked to value old books. However, it is not advisable to offer such a service:

1 Staff are unlikely to have detailed knowledge of market prices
2 Valuations can cause ill feeling, particularly if the price suggested is not realized or the item turns out to have low market value
3 Ethical concerns, see Chapter 6.

Services may find it helpful to state on their web pages that they do not offer valuation services, and offer other suggestions, for example a link to *Your Old Books* (Rare Books and Manuscripts Section, 2006), or the National Library of Scotland's Rare Books for Beginners website. However, they should avoid suggesting a particular bookseller or appraiser for valuations. Librarians should also exercise caution in answering enquiries that relate to market value, for example whether a signature in a book is that of the author (increasing value thereby). Association of College and Research Libraries (1992) remains a useful standard for these issues. However, valuations could be a useful element in outreach, for instance offering access to experts at events (for UK readers, the 'Antiques Roadshow' element).

People are also likely to ask Special Collections staff for advice on caring for their own old books or documents. This is a great chance to improve collections care and raise awareness of Special Collections, although, again, librarians should avoid recommending particular bookbinders or suppliers of archival materials. It may be advisable to point readers in the direction of the above titles or other resources suggested in this book, rather than trying to answer individuals' questions in detail.

Improving services to users

It is easy, particularly in a busy service, to let services continue as they have always done. However, the fast pace of changing user needs and technology means it is worth reviewing them regularly.

Systems and record-keeping

Key points:

1   Develop systems that work for your library, keeping track of enquiries to monitor progress and allocate work, and for statistical purposes. A spreadsheet may work well; larger services might investigate customer relationship software.

2   Records relating to access to collections may need to be kept indefinitely, for security reasons and because Special Collections links can be long term. These issues should be included in any retention schedule.

3   If the collections are subject to freedom of information legislation (see Chapter 6), particular timescales and procedures will be required for such enquiries, for example reply within a set number of days.

Statistics and performance indicators

It is essential to keep statistics relating to the above services to enable librarians to see patterns and monitor the impact of activities such as cataloguing projects and provide information for managers and funders about activities. However, keeping statistics is a balance between the data that it is practical to gather, and data that will be useful. There is no point in creating a complex system that no one has time to complete properly.

The measures used by a parent library will probably not be suitable: enquiries, visits and other activities in Special Collections will bear little resemblance to such encounters in an open access environment. Footfall alone is an unhelpful figure in isolation, particularly if physical visits are in decline. Remote and virtual services mean many readers do not need to visit. Virtual visit figures should not be limited to the corporate website, but take into account views of blogs, Flickr images and other online digital assets.

Measures devised for archives services have much to offer Special Collections, for example the Public Services Quality Group (2003) draft performance indicators for archives. The Public Services Quality Group (PSQG) run regular surveys of visitors to UK archives, which Special Collections services may be eligible to join. Another PSQG document, Mander (2008), may also help in benchmarking access and services against standards. The Archival Metrics Project is creating toolkits to help archivists assess performance (see Yakel and Tibbo 2010). Whittaker (2008) suggests and discusses the role of the library management system circulation module in Special Collections metrics.

Targets and agreements

Special Collections services do not fit well into targets set for wider library services: for example cataloguing early printed books requires far more skills and time than downloading records for new textbooks, although they can be useful as part of effective management and customer care, for example aiming to reply to enquirers within a set period or giving new staff something to aim at. However, targets are problematic if not part of a good management regime, i.e. people work to them rather than looking at the wider picture, to the detriment of the service.

Libraries, for example in UK universities, are increasingly committing to agreements that set targets or standards in customer care, for example:

1 **Customer charters** that outline what the service offers and the behaviour expected of the user in return.
2 **Service level agreements** (SLAs) agree a defined level of service.

Special Collections need to ensure that their particular users and services are fairly covered; however, note for example that Sheffield University's Special Collections section of the library's SLA does not commit the service to anything beyond what might be expected.

Feedback and complaints

The complexity of Special Collections issues and the human factors mentioned above mean that sometimes complaints may arise.

1 A complaints procedure should be in place, publicized online.
2 Apologizing and taking quick action can often stop a complaint getting out of hand.
3 Get it in writing. Keep notes, and ask complainants to send written complaints.

When interactions with users go badly, even if they do not complain, reflecting on the possible reasons for the problem is worthwhile. Was it an interpersonal clash, a mismatch of expectations, a problem with procedures or information? More on feedback and communication with users in Chapter 8.

Conclusion

Managing Special Collections services is about balancing the often irreconcilable needs and motivations of service users with the staff and resources available. It is also about ensuring that staff are empowered, trained and encouraged to help. The services offered typically include enquiries, research in the reading room, group visits, reprographics and, increasingly, virtual services. All need to be reviewed regularly to ensure they are effective and meet user needs. The next two chapters consider users from marketing and outreach perspectives.

Further reading

Spaces: Kitching (2007) on UK archive buildings (many case studies) and Pacifico and Wilsted (2009) on archives and Special Collections facilities. See also the Public Services Quality Group (2003) performance indicators, Khan (2009) and Stewart (2010) for academic library buildings, McCarthy (2007) on working with architects, checklists in Sannwald (2009) plus useful case studies including historic buildings in Dewe (2009). The website Designing Libraries is an information resource about library design, including Special Collections issues.

Mobile: for a general introduction to mobile services, see Griffey (2010).

Examples and case studies

British Library's Treasures Gallery app, www.bl.uk/app

Hull History Centre, www.hullhistorycentre.org.uk

National Library of Scotland's John Murray Archive, www.nls.uk/murray-app

North Carolina State University's 'WolfWalk', www.lib.ncsu.edu/wolfwalk

Quadmented, www.layar.com/layers/quadmented

Research service – Borthwick Institute for Archives, The University of York, www.york.ac.uk/library/borthwick/research-support/research-service

Sheffield University Service Level Targets, www.shef.ac.uk/library/sla/services15.html

Useful websites

Archival Metrics, www.archivalmetrics.org/node/10

Designing Libraries, www.designinglibraries.org.uk

National Library of Scotland, www.nls.uk/collections/rare-books/beginners

Public Services Quality Group, www.archives.org.uk/si-psqg/public-services-quality-group-psqg.html

8
Marketing and communications in Special Collections

Introduction
In this chapter we cover:

1 Marketing for Special Collections: an overview of the marketing mix.
2 Commodity/product and marketing themes.
3 Cost/price and convenience/place.
4 Communications/promotions, including key channels: websites, the press, exhibitions, social media and advertising.
5 Feedback and market research.

Other chapters relate to aspects of marketing Special Collections: metadata in Chapter 5, user services in Chapter 7, education and outreach in Chapter 9, and fund-raising and advocacy in Chapter 10.

Marketing in Special Collections and libraries is often equated with promotion (e.g. producing leaflets), but promotion is just one element of marketing. Marketing is about every interaction a library has with its users, defining and meeting their needs. All Special Collections librarians and other staff are involved in marketing, whether they realize this or not, and even if the organization employs marketing staff.

Librarians sometimes worry that marketing will lead to an increase in use: a concern if services can barely cope with existing levels of enquiries and visits. However, good quality communication by libraries means better informed Special Collections users who need less individual attention. Increased use can help librarians acquire funding and resources, diminishing use and hidden collections lead only to stagnation and threat.

The Special Collections marketing mix
This chapter follows the structure of the **marketing mix**, which in marketing theory is a set of elements to be considered in marketing a product or service. This version is the user oriented 'four Cs': Commodity or Customer Value, Cost to the customer, Convenience to the Customer, and Communication (Lauterborn, cited by De Saëz 2002).

Commodity: the Special Collections offer

Special Collections can offer users the following:

1 **Collections**. Libraries have little control over the collections they have inherited and acquiring appealing new material is not easy (as discussed in Chapter 4). However, the rich content of existing collections can be adapted and remixed to appeal to users; suggestions appear below.
2 **Services**. Some users will use Special Collections regardless of service quality, because they need access to a certain item or collection. However, they may not get the most from the experience; others may go elsewhere.
3 **Expertise**. Special Collections work is not just about making available whatever collections people ask to use. Staff are uniquely placed to add value to the user experience by acting as nodes of expertise, bringing together the collections, their stories and the people who use them.
4 **Messages**. The mission, but expressed informally for different audiences. Consider the idea of the **elevator pitch**, an informal sentence or two to explain the mission to new acquaintances. There are also many messages within the collections.

Marketing messages

Librarians need to find angles from which to approach particular objects or collections to help audiences relate to them. Here are some suggestions that are well suited to Special Collections and which can be adapted to various audiences and methods.

'Treasures'

This approach highlights key objects in Special Collections: their visual appeal, historical significance or links with famous people. Ideally they should be set in context and their significance explained. 'Treasures' can be the basis of a publication, permanent or temporary exhibition, a monthly feature on a website, even an app (see Chapter 7). Chapter 9 includes a case study about treasures being taken on tour in remote parts of Australia.

Record-breakers

It seems to be human nature to be drawn to extremes, and Special Collections can yield all kinds of examples: oldest, largest, smallest, most expensive, first, last … There is also the 'wow factor' of size and scale: the sheer size of collections or number of users may impress.

Record-breakers can be significant as well as curious. Witness the attention paid to the first printed texts produced in particular countries: these are 'firsts' but can also inform the reader about culture and society. See for example the rich story of the 1796 playbill from the Sydney Theatre held by the National Library of Australia: the first item to be printed in that country. Its citation on the UNESCO Australian Memory of the World

Register explains that it was 'produced by printer George Henry Hughes on the first printing press in the new colony, a wooden screw press brought to Port Jackson by Governor Arthur Phillip but not used until 1795' (www.amw.org.au/register). The item also has interesting provenance: it is annotated by Philip Gidley King, later the third Governor of New South Wales, who took it from Australia. Eventually it became part of a scrapbook held by the National Library of Canada; in 2007, Canada gave the Playbill to Australia.

Events and other key dates

Special Collections marketing often exploits links with events and dates. Most could be used for any campaign from a few tweets up to a major programme. If other parts of the organization or other libraries are celebrating the same events, all benefit from cross-promotion. Seasons and holidays are useful for blogs and temporary events (see Chapter 9 for a case study on using holidays with student appeal). Other possibilities include:

1 **Anniversaries**, which are well suited to major exhibitions and programmes of events and offer great opportunities for collaboration:
   — Local. Key date of someone significant or founding of the library/organization, for example Gilding the Lilly celebrated 50 years of Lilly Library at Indiana University in 2010 by showing gilded medieval manuscripts. Such events are particularly useful for internal marketing.
   — National or international – dates of historic importance. These offer great opportunities for partnerships and cross-promotions, for example many events in 2011 on the anniversary of the King James Bible, including the exhibitions Manifold Greatness, by the Folger, Bodleian and Harry Ransom Center, and Great and Manifold Blessings at Cambridge University Library.
2 **History days and months**, for example Black History Month, International Women's Day and Women's History Month, Lesbian Gay Bisexual Trans History Month, offer useful pegs for demonstrating commitment to diversity (as discussed in Chapter 6) and interpreting collections in new ways.
3 **Awareness-raising campaigns** based on libraries, archives or history are also excellent opportunities, offering promotional toolkits and other support, for example Heritage Open Days, Archives Awareness/American Archives Month, Local History Month.
4 **Current news stories**. Special Collections can add historic context and human interest to stories in the news. Stories that have a historic resonance and which have some lead time are easiest to use, for example many libraries used the 2011 royal wedding to showcase objects from their distinctive collections.

Stories and people

Special Collections are about the people who wrote, made or owned the materials. Their stories lend themselves to all kinds of marketing activities. Librarians can write biographies, or tell the stories of particular events. This approach works for all kinds of people and ways of communicating. It may also be useful for encouraging others to tell the stories, thereby enriching the collections.

Curiosities

Users are often intrigued by the more bizarre and memorable items in Special Collections. Who could forget an anthropodermic book (bound in human skin – not uncommon in Special Collections), the 'Monk's Blood' manuscript (at the University of Wales) or a man-trap (the Brotherton Library)? These excite users and the media alike.

However, a note of caution: librarians need to be wary of implying (especially to senior managers) that Special Collections is a dumping ground for random objects rather than a key resource for education. Quirky objects with significance are particularly useful: for example J. B. Priestley's collection of tobacco pipes and accessories in his archive at Bradford University is actually highly relevant to his writings and personality.

Cost and convenience: accessing Special Collections

These elements of the marketing mix concern the ways in which the user accesses collections and services. If they perceive the cost of engaging with Special Collections to be too great, or if the transaction is too inconvenient, they will not pursue their interest.

Costs can be direct, for example photocopying charges, or indirect, for example the user's time and expense in dealing with the service or travelling to visit. There is little to be done about geographical location unless the service is relocating, but virtual collections and services can reach readers for whom the journey would not be convenient. Cataloguing in particular makes access much more convenient, enabling potential users to discover remotely whether collections meet their needs.

However, managing this part of the marketing mix is not just about the reality of how much it costs or how convenient it is to access Special Collections. The user's perception of cost and convenience is what matters and needs to be addressed via the communications methods below. We also discuss how new audiences perceive the barriers to accessing Special Collections and some ways to help in Chapter 9.

Communication: sharing Special Collections

The communication or promotion element of marketing is how potential Special Collections users find out about the above 'commodities' and the cost and convenience of accessing them. It also involves finding out what users make of these things.

Effective communication needs to contain the right information for the audience and be presented in the right medium and tone. Special Collections librarians need to adapt language and other factors for different audiences, for example using business jargon or the technical terms of digitization where appropriate, but also understand when more simple language is needed, for example for outreach to schoolchildren (more on advocacy and outreach in later chapters). This is not a call for 'dumbing down': sometimes specialist language is needed to describe things and ideas in Special Collections such as the parts and processes that created medieval manuscripts.

Understanding the **call to action** is vital: how do you want users to engage as a result of your communication? Engagement with Special Collections can be seen as a pyramid, in which people move up levels of involvement, from awareness that the service exists to active lifelong engagement with it. Not everyone has to move all the way up the levels for marketing to be successful. Engagement at a lower level may be just as worthwhile (see Figure 8.1).

Here are some communications channels that Special Collections should explore.

Working with mass media

Newspapers and broadcast media reach huge audiences and often feature stories concerning heritage and education; they therefore have much to offer in promoting Special Collections. Special Collections usually interact with journalists via press releases, though journalists may get in touch with particular enquiries.

Typical media stories about Special Collections are: the finding of an important hidden item (even if it has been catalogued for many years), the opening up of hidden collections, theft or other damage, selling off rare books, or new acquisitions, especially if they involve famous people or large sums of money, or reviews and articles based on major exhibitions.

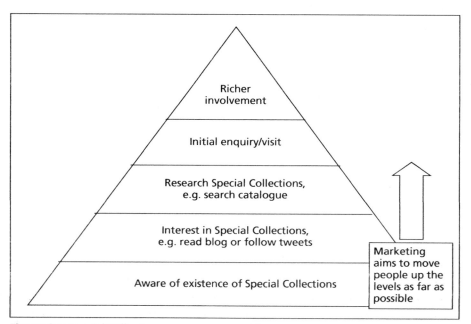

Figure 8.1 *Special Collections awareness pyramid*

Risks of media coverage

1 **Negative publicity**. Stories of theft, disposals, etc. reflect badly on the library. However, if the error was long ago and has been put right, bad publicity can be used to bring benefits, as Durham University did in the Chapter 2 case study.

2 **Ethics**. Real stories are more complex than can be fitted into a press release or short news story, leading to accusations of 'dumbing down'. Librarians need to try to keep stories as accurate as possible within the demands of the media.

3 **Long-term effects**. It used to be easy to dismiss a harmful news story as 'tomorrow's chip wrapper'. Now stories remain online indefinitely and are read by a larger international audience than might have read the printed paper. To counteract this, responsible newspapers offer right to reply and will correct online stories.

4 **Adversarial approach**. While most Special Collections coverage is positive, especially on local news channels, watch out for more controversial situations when the interview is set up between two opposing views. Likewise, an antagonistic interviewer or a difficult final question can flummox an inexperienced person.

Making the most of the media

However, by understanding risks and thinking about the following key points, librarians can make the most of their media coverage.

1 **Know what makes a news story**, for example what works for a particular newspaper or channel, what interests its readers and its journalists, and understanding what kind of story is being offered. Local newspapers and radio stations are often looking for good news stories and may need material at short notice. Building links with individual journalists can result in mutual benefit.

2 **Understand the pressures**. Journalists operate on short timescales, to a news agenda. They will usually wish to follow up that day, and if that is not possible or a more interesting story emerges will drop the piece. They also tend to gather far more information than will be used. Don't take this personally! There will be other opportunities.

3 **Work with the press office** (if your parent organization has one). Press offices can be strict about who is allowed to contact and speak to the press, to protect the organization from damaging stories. If the librarian can persuade them of the value of Special Collections (e.g. helping with images and organizational history) and that they understand the issues, then an effective relationship can be built.

4 **Learn how to write a press release**. This is helpful even if there is a press office, as sending them a basic press release will save time. Press releases have standard structures and content, for example an appealing lead in and a quotation from someone important. They have to answer basic questions – Who? Why? When? – and include key information about funders or other third parties, in a limited number of words.

5 **Cope with questions on broadcast media**. Know the message to be conveyed and keep it simple and positive. Any question asked should be answered but taken by a 'bridge' to repeat the message. This is harder than it sounds when under pressure! If media training is offered (e.g. by the press office), it is worth taking.

Developing Special Collections web presence

First we consider 'official' Special Collections websites, which vary depending on their relationship to a wider organization.

Special Collections that are part of a research library, university or other big organization will have a site that is part of a larger corporate one. Such sites are likely to be managed by experienced staff, and comply with the basics of good and legal web design.

However, difficulties can arise. Special Collections users may be distinct from users of other parts of the website, and staff are likely to wish to put all kinds of material on the web: 'Descriptions of manuscripts, finding aids in HTML or PDF formats, Encoded Archival Description findings aids, short-title lists, and home-grown databases ...' Dowell (2008), not to mention images, films, podcasts ...

Special Collections may also feel constrained by the organization's understandable need to protect corporate identity and manage responsibilities under equality legislation. Corporate web pages are increasingly managed by cascading style sheets, templates and content management systems, which restrict scope for design and visual creativity by individual departments. Librarians need to work with their systems colleagues to ensure that the needs of Special Collections users are considered.

The use of corporate language and structures is often a problem on corporate sites. Ideally the content (even if not the design) of pages should be created by those who know the audience concerned. Special Collections users are probably not interested in management structures, but want to know about collections, opening hours, directions and who they need to contact.

Dowell (2008) gives an overview of the literature and discusses the redesign of the Lilly Library website, including focus group work that offers interesting insight into user perceptions of specialist terms, for example would a set of papers include photographs? Walton (2008) surveys how finding aids and other information about manuscript collections are appearing online in the US and Canada.

Smaller independent libraries often have either no internet presence or web pages with dated design and structures. In the one case the library is invisible, in the other the web presence is not doing it justice. Such libraries will not necessarily have specialist staff and need to find sustainable ways to enhance their web presence. It is increasingly possible to develop an effective web presence relatively cheaply and without specialist skills, for example by using blogging software such as WordPress, which requires little knowledge of code, to create traditional web page structures.

Whatever their web situation, librarians are advised to try to get as much rich, interesting, accurate content onto their organizational web as possible. This helps to make the service less costly and more convenient for readers to access, resulting in fewer enquiries about basic matters that could easily be covered on the site. Although, as we will see, social media has enormous potential, traditional web pages seem trustworthy and official in a way that social media cannot, and reach older or less digitally aware users who are more comfortable with the traditional web.

Exploring social media

Also known as **social networking** or **Web 2.0** (the latter also includes other interactive developments such as e-commerce). Web or mobile social media sites allow users to interact with each other and the site, in real time. Activities include blogging, micro-blogging (Twitter), social sites such as Facebook and LinkedIn, and video and image sharing sites such as YouTube or Flickr. These sites have enormous worldwide appeal, offering the potential for reaching out to audiences in new ways. Social media is generally free to use, widely available and intuitive in design.

Risks

Although social media seem simple and informal, as much planning is needed as for more formal communications channels. Issues include:

1 **Professional or personal**. It is important to be clear what you are trying to achieve, and on whose behalf you are speaking. If you are writing as yourself, decide how much of your personality and personal life you wish to reveal. Staff may keep their personal and professional personae distinct. However, these media work best with a little humour and humanity – an approach based solely on press releases and official communiqués is dull and would work better on the corporate web.
2 **Privacy, ethics and law**. The informality and fun of social media make it easy to forget that they are not private spaces. Data protection and copyright laws still apply. Criticizing and making fun of users who could easily identify themselves is risky. Social media inputs are visible to search engines: a funny tweet that made sense in context of everyone else's funny tweets may look quite different on the Google results page.
3 **Preservation**. If putting unique material or particular effort into social media sites, back them up: sites may be hacked or cease to exist. Devise a graceful exit strategy for a site that will not be maintained: the web is full of neglected blogs.
4 **Hostility**. Some users are hostile to social media, seeing it as aimless wittering (which it can be!). It is easier to direct such users to a blog if you call it an exhibition or web page instead. It can be more difficult to deal with hostile colleagues or management, particularly when they wish to restrict social media use. However, 'movers and shakers' in the organization are probably already using these media and they are becoming part of marketing strategy.

5 **Feedback**. Part of the value of social media for Special Collections is the chance to interact with others and get feedback. However, a policy on comments and other hostility is needed, for example moderating blog comments to remove spam and anything offensive.

6 **Service continuity**. Social media tends to assume those involved are individuals rather than corporate bodies, although this is changing, for example Facebook offer pages to organizations. The service may therefore be relying on individuals' accounts to maintain important communications. When staff leave or are away, it is important to have procedures for maintaining key social media.

Advice for social media

- A less formal tone than the corporate web works better.
- Experiment, play and try new things. There are no limits.
- Be courteous. Follow back, re-tweet, thank people.
- Share. If you find something interesting, let others know.
- Learn from others who are more experienced.

Suggestions for social media use by Special Collections
Blogs – inform and reflect

Blogs offer more scope for sharing rich, interesting detail about collections than institutional web pages. Unlike web pages where outdated entries are not appropriate, there is no expectation that old posts be removed. Hence blogging is a wonderful way for project workers to share their projects as they happen, making users feel more involved. We discovered the Cambridge University Tower Project in Chapter 3: contrast the light-hearted tone of the project blog with the formal University pages about it. Most of the projects mentioned in this book make effective use of blogs. The blog can also sustain a project beyond its formal lifespan, as we found with another case study, PaxCat Project: the reflections of our project archivist on the nature and history of peace campaigns remain popular two years on.

The reflective blog gives individuals a platform to share their views, for example on professional matters. Blogging can help build skills in natural, relaxed writing. It is particularly helpful for librarians who need to write for the public and can find it difficult to break with corporate writing styles. However, it is easy for bloggers to lose momentum, particularly if they started for the sake of having a blog rather having something to say. If a blog is no longer being updated, it should be elegantly wound down and maybe archived rather than being left as a fossil.

History today

The immediacy of blogging and micro-blogging make them perfect for historical projects in real time: low-cost and engaging ways to share with new audiences. Special Collections are full of historic material with dates that could be shared in this way, such as diaries, letters or logbooks. See, for example, two excellent Twitter projects based on the Second World War: the West Yorkshire Archives Service tweets air raids as they happened and the National Archives shares news from the War Cabinet Papers (see 'Examples and case studies' below). Embedding war news within people's modern data streams helps users understand how it felt at the time. When choosing a project, librarians need to be aware of copyright and data protection as with all publication, and make sure that they can sustain the project over the chosen time span.

Sight and sound
Social media offer great scope for sharing non-text media. Most blogging software can handle images, video and audio, and there are many specialist sites for particular media, full of users hungry for new content, e.g. Flickr, YouTube. Such sites are also ideal platforms for crowdsourcing and training.

Professional development
Special Collections staff can find social media invaluable in professional development and networking, for example by following 'mavens' or 'hubs' (people who are expert in a particular topic and share information from many sources). LinkedIn is the professional Facebook, offering links to many people in commerce and marketing who do not use other sites.

Service continuity
It is easy to add information to social media from any device and on the move, so they are ideal for posting news of changes to or problems with services, especially in emergencies. However, they are vulnerable to network issues so should not be absolutely relied on.

Understanding exhibitions
Exhibitions offer a way for larger numbers of people to encounter Special Collections than would be possible using the standard services. Many Special Collections have exhibition space, ranging from a case or two to a whole gallery. There are also opportunities to display outside library space, create joint displays or loan materials to other organizations, and, increasingly, possibilities online. Exhibitions can be based around ideas like those above, or highlight a new accession or completed project.

As with all marketing and communications, the curator needs to consider the audience, message, how to convey the message, and how the audience will respond and get involved. The curator need not necessarily be a librarian: exhibitions using Special Collections may be curated by academic staff, other experts or other groups as part of outreach (see Chapter 9), bringing different voices and ideas to the interpretation of the collections. Seeing exhibitions as part of a programme of events on the theme of the display reinforces the messages and enriches user experience, for example talks and blogs by curators, linked publications, expert lectures and merchandise.

Major exhibitions take years to plan and involve many staff; even smaller exhibitions require time and expense. Effective project management can help: particularly in highlighting risks such as work to be done by external firms.

Originals vs facsimiles

Original materials have so much to offer in exhibitions (their power is discussed in detail in Chapter 9). Sometimes, however, risks of light damage, theft, etc. may be too high and facsimiles used instead. This is not an easy option: copyright issues must be considered and extra time allowed for permissions, image capture and printing. For exhibitions in locations that would not be suitable for display of originals, for example schools or theatres, it may be worth developing loanable facsimile exhibits on boards or stands that can be loaned without worry.

Online exhibitions

It is now possible to create high quality exhibitions online, as stand-alone displays or to accompany physical exhibitions. Curators of physical exhibitions should seriously consider creating an online version, as it opens up the work to wider audiences, for longer periods, and reinforces the messages of the physical version. However, there are key differences between online and physical audiences and delivery:

1 **Context.** A visitor to a physical exhibition has decided to visit it (or at any rate the place in which it is displayed). They will see the exhibition as a whole. However, an online visitor may reach an individual exhibit directly from search engine results. Hence online exhibits need more explanation with each object than physical ones do.
2 **Scope**. An online exhibition can link to catalogues, web pages or any other source that helps illuminate the story of the exhibits. If required for context, more text can be associated with the images without overwhelming them.
3 **Time**. Unlike most physical exhibitions, online exhibitions can continue indefinitely, so the effort put into the original curation reaps rewards for longer. However, like any digital asset, online exhibits need care to make sure they remain online and working effectively. Online exhibitions do not have to be loaded all at once; the weekly or monthly reveal can create a long-lasting asset that has time to build awareness.

There are several options for creating and hosting online exhibitions, for example Omeka, a free open source platform for publishing collections online. Blogging software such as Wordpress or Tumblr can work well, especially for displays that add new items regularly. The right platform for a particular exhibition will be:

• **suitable** for the balance of text and images required

- **sustainable**. Either hosted in-house or on a well-established source that has clear back-up procedures. Ensure the exhibition is treated as a digital asset in emergency planning
- **manageable** with the staff and other resources available
- **accessible**, for example will work on various browsers and mobile devices.

Loaning

Loaning Special Collections to external exhibitions opens up new audiences and offers exposure beyond what their home service can provide. However, risks include:

- **theft/vandalism** while on display
- **theft or damage** in transit
- **environmental damage** while on display
- **fire, flood and other emergencies** while on display.

We mentioned the need for a policy on exhibition loans as part of the preservation policy in Chapter 1. This specifies standards such as BS 5454:2000 that must be met and outlines policy on fragile or particularly valuable items, which might not be loaned at all, or not by particular means of transport, for example vibrations during aeroplane travel might dislodge pigment on manuscripts.

Organizations applying to borrow Special Collections materials should be asked for details of the nature and timing of the exhibition. Conditions of loan should be agreed, covering issues such as insurance, expenses, facilities and who is authorized to handle the materials. A facilities report may also be required, outlining security of cases, room and building, environmental levels and controls, and emergency capability. Transit is a particularly risky time for collections items; Resource (2003) includes good advice on choosing a courier.

More promotional channels
Advertising

Advertising is a form of promotion: paid-for campaigns such as advertisements in the press, broadcast media or billboards. This is probably is too expensive for most Special Collections, who will find press releases a more productive way to reach the mass media. However, there may be niche publications, television channels or websites that enable a service to reach a particular audience.

Branding and corporate identity

Corporate identity and image are about the values and message put forward by a service. Branding is a way of creating powerful identities with their own images. It includes naming, slogans or tag lines, and developing logos. A brand can have its own Twitter account, website and other publicity. Like the marketing messages above, it humanizes, simplifies and makes memorable the complex reality of collections and services. Branding is useful for Special Collections because:

1 Services may be hidden in a management structure featuring acronyms and meaningless names; effective branding brings them out.
2 A project that might not appeal to all potential users can be given a separate identity and quality to keep it distinct from the wider service.

While large-scale branding needs the input of marketing experts, even a small project will benefit from an appealing and memorable name.

Libraries have a strong identity, as do Special Collections (or, at least, rare books and archives). Some of these ideas may be negative, and relate to dated views of library service (dust, ssshing), but there are also positive aspects: libraries embody values of free speech, accessibility, education and knowledge. They are trustworthy. Corporate identity and branding need to build on such positive associations, and try to turn round, play with or ignore the negatives.

Merchandizing

One way to build a brand is through merchandizing, from a few postcards in the porter's lodge to a large retail operation as found in major museums and libraries. The latter is of course a business specialism in itself and libraries are advised to employ experts. When creating products, it is important to have clear objectives: who is the target audience? Is the product to raise awareness or generate income? All the elements of the marketing mix need to be considered. Merchandizing should be:

- cost-effective
- relevant to collections
- appropriate for Special Collections
- ideally, witty, engaging, fun or appealing
- desirable to the target audience, for example if school parties visit, children will wish to buy pocket money gifts
- not time-restricted. Calendars and diaries can be risky.

There is more on income generation in Chapter 10.

Direct mailing

Contacting people directly by email or other means is a powerful way to reach them, for example to publicize the latest newsletter, exhibition or event. However, if badly handled, it is also a way to annoy them. This area of marketing is regulated; for example in the UK, the Privacy and Electronic Communications Regulations apply to marketing by electronic means such as email. In particular:

1 Consent should not be assumed: people must agree to receive mailings.
2 Direct mail should always include details of the sender and a simple way to opt out of receiving it.

To manage this process, mailing lists should be created of people who wish to hear from Special Collections, which record their details and the nature of contact and can be easily updated. Depending on the scale of the operation, lists can be managed using spreadsheets or databases, online software such as Mailchimp, or specialist customer relationship software. Direct mailing is also essential in fund-raising from individuals, discussed in Chapter 10.

Researching user needs

This is the other side of communications: how users let Special Collections know their views on the collections and services offered. Many of the channels mentioned above allow users to have their say, for example exhibitions include visitors' books, social media are by their nature interactive, websites can contain feedback forms and contact details. However, these may not be enough to give librarians the information they need: here are other useful techniques.

Finding out about users and potential users is more difficult for Special Collections than for some general library services, because many users may visit only once and the potential audience is so wide. Friends' groups (see Chapter 10) may be useful though of course may not necessarily represent other users. **Market segmentation** can help. This is the process of splitting users into groups depending on their needs and elements of the marketing mix. Groups can be split by commodity, place or price, and by which communications channels appeal to them. For example, one could consider all potential users of a particular collection, people who live locally or users of a social media platform.

Market research is the way in which users are asked their views. It is another specialist branch of marketing, with its own experts and techniques. Major research is best commissioned from such experts. Smaller projects done in-house need effective planning:

* defining the issue to be researched
* devising an effective method (for the right audience)
* gathering data
* analysing data
* presenting the findings to management and users
* taking action based on the findings
* letting users know action has been taken.

Some useful market research techniques for Special Collections:

1 **Observation**. Watching or recording how people interact with services, for example how long they remain on web pages and where they go next, or how they behave in

an exhibition or reading room space. Mystery shoppers are useful for testing services with fresh eyes.

2 **Surveys/questionnaires**. These must be well designed to produce useful information. They might include forms that pop up on a website, paper forms in the reading room or questioning by a person. Online software like SurveyMonkey makes it easier to create online surveys. Surveys should be piloted first to weed out ambiguities and care is needed in creating questions, for example whether to use yes/no, a range of options or free text. Special Collections in larger organizations need to be mindful of other market research that may be going on so users don't get survey fatigue. It may be useful to incorporate questions concerning Special Collections into wider surveys and market research, but this should only be done where it will elicit useful information.

3 **Focus groups**. A small group is gathered to discuss ideas or to carry out particular activities, while being observed and recorded. Incentives (from biscuits to iPods) may help, especially for students. Creating and facilitating such groups is a skill and requires planning. Focus groups are useful for more complex feelings and ideas that a questionnaire format cannot capture, or for seeing how people interact with a particular technology (e.g. Dowell 2008).

Conclusion

As this chapter deals with the details of marketing Special Collections, it has emphasized particular promotional methods and channels and offered many examples to inspire readers. These include web pages, social media, the mass media and exhibitions. However, it is most important to understand how promotion fits into the marketing mix for collections and services, and to remember that gathering information from users or potential users and finding out about their needs is as important as telling them what is available.

Further reading

Many marketing textbooks exist aimed at librarians, archivists, museum staff and other non-profit workers, for example De Sáez (2002), an excellent introduction to marketing theory for librarians.

Social media: Theimer (2010) and Whittaker and Thomas (2009). The volumes in the Neal-Schumann/Facet 'Tech Set' cover key social media topics for librarians, for example Crosby (2010) on blogging in libraries, Hastings (2010) on micro-blogging (Twitter, Tumblr). Social media themselves are full of advice and support.

Exhibitions: Milne and McKie (2009). For exhibition loans, see McIntyre et al. (2000) and the Association of College and Research Libraries (2005) guidelines (currently under revision).

Examples and case studies

Gilding the Lilly, http://newsinfo.iu.edu/news/page/normal/15851.html

J. B. Priestley Archive, www.bradford.ac.uk/library/special/priestley.php

King James Bible exhibits, www.manifoldgreatness.org; and
    www.lib.cam.ac.uk/exhibitions/KJV/index.html

Monk's Blood Manuscript, www.tsd.ac.uk/en/rbla/onlineexhibitions/thomasphillipsexhibition/
    13th-16thcentury/petrusdecapua

Sydney Playbill, www.nla.gov.au/news/story.php?id=391 and www.amw.org.au/register

War Cabinet, http://twitter.com/#!/ukwarcabinet

West Yorkshire Archives Service, http://twitter.com/#!/WR_ARP

Useful websites

CILIP Publicity and Public Relations Group, www.cilip.org.uk/get-involved/special-interest-
    groups/publicity/Pages/default.aspx

Mailchimp mailing list software, http://mailchimp.com

Omeka, http://omeka.org

SurveyMonkey survey software, http://surveymonkey.com

The Wikiman, http://thewikiman.org/blog (blog on marketing libraries)

9
Widening access to Special Collections

Introduction

This chapter looks at widening access to Special Collections beyond the standard services to traditional groups of users outlined in Chapter 7, reaching out to market Special Collections to new audiences. It should be seen in light of the ideas and techniques presented in Chapter 8. It will:

1 Explain why Special Collections are trying to widen access.
2 Discuss issues and obstacles in widening access.
3 Look in detail at Special Collections work with two groups of non-traditional users: undergraduates and school-age children.
4 Introduce other possibilities for widening access.

Widening access is often known as **outreach**. It is becoming more significant in Special Collections work: libraries are recognizing how valuable Special Collections can be in making their organization distinctive and helping with lifelong learning. Other terms associated with widening access are **audience development**, 'identifying who you want to engage with your heritage project, and taking proactive steps to attract and retain their interest' (Heritage Lottery Fund website, www.hlf.org.uk) and **community engagement**, in which universities and other organizations try to work more closely with local people.

Why build new audiences?

Special Collections often lack time and resources to manage existing readers, not to mention preservation problems, hidden collections and other pressures. The activities in this chapter are, as all commentators observe, highly labour-intensive. So why are librarians keen to reach out to new audiences?

Proactive way to develop service

The Special Collections world is changing, thanks to mass digitization of older texts. Librarians cannot assume that the same groups will continue to wish to access collections in the same way. Rather than watching traditional use decline, why not seek new audiences and explore new ways of using collections?

Advocacy

Chapter 10 explains that Special Collections must demonstrate their value to their institution by showing how they contribute to its mission:

1 Special Collections in universities can do this by emphasizing their work with students, increasingly central to their parent organization's mission.
2 Special Collections can offer any parent organization a way to reach beyond their walls into communities, thanks to their range of compelling materials and stories.

Not to forget, of course, that the more people who understand and appreciate Special Collections, the more support they will receive for their work in future.

Moral imperative

In addition to these pragmatic arguments for encouraging wider access, there are moral arguments. Why should material whose care is financed by the public be inaccessible to the public? Or, as Torre (2008) puts it, 'Why should they not benefit from rare books?' Visser (2006) quotes Roberts: 'the political and intellectual climate in which we now live, whether we like it or not, will make it increasingly difficult to house our special collections in ivory towers'. This climate includes the free, easy availability of information online and the influence of freedom of information legislation.

Issues in widening access

However, there are challenges in increasing access to Special Collections.

Building relationships

The audiences discussed in this chapter may not use the standard marketing channels for Special Collections we saw in Chapter 8. They may be most easily reached by forming links with people who work with them regularly, for example academic staff and subject librarians for undergraduates or teachers for schoolchildren. Such individuals, like librarians themselves, are very busy and face conflicting pressures. Marketing Special Collections to them involves understanding these pressures and developing ideas that will help them help their students, as we will see later in this chapter.

Capacity: time and skills

Building relationships with these helpful people takes time, as does researching the audience, organizing, planning, running and assessing the activities offered. Teaching and outreach also require skills new to many librarians, for example handling large, possibly unruly or exuberant groups.

Many Special Collections have created roles for staff that concentrate on undergraduate teaching or community engagement, often known as education officers. These individuals will have the time and skills to make links and plan effective sessions and have experience of working with similar groups. However, it is important that teaching and outreach are not left entirely to them, especially if their post is temporary. A close relationship with other staff, possibly by joint teaching, will ensure that the education officer has the information about collections and other support they need.

In smaller libraries currently unable to employ a specialist, capacity can be built gradually, for example by working with more experienced institutions on a project. Museums are a particular source of good practice and may be keen to find partners. Another possibility is to target the keenest academic staff or the groups of students who would gain most from Special Collections, for example those studying history. Note that funding bodies are often keen to support outreach, indeed its presence in a project may be an essential requirement.

Objects and preservation

The Special Collections objects themselves should be at the heart of outreach activities wherever possible. They have a physical presence, tactile nature and even smell completely different from modern printed sources, let alone digital materials that flatten and homogenize diverse physical formats. The great age and historical associations of many Special Collections objects add to their magic. A medieval manuscript may be the oldest object many young people have ever seen, let alone touched. As Allen (1999) says of a rare book, 'without moving an inch, it has within itself the power to "move" all the students in the room toward it, both physically and intellectually'.

However, Traister (2003) makes a vital point about the use of physical objects in outreach:

> What, after all, does it mean for a class 'to see' such materials? Is the sight of a First Folio worth a thousand words about it? ... Practical as well as intellectual questions need to be asked ... what does 'showing' the First Folio to a class of students mean? May members of the class touch the book? turn a leaf? look at the endpapers? examine the binding?'

It is therefore essential to decide how visitors will interact with physical objects before the session begins. A balance between preservation and learning needs is required. The rules for the session need to be made clear and the intermediaries informed before the visit. Otherwise, as Traister observes, misunderstandings can result. Standard rules about food, drink, use of supports and other equipment should be maintained. It makes sense to avoid using fragile, damaged or dirty materials. If these are used for any reason, they should only be handled by the librarian. The rules should be explained 'so that students will understand why it takes a little extra effort to use these materials and that the effort is well worth it' (Taraba 2003).

The **handling collection** is a useful idea borrowed from museums: a collection that mirrors the main collection or illustrates particular topics, gathered for educational purposes and above all for learners to handle. It offers the magic of real objects while protecting the originals in Special Collections. For example, 'in the special collections department at CU-Boulder, fourth graders studying Medieval manuscripts may not handle the manuscripts but are encouraged to handle modern models of wax tablets and limp vellum bindings, as well as samples of parchment and rag paper, quills and lead type' (Visser 2006).

Digital innovations such as augmented reality (see Chapter 7 and below) may be able to combine access to the physical objects with rich online information.

Spaces

The ideal: separate space(s) near Special Collections storage, which does not impinge on standard reader services and offers modern teaching and learning facilities for groups. Any new build or refurbished Special Collections service should include such areas, which are also useful for launch events and other social activities.

If this is not possible, depending on numbers, it may be possible to use a reading room, which offers security for collections, the rich experience of seeing them *in situ* and control of the situation by staff. However, such sessions may disrupt normal services, and the reading room may not be large enough or laid out in a suitable way. Otherwise, in a university setting, regular teaching spaces could be used, though the experience will be slightly less rich for students as it will involve a familiar space. As with so many Special Collections issues, there is no right or one answer, but a range of solutions involving various compromises.

Widening access is not always about physical access: later we consider online and distance learning methods. For libraries with major space concerns, these offer a route to outreach until improvements can be made.

Barriers

Special Collections can be intimidating environments to those who are not used to them. Witness Torre's (2008) experience:

> I had avoided visiting [the rare book room] alone because of the slips that required a person to cite their research purposes for being there … I regarded the slips as eliciting a defense as to why I deserved to handle anything in the collection at all.
>
> The rare book room itself was stunningly intimidating because of its lush and extravagant appearance. The door was a heavy glass one that seemed just heavy enough that it permitted you to turn away, believing it locked or that you really were in the wrong place. It was located, like most rare book rooms, in an out of the way part of the library. You had to take the elevator to a special floor just to get to it. The floors were covered in an array of splendid rugs, high leather backed chairs, and paintings of dead white males, hovering among the walls.

This account highlights two kinds of barrier to widening access. They do of course, as in this case, overlap.

1 **Physical**. Like this one, some services intimidate because of their grand appearance. Many more within general libraries are located in remote spaces. Issues include the exterior design, interior layout and poor signage.
2 **Managerial**. Procedures that seem sensible precautions to librarians (asking why individuals wish to access material) are off-putting to users and prevent many from gaining access. Traister (2000) is a classic, provocative article on practices in some US research libraries; the author argued that they had gone way too far in setting preservation above access, effectively excluding almost everyone. There have been many follow-ups and reflections on this original piece.

Both kinds equate to negative marketing to particular audiences. The message they receive, as the Torre quote shows, is that the service is not for them.

So what can librarians do about this? The first step, as with so many matters, is to understand that the barriers exist. It is not enough to argue that if the service is open to the public, that it is accessible to the public. Working with intermediaries cuts through the barriers: if a group is brought by someone they know and trust, the environment and procedures will be less of a concern. There may of course be barriers towards developing the relationships with the intermediaries, but as fellow professionals with shared interests, these will be less serious.

The location and nature of Special Collections space are difficult to change. However, reviewing the layout of spaces and signage may help. Taking the service beyond the space by exhibitions in other parts of the library, other organizations and online will make a difference. Access procedures should be kept under review, not only as to whether they are necessary, but also how they are explained to potential users.

Closed access

This is another barrier, requiring readers to master the use of catalogues and finding aids or to be able to articulate their needs effectively to library staff. Users may be familiar with the idea of browsing in a library and find closed access restrictive and puzzling. Given the issues raised in Chapters 1 and 2, it would be inappropriate to make most Special Collections physically browsable. Ways in which this barrier could be reduced therefore include:

1 Making finding aids easier to use and more powerful. Some new developments discussed in Chapter 5 do just that.
2 Pre-packaging and intermediation by librarians. This may include creating learning objects, as we will discuss later, or simply sharing information about Special Collections in more informal ways, for example via blogs. Librarians need to

present themselves to users not as dragons sitting on treasure (Traister 2003) but as companions and guides in finding out about collections.

Nature of collections

The nature of the Special Collections will affect the outreach that can be offered. Large research libraries can probably offer collections in support of any subject or project that could be imagined. Special Collections with more narrow strengths will need more careful consideration about outreach, but there are sure to be possibilities. The collection development policy (see Chapter 4) could include outreach potential as a factor in materials choice in future

Two key audiences for Special Collections

We now consider in more detail two key audiences. Most writing about Special Collections outreach has concentrated on undergraduates and school-age children, for the reasons discussed above. We will also discuss briefly other possible audiences. Although it is convenient to treat them as uniform groups, remember that there are many different types of undergraduates and children, who will have different knowledge, ideas and preferences that will need to be considered in planning.

Working with undergraduates in Special Collections

Introduction

Recently, Special Collections librarians in universities have actively welcomed undergraduates, encouraging them to engage with collections. This is in contrast to traditional practice in which such collections have been seen mainly as the preserve of academics and researchers (though there are early examples of such outreach).

Alongside the general factors mentioned above, this change has been driven by the changing nature of undergraduate teaching and learning, which is becoming more group and project-based. Special Collections lend themselves well to these more flexible, active and research-led methods and students (certainly in the UK) are increasingly keen to work with primary sources for their dissertations.

This section assumes that the Special Collections concerned belong to the university, but Special Collections in other institutions can be valuable resources for undergraduate learning. Existing channels could be used, for example many English cathedral libraries have links with local universities, or suitable project funding might be found. Witness for example the Brooklyn Historical Society, which received a US Department of Education grant to create a model for collaboration with higher education. The programme, Students and Faculty in the Archives (SAFA), will work with five local universities, enabling students in history, photography, architecture and other subjects to encounter the Society's archive collections with the support of their tutors.

Issues

Alongside the outreach challenges above, there are extra issues to consider when working with undergraduates.

Developing effective teaching sessions requires time and planning. They need to take place at the right time of day, week, academic year and stage of learning, be pitched at the appropriate level, and fit into the course structure. Otherwise, sessions may be poorly attended and unhelpful to students.

To ensure sessions meet these requirements and to reach the undergraduates, collaboration with academic staff is essential. However, in institutions where little teaching using Special Collections has been done, it can be difficult to engage academic staff and persuade them of the value of teaching in this way. It helps to find academic champions within a department who will encourage others to become involved and to seize any opportunities that become available, or to go through subject librarians if they already have good links within the department. Likewise getting to know departmental administrative staff can help with timetabling and other practical arrangements.

It is vital to establish how teaching will be carried out and who will deliver it. In any case, both groups have a part to play. Librarians offer their detailed understanding of the collections and awareness of preservation matters, faculty know what students are being taught and their learning needs at different stages. See Bond and Butler (2009) for the challenges faced by a collaborative project between a librarian and a professor to teach book history at Washington State University.

Engaging undergraduates with Special Collections

Special Collections staff will be familiar with talking about treasures to small groups who are already interested. This approach has its uses for students, particularly those who are already engaged in relevant study. However, a standard presentation by the librarian may not be the best method for many students. Krause (2010) surveyed 12 archivists who were experienced in working with undergraduates. They reported that in response to student needs, they had moved from traditional lecture-based 'show and tell' to more effective active and visual methods of bringing Special Collections to groups. Such approaches can go beyond the wow factor of beautiful, old or interesting material to engage with the details of its making and meaning.

The literature of learning styles is beyond the scope of this book, but it is worth remembering that the ways staff prefer to learn may not be the ways students or other visitors do. Offering a varied experience with a range of activities and senses may help reach more people. Consider for example:

1 **Visual impact**. Using objects with immediate visual appeal: attractiveness, age, gilding, colour, scale, as different as possible from typical books and other items familiar to students. Use of a historic reading room or other space enriches the experience.

2 **Practical**. Showing students how collections were created may help them to understand them better. Levy (2005) suggests teaching students studying the history of communication to use a hand-press, bind a book and try calligraphy. Students may also learn by trying basic conservation and digitization activities.

3 **Group work**. There are many ways to work with students in groups, for example see below for the Cephalonian method. Students can learn from exploring an object as a group and then discussing it. See Gardner and Pavelich (2008).

4 **Games**, for example guessing the age or nature of materials, putting them in order (oldest, etc.) can work well. The size of groups needs to be limited, the games need to be simple to explain, and the exercises should be designed so students have a chance of finding the right answer.

5 **Competition/awards**. This element can encourage students to explore Special Collections, for example book collecting contests, essay or creative writing prizes, fellowships or other awards, scholarships.

Introducing online and distance learning

Online outreach loses the magic of contact with objects we mentioned above. But it can reach great numbers of people who could never visit Special Collections for time or geographic reasons. It can also be used to attract teachers and others who may visit later, and to reinforce what has been learned during a session. Information can be made available without time or space constraints, and used and adapted indefinitely. A few online methods:

1 **Virtual Learning Environments** (VLEs) or other course delivery software. Students and schoolchildren will know and respect this source, and it enables material to be precisely targeted at particular groups. However, access is restricted beyond those groups; some material might be better on the web.

2 **Mobile technologies** introduced in Chapter 7 offer many possibilities for enriching the learning experience. See for example, the SCARLET Project, funded by JISC and based at the University of Manchester, which will use augmented reality to enable 'students to experience the magic of original materials, whilst enhancing the learning experience by "surrounding" the object with digitized content; images, texts, online learning resources and information on related objects held in the Library and elsewhere' (www.jisc.ac.uk/whatwedo/programmes/elearning/ltig/scarlet.aspx). This exciting project will produce a toolkit to enable other librarians to do similar work with their collections. Such technologies will be familiar to students and help them engage with the original objects.

3 **Learning objects and curriculum packets**. Small, self-contained learning resources are an excellent way to reach teachers and to offer online learning in a managed way. Witness the objects produced by Nottingham University's Special Collections and Archives, which include units offering guidance on how to research

using Special Collections and objects based on original documents aimed at A-Level plus, for example the writing of a short story by D. H. Lawrence.

4 **Collaborative spaces**. Use of wikis and social media can add an extra, interactive dimension to online learning.

Ways to use Special Collections with students

Induction

Also known as **orientation** or **familiarization**. Useful as a taster before a longer course, or as a slot within the training offered by subject librarians to all students, it builds on standard practice in dealing with any new Special Collections user. Aiming to introduce students to Special Collections at the university and ensure they know how to make effective use of them, it might cover:

- nature of collections: strengths, star collections
- how to find out more: catalogues, web pages, etc.
- practicalities: opening hours, how to book appointments, what to bring (and not to bring), etc.

This approach should meet the needs of students who are already have an active interest in Special Collections, maybe having encountered them before. However, it may not engage the less experienced. The Cephalonian approach to induction could work well for Special Collections. This involves students by having them ask questions from coloured cards – they can be funny or quirky, for example: 'What's in the cage/tower (if you have one)? What's the oldest book? What are the gloves for?'

Information literacy

This is 'the ability to find, use, evaluate and communicate information' (LILAC, www.lilacconference.com). This is an increasingly vital skill for students when so much information, of varying quality, is so readily available, and when universities are working to enhance students' transferable skills for employment.

It is not always realized that Special Collections can play a part in teaching information literacy. Witness, however, two of the performance indicators for information literacy in Association of College and Research Libraries (2000b):

The information-literate student …

- 2e. Differentiates between primary and secondary sources, recognizing how their use and importance vary with each discipline …
- 2f. Realizes that information may need to be constructed with raw data from primary sources.

These are the very stuff of Special Collections work.

However, it can be difficult to move information literacy teaching (with or without Special Collections) beyond traditional library skills teaching. Academic staff may not grasp the complexity of what students need to learn, dismissing information literacy as 'electronic, introductory, and teachable in a single visit' (Mazella and Grob 2011). These authors collaborated on a course for English majors intended to improve information and critical thinking skills by focusing on enquiries and research. Working with students as researchers creates new, positive relationships between them and academic staff and librarians, as was found by the Angel in the House research-based undergraduate module at Bath Spa University. Such courses encourage students to develop as researchers rather than passive learners.

Understanding primary sources

An understanding of primary sources is the basis of studying the humanities. Special Collections materials, even if actually printed or published, offer a wealth of such materials. They can support learning in history of all kinds, art, design, music, geography, archaeology … This goes beyond the traditional humanities subjects: almost any academic subject has historic origins that might be illustrated using Special Collections, for example physics (first edition of Newton's *Principia*).

Special Collections can help literature students by giving them an idea of the creation and transmission of the texts studied. Literature students may think of the modern paperback or study notes as the text; to see how it appeared to its creator and its first readers is a thrilling experience. Witness this oft-quoted comment in Gardner (2006):

> Even the coolest undergraduates describe workshops with the literary collections, which take place under the supervision of experienced curators, as 'magical' and one student studying Daphne du Maurier's Rebecca, memorably described du Maurier's original typescript as 'the big gun': 'It's like that's when you get your [white] gloves on! It's like the big hitter, the one everyone was looking forward to when it was going round the circle.'

McCoy (2010) discusses the China Missions project, in which students studied and formed questions on particular letters from missionary priests in China. Points to note: use of unexpected images to intrigue (priests on motorcycles!) and how the students came to sympathize with the individual whose letter they studied. The article contains interesting reactions from students over the course of the project. Not all were positive, finding the lack of results and the frequent dead ends frustrating. However, this engagement with the sometimes disappointing reality of historical research takes work with Special Collections beyond looking at treasures into a deeper understanding of the material record of history.

The nature of objects

Students can also engage with the physical nature of Special Collections materials, their structure, production and meaning. Universities that teach the history of the book, communication and media studies will find Special Collections perfect for illustrating the subjects in physical form. Students of librarianship, information studies, archives and museum management will also benefit from the opportunity to see examples of historic communication. Such universities are also likely to have postgraduates and faculty specializing in aspects of communications history (e.g. printing or bindings) who are keen to work with librarians on teaching these subjects.

Using ephemera and artists' books

New or unexpected formats such as ephemera, private press and artists' books can help enliven learning for students.

Gardner and Pavelich (2008) explore the value of teaching undergraduates using tickets and other advertising for the 1893 Chicago World's Fair, plus other ephemera. The resemblance of ephemera to materials with which students are familiar in their own lives helps them to grasp what it teaches. This is particularly true of ephemera created by previous students in the university archives, like the materials they are creating in their own careers. Ephemera also enable librarians to explore with students the reliability of historical evidence, for example did a concert advertised on a flyer actually happen?

Taraba (2003) explains the uses of artists' books: they 'invite the reader to touch, to interact with the book, to read it and figure it out. Many students find artists' books immediately captivating and more accessible than some of the traditional rare books in the collection.' Their appeal differs from the 'sacro-power' (Allen, 1999) of manuscripts and rare books: they are often created with wit, humour and irreverence, and are in modern language. The response may be delight rather than awe. Taraba also notes that artists' books often engage with older texts, offering students a bridge to help them reach the more difficult older work, for example 'Laura Davidson's Ideal City which uses the image of the fall of Babylon from the Nuremberg Chronicle to stand for Boston ...'

Inspiration

Special Collections are full of materials that could inspire a creative response in students, as part of their courses or a personal interest. Think creative or life writing, art, design, fashion, theatre, performance or computer gaming. The inspiration could be the visual or other sensual aspect of the objects (e.g. cockled parchment), the stories they contain, for example provenance, or some aspect of the Special Collections experience.

Working through others such as tutors or artists/writers in residence will help librarians to think about which materials to offer. Encourage groups to create their own response to collections by producing work based on them, for example their own artists' books or ephemera.

Special Collections can help not only with ideas for creative work, but show students how other creative people developed their skills. For instance, the papers of writers, as

Gardner (2006) observes, can show students how even the greatest finished literary works are created through drafts, giving them more confidence in their own work. Pavelich (2010) outlines 'five examples of creative writing sessions hosted in the Special Collections Research Center of the University of Chicago Library: historical fiction, editorial interventions, drafts, versions, and self publishing and alternative book forms'.

Curation

Asking students to curate an exhibition builds many transferable skills, for example group work, understanding of objects, organizational skills, marketing and design. However, it can be challenging for students and demanding for staff to facilitate it, as Bond and Butler (2009) explain. If space is an issue, the exhibition could be electronic. The choice of collection is crucial: it needs to have enough scope for students to feel they are making choices but not overwhelm them. Treasures of printing or the University's material relating to past students seem to work well.

Special Collections can also offer training in how to create exhibitions more generally, to students studying subjects such as art or museology. For example, Cardiff University offers a workshop on exhibitions taught by Special Collections staff, conservators, academic staff and, sometimes, external partners such as local museums.

The dissertation

Students often engage with Special Collections for their dissertations. This offers them exciting opportunities to carry out original research, often on material that has not been consulted by other scholars.

Special Collections can help in two ways:

1 Offering subjects for student research. It may be helpful to students to pre-package good ideas for themes or topics, for example see the University of Reading 'history explorer'. This directs students considering dissertation topics towards areas that Special Collections can support.
2 Advice on how to use primary sources in research. Some students will wish to use materials held elsewhere, but their local Special Collections staff can still help them to approach this work to get the most from the experience.

Case study: love and fear in the stacks

This illustrates two key points: engaging undergraduates does not have to be only about what happens in class, and many of the suggestions in Chapter 8 can be adapted for new audiences.

Summerfield Hammerman et al. (2006) outline a programme of fun holiday-themed events during study breaks at the University of Chicago. This bright idea worked round the problems of limited finance and staffing, plus preservation issues. The events were:

1 Love in the Stacks (Valentine's Day) featured romantic materials including Victorian Valentine verse.

2 Things that go Bump in the Stacks (Hallowe'en) included a first edition of Mary Shelley's *Frankenstein*, Defoe's *A System of Magick* and a parlour book of illusions.

Separate seasonal food treats were offered nearby, but obviously not allowed near the displays. The events were an overwhelming success. Note that they used a standard Special Collections message (holidays) and that the holidays chosen are particularly enjoyed by and relevant to young people. Both the appeal of food and its risk to collections were highlighted. Such events could be enhanced by the use of social media.

Working with schools in Special Collections
Introduction
It can be difficult to make links with teachers, who are of course busy people. Using existing contacts helps, for example teacher trainers or museums, as does knowing the demands placed on teachers. This makes it possible to package the idea of working with Special Collections as a solution. Special Collections are best placed to do this where schools are encouraged or required to develop students' use and understanding of primary sources as part of information literacy. Such requirements may be supported by funding schemes to help teachers use historic material, for example Teaching with Primary Sources grants from the Library of Congress. Creating online packages of teaching resources directed at teachers' needs appears to work very well: see for example Archives Alive! at Newcastle University, which offers teachers ideas based on themes including the history of cholera and creative writing. They are then encouraged to visit the service for more, including handling sessions, source evaluation, A Level study sessions, and a cholera investigation.

Engaging schoolchildren with Special Collections
The points made about work with students also apply to working with younger people. Similar topics seem to appeal, and the methods that work for undergraduates will work for younger audiences: keeping things visual, hands-on, exciting, competitive.

However, teaching younger children is challenging, for example attention spans are likely to be shorter and language needs to be simpler. Material chosen needs to be appropriate to the age of the children. There are of course also legal issues as discussed in Chapter 6.

In light of this, successful visits by younger children to Special Collections require pre-planning by librarians and teachers to ensure age-appropriate and appealing content, along with supervision by teachers and other helpers during the event. The use of a handling collection, as suggested above, may take some pressure off staff and helpers, as damage done matters less.

Given these issues, plus space problems, some libraries may decide that they can only manage visits by older children. However, they can still bring Special Collections to younger children by working with teachers, for example:

1 In workshops (e.g. making books, calligraphy or other useful classroom activities). These skills can be cascaded to teachers and thence to many more children than the library could have handled directly. Visser (2006) mentions a book arts project that taught 200 teachers and thereby reached 26,000 children.
2 Bringing in the expertise of teachers or student teachers to use Special Collections to create learning packages, as we saw above, and below.

Librarians can learn a great deal from Special Collections and museums that exist to work with children. Witness for example the activities at Seven Stories in Newcastle, home to children's literature archives, or the Roald Dahl Museum and Story Centre.

Here are two case studies that illustrate the many ways Special Collections can work with young people.

Case study: cartoon creations

Robb (2009) describes the Opper Project, a successful collaboration (funded by a private donor) between the Ohio State University Cartoon Library and Museum and the University's History Teaching Institute (HTI). The project produced learning packages for schools based on editorial cartoons, a fun, visual way to help students understand history. Graduate students mined the collections for suitable images and teachers created the packages, in return for honoraria and educational credits. The site proved very popular with teachers and the methodology was later used with another Special Collection at Ohio. The project seems to have been based on two sound principles:

1 Understanding the barriers to access for the intended audience: even though the collections were catalogued or digitized, they would still be hidden from busy teachers who need someone to package the content in helpful ways.
2 Using an existing strength: the HTI worked with local teachers, so staff understood their needs and had the right contacts to recruit the teachers needed to make the project happen.

Case study: bright young things

Year 10 students from a school in Manchester created an exhibition of lighting designs, which were shown with the artworks and books from Manchester Metropolitan University Special Collections that inspired them. The sessions were facilitated by a designer who was an alumna of the University and fitted into the General Certificate of

Secondary Education (GCSE) Design and Technology curriculum. Each student was asked to design a light for home use for a specific function and space. The project was funded by the V&A under a national scheme, Design for Life, which seeks to use designers and collections to engage young people in design. Note the:

- use of the unique selling point of these Special Collections: design
- fit with national aspirations to get more students into design and into a particular curriculum slot
- use of the external expert to facilitate the work
- specific brief given to the students.

Exploring new audiences

Alongside these two key groups, there are many other groups to whom Special Collections could reach out: families, community groups, people in retirement homes … The points made earlier about visual, hands-on and above all fun activities apply even more when engagement with Special Collections is not part of a course of study. This is an area in which wider initiatives such as Heritage Open Days and the other marketing themes mentioned in Chapter 8 are particularly useful: these enable librarians to interest the media, which in turn may reach the target audiences. Again the use of intermediaries with the right contacts can help.

Inspiration and advice can be found from other heritage professionals who work extensively with communities, for example museum staff and local studies librarians. Useful sites that outline the range of possibilities include My Learning, CILIP Local Studies Group, and the National Co-ordinating Centre for Public Engagement, which exists to help universities work with communities. Librarians based in universities and other large organizations might form partnerships with colleagues who are also engaging with the public. Friends (see Chapter 10) and volunteers may also be able to assist in this area.

A few suggestions:

1 **Open Days** (tying in with national initiatives or with particular themes, for example An Apple a Day at Reading University and the Museum of English Rural Life displays apple-related Special Collections at an event that promotes English apples in a fun way for families).
2 **Summer schools** and other in-depth learning opportunities enable people to engage in detail with Special Collections and experts.
3 **Reminiscence therapy**: Special Collections with 20th century holdings might help assemble collections to help people with dementia through familiar objects and activities.
4 **Community-generated collections and metadata** (see Chapters 4 and 5). Working with users to create resources generates a more equal relationship between staff and the public and may help to bring down barriers to access.

5 **Volunteering**. Helping build skills is a way for Special Collections to develop the profession for the future and to engage with local communities. Many grant-giving bodies require or encourage funded projects to involve volunteers from the community.

6 **Roadshows**: taking collections to people, as in the following case study.

Case study: travelling treasures

This case study shows that with imagination and financial backing, it is possible to overcome barriers to access while continuing to care for collections. Tidy (2008) wrote about a project that took rare books and other treasures from the State Libraries of Victoria, in Australia, on tour to rural parts of the state. Geography (sheer distance) limits access to exhibitions of these treasures for many people. Supported by philanthropy, the project took rare items to thousands of people in schools and public libraries to towns across the state. The displays were supported by lectures and events. Among the items chosen were rare books such as Hooke's *Micrographia* (mentioned in Chapter 3) and significant archives, for example Margaret Ingham's diary that survived a shipwreck. Preservation and security were maintained: the items were carefully guarded and locked in confidential locations at night.

Managing assessment and feedback

Relatively little work has been done on this aspect of outreach in Special Collections. Two recent surveys (Krause 2010 and O'Gara, Walters and Putirskis 2010) find that most assessment is informal, based on simple forms and tally marks, or squeezed into statistics created to measure the work of general libraries. These surveys are based on US libraries but the findings would probably be borne out by other Special Collections.

Basic feedback might include asking learners how they felt about the session and what they learnt. This is easily done using feedback forms or polls embedded in the VLE or other online survey methods. Audience reaction software (e.g. Qwizdom) allows the trainer to poll a class and get instant results to show. However, it is much more difficult to go beyond this to see how learners find the visit useful later on; this may be something the learners themselves find hard to articulate.

As the O'Gara piece notes, this is a serious problem. We may know anecdotally the value of outreach, but Special Collections need to find ways to measure and evaluate this in order to make the case for resources to support it. As mentioned in Chapter 7, the Archival Metrics site offers a toolkit to study use by student researchers, and see Yakel and Tibbo (2010).

Conclusion

Special Collections librarians are actively trying to improve access to collections for undergraduates, schoolchildren and other new audiences. Collections can be used for teaching information literacy, subjects and other skills to undergraduates. These activities are rewarding but require a great deal of planning and development to be worthwhile. Barriers include psychological and physical obstacles and concerns, capacity, and relationships with faculty and other key people. This chapter has shared research and good practice from many Special Collections librarians working in this challenging but exciting area.

Further reading

In addition to the many articles cited, a forthcoming Association of College and Research Libraries publication entitled *The Past is Portal: teaching undergraduates using special collections and archives* will be invaluable.

Examples and case studies

An Apple a Day, www.publicengagement.ac.uk/how/case-studies/apple-day

Angel in the House, Bath Spa University,
www.english.heacademy.ac.uk/explore/publications/casestudies/linking/angel.php

Archives Alive!, http://archivesalive.ncl.ac.uk

Bright Young Things at MMU, www.specialcollections.mmu.ac.uk/exhibitions.php

Exeter University Special Collections teaching,
http://as.exeter.ac.uk/library/about/special/using/teaching

Nottingham University Manuscripts and Special Collections Learning Objects,
www.nottingham.ac.uk/manuscriptsandspecialcollections/learning/introduction.aspx

Roald Dahl Museum and Story Centre, www.reoalddahlmuseum.org

SCARLET Augmented Reality Project,
www.jisc.ac.uk/whatwedo/programmes/elearning/ltig/scarlet.aspx

Seven Stories, www.sevenstories.org.uk

Students and Faculty in the Archives at Brooklyn Historical Society,
www.brooklynhistory.org/exhibitions/safa.html

University of Reading 'history explorer' dissertation advice,
www.reading.ac.uk/web/FILES/special-collections/historyexplorerintroandsubjectlist.pdf

Useful websites

ALA Special Collections teaching strategies, http://connect.ala.org/node/85063

Archival Metrics, www.archivalmetrics.org

CILIP Local Studies adult learning case studies, www.cilip.org.uk/get-involved/special-interest-groups/local-studies/inspiration/pages/adult-learning.aspx

Higher Education Academy, www.heacademy.ac.uk/home

LILAC (information literacy), http://lilacconference.com/WP/

My Learning (UK), learning resources from museums, libraries and archives,
www.mylearning.org

National Co-ordinating Centre for Public Engagement, www.publicengagement.ac.uk

Teaching with Primary Sources Program, www.loc.gov/teachers/tps

Quizdom, www.quizdom.co.uk

10
Influencing and fund-raising for Special Collections

Introduction

Finally we consider fund-raising and influencing, without which none of the other Special Collections activities in this book would be possible.

This chapter will:

1 Introduce advocacy.
2 Introduce fund-raising and explain its importance.
3 Outline fund-raising issues.
4 Discuss sources of Special Collections funding: public programmes, trusts and foundations, individual giving, sponsorship and income generation.
5 Consider fund-raising strategy.

Introducing advocacy

A common problem for Special Collections, especially in large organizations, is that they do great work in the areas we have discussed, for example offering excellent services to their users, but their senior managers and other stakeholders are not aware of this or do not value their contribution. This puts the service at risk of cuts and other harm. To survive, let alone develop, Special Collections services need to maintain or enhance their share of central funding and other resources. Special Collections librarians need to shout about their achievements and excellence, about the positive contributions they make, in ways that will make sense to internal and influential audiences. This is known as **advocacy**. Advocacy is also about influencing external organizations and governments in relation to the sector. This process is sometimes called **lobbying**, especially when dealing with governments.

As with all marketing, advocacy entails finding out what matters to the audience and making sure they know you offer it, i.e. explaining Special Collections activities in language and ways that align with the organization's strategy.

While Special Collections face many threats, they are also in the most powerful position they have ever been. In universities, they offer 'the equivalent of unique laboratory facilities that attract faculty and research projects' (Pritchard 2009): unique materials that are entwined with the story of the organization, unique selling points in a time when institutions must compete more than ever. The digital technologies discussed throughout now allow us to do so much more with collections than ever before, bringing them to huge audiences and doing incredible new things with the data and stories they contain.

Often advocacy is only considered when a service is under threat. It is more difficult to market in such a situation, when the audience have already made decisions. They need to be brought up the many levels of the triangle we mentioned in Chapter 8 very quickly, from being completely unaware or even hostile to being engaged and supportive. This is very difficult. It is better to identify key people in less difficult times and build ongoing relationships to help them understand how Special Collections are an asset to the organization. Note that advocacy is needed even when dealing with other librarians, who may have little understanding of Special Collections. They may for instance emphasize physical footfall (historically a useful figure in a general library, though less so in the age of e-resources) without realizing the importance of remote or virtual use in Special Collections.

Given its importance, internal advocacy should pervade policies and practice in the same way as preservation or legal issues. The Association of College and Research Libraries (2006) advocacy toolkit suggests that it be included in Special Collections strategy, job descriptions, training plans, marketing plan, etc. The toolkit also advises librarians to seek out and plan for situations in which they can put their messages across, for example at committees.

However well librarians do this, however, collections and services can still be threatened. We discussed in Chapter 4 the sale of valuable items or collections by the owner or by the library. Staff may be cut, for example losing the rare books librarian and expecting the archivist to take over their work. Even worse, we are seeing the replacement of professional staff with volunteers and even service closures, particularly of public libraries and record offices.

So what to do? Much depends on the nature of the threat. If the threat is from outside, for example owners wishing to sell deposited collections, the library or parent organization is likely to help Special Collections. This book includes several case studies of libraries that successfully saved material from sale, for example the Broadlands Archives in Chapter 4. These involve intensive fund-raising and marketing to raise awareness and funds in time.

Threats from inside, such as sales, redundancies or closures, are even more difficult. Staff are often bound by their conditions of employment from publicizing or campaigning against threats (e.g. staff in national or other public sector libraries are civil servants and therefore bound by the Civil Service code, which prevents them from trying to frustrate government policies or publicize decisions). This is where effective relationships can help: outsiders who are already supporters can champion the service and get campaigns under way. Useful individuals and organizations include professional associations, Friends' groups (discussed under fund-raising), trades unions (especially regarding staffing matters) and pressure groups. Social media is opening up new ways to campaign, though traditional methods such as the broadcast media remain essential.

More help: Library association websites include plenty of advice on advocacy. The CILIP RBSCG website includes a paper defending the role of the rare books librarian. The ALA's bibliography is recommended. Voices for the Library campaign includes useful arguments and advice on opposing closure. Welburn, Welburn and McNeil (2010) offer guidance on advocacy in academic libraries.

A note on persuasion

Throughout Special Collections communications, librarians will be seeking to persuade others to think or do particular things. Sometimes these might be things to which the person is inclined anyway, but often they are difficult or demanding, for example to donate money or reverse a policy decision.

It helps to understand what persuasion is and the different ways in which it works; Association of College and Research Libraries (2006) is a useful introduction. When creating a presentation or written piece that seeks to persuade, it is essential to make sure that the form of persuasion used is right for the target audience. The arguments used to persuade a Friends' group, people who already care about and are engaged with the service, might be very different from those used to persuade senior managers. The former might be persuaded by evidence of a threat to something they value, the latter are likely to be more convinced by arguments referring to cost-effectiveness, strategic considerations or legal obligations.

Facts and figures are essential to back up arguments. When deciding the performance indicators to collect, making the case internally should be one of the considerations. Ideally these should go beyond numbers to consider impact. Think about how Special Collections staff add value to collections. What happened as a result of a visit to Special Collections? Evidence of savings/efficiencies is particularly useful, for example how much time did Special Collections save the marketing department by putting historic images of the library online?

A note on awards

Schemes or awards that recognize quality in Special Collections may help to demonstrate value to management, users and potential funders. They may also raise the standard of collection care, offer access to special funding, and are useful opportunities for raising Special Collections profile. For example, in England, the **Designation** scheme identifies 'the pre-eminent collections of national and international importance held in England's non-national museums, libraries and archives, based on their quality and significance' (www.mla.gov.uk/what/raising_standards/designation). The scheme has designated over 130 collections, including Special Collections such as the Mingana Collection of Middle Eastern Manuscripts at the University of Birmingham, which later received JISC funding to improve electronic access to the manuscripts via the Virtual Manuscript Room project.

A note on 'inreach'

Influencing within an organization is not just about reaching powerful senior decision makers. Other people may not be high in the hierarchy but may have a considerable impact on Special Collections services and collections, for example administrative staff, porters, security guards, switchboard workers, cleaning staff. Such colleagues may be the first people that a visitor encounters or may be in a position to see and react to a water leak, fire or theft that may harm collections. They may also be interested in or have something to contribute to the work of Special Collections. As well as thinking about new audiences externally (outreach), Special Collections communications plans should also therefore remember non-traditional audiences internally (which could be called inreach).

Introducing fund-raising

Fund-raising is a form of marketing with a distinct objective, call to action and set of techniques. We discuss it separately because of the level of detail required, but it works like other forms of marketing: understanding audience needs and adapting what is offered to fulfil them.

Like marketing, fund-raising is often misunderstood in academia and heritage organizations. It may be seen as pushy and cynical, judged by the intrusive methods used by some fund-raisers. There are many ways in which Special Collections can raise funds without resorting to such practices and fund-raising is two-way: the library receives funding, but the person or organization giving funding receives some tangible or intangible benefit in return.

Fund-raising is also seen as an academic matter, about applying to funding councils, with writing grant applications as the essence of fund-raising. High quality written applications are essential to tap funding from funding councils and other organizations. However, even for these, the relationship should be wider than just the creation of a large document; and it is advisable to consider raising funds from other sources rather than relying solely on such bodies.

Many Special Collections librarians do little or no direct fund-raising, as their library or parent organizations employ development or alumni relations specialists. However, librarians need to work closely with such colleagues to ensure that they have the information they need. Even if Special Collections is not necessarily always a fund-raising priority for these staff, any help offered in gathering information, images, etc. to help will pay off in good relations that will assist Special Collections in future.

Special Collections librarians can learn about fund-raising from a wide range of organizations, not just libraries; especially the arts sector and charities. As with other types of marketing, it is helpful to think about fund-raising methods encountered outside libraries, for example who is the campaign aimed at? What is the message? Does it work? And, most importantly, could it work for Special Collections?

Why fund-raising matters

All Special Collections librarians should understand how their organization is funded. Otherwise, they can appear naive and uninvolved with their organization. If they show such understanding, they are more credible and are better placed to seek funding at the right time from the right source.

Most libraries have some form of core funding, some of which reaches their Special Collections. It may come from top-slicing (a share of departmental income taken to support central services), subscriptions, a share of a central budget, or endowments.

However, such funding is vulnerable to cuts and other changing economic circumstances. For example, in academic libraries, when electronic journal prices rise, Special Collections acquisitions budgets may be reduced because they are discretionary: there is less choice about supplying essential journals. Advocacy may help Special Collections to keep its share, but sometimes there is simply no scope for this. Libraries with endowments are in a stronger position than those without, but the income from endowments may fluctuate considerably: at present returns are low.

In any case, core funding is seldom adequate for everything a Special Collections service may wish to do. At best, it maintains basic staffing levels and activities. Libraries must consider external fund-raising for other desirable activities, for example to purchase new materials, or, as we have seen, materials already held on deposit. Major projects such as cataloguing, digitization, exhibitions, conservation or developing better storage and user facilities generally require external funds.

Understanding fund-raising issues

Core funding is under even more pressure now, as public sector institutions face major cuts. Fund-raising, especially philanthropy, is being suggested as a way to bridge the gap in funding. However, fund-raising techniques do not offer easy solutions to funding problems in Special Collections. Here are the key issues.

Capacity (and collaboration)

Raising large sums of money requires a great deal of staff time and effort. A librarian fund-raising as part of a diverse range of duties with no extra support might be able to raise £4000 or even £40,000 in a year, but not £4 million. This basic fact is not always understood by senior managers. Also, once the money is received, spending a large sum in a public sector environment requires resources, for example recruiting a new member of staff requires time and expense in grading, advertising, selection, etc.

Ideally libraries will build their fund-raising capacity by understanding how much it costs to raise funds, setting realistic targets, and planning ahead to ratchet up capacity. Initial income might be better invested in more fund-raising rather than spent directly on services. Capacity can also be built through collaborating with other services, for example a small library can enhance a funding bid led by a more experienced service by bringing different collections or audiences to the project.

One of the most exciting examples of collaboration is the Philadelphia Area Consortium of Special Collections Libraries (PACSCL), which has 35 member libraries. PACSCL has supported its members in improving access in many ways, tapped funding from public organizations and trusts, and is currently involved in a major project to catalogue hidden collections in the city; activities that would be much more difficult for individual libraries to carry out alone.

Time

All fund-raising is constrained by time factors. Time is needed to build relationships with potential donors. A funding body may meet only once a year to assess applications or there may be deadlines to meet when applying for, or spending, grants. As noted above, it may take time to recruit new staff or source new equipment. Libraries need to be aware of these factors and develop fund-raising programmes before their situations become desperate. Understanding how funders operate means that requests or applications will be planned and made at the best time.

'The fund-raising landscape'

Just as it helps to understand how the parent organization is funded, so it helps to know who funds the funders. At present, the pressures on parent organizations that are leading to cuts in core funding for Special Collections are also affecting trusts, foundations and wealthy individuals who might provide alternative funding. When returns on investment are low, endowments suffer and there is less to give out.

Restrictions

Most sources of external funding for Special Collections restrict how it is spent. Funding bodies have to be precise about what is funded and what is not in order to achieve their aims. Individual givers support activities or collections that appeal to them (e.g. conservation work or acquiring an object of interest) but may not wish to support other activities. Such restrictions mean that the purposes of the funding available does not always match Special Collections spending needs. To cope, libraries need to be creative in finding funders whose interests are a good enough match for their strategy, and to seek funding from a range of sources.

Competition

Fund-raising is competitive. Other libraries, archives, museums, art galleries, universities, etc. face the same financial pressures and seek funding from the same sources. Libraries need to:

1 Concentrate on funders with the best fit and where the library has a good chance of success.
2 Ensure that applications and other contact with the funders are high quality and meet their requirements.

3 Find funders who have a particular relationship with the service. These include university alumni, collection donors and users, and trusts specific to a particular collection.
4 Understand who your competitors are, locally, regionally, nationally and internationally.
5 Collaborate with competitors, for example with local libraries or those with related collections, for one-offs or as part of a consortium. Many funders favour partnerships, and building capacity in this way can make for better projects.

Mission creep

This happens when projects are carried out because funding is available, rather than because they are part of library strategy. Result: time and effort being put into non-core projects while the central mission suffers. Strategy needs to be planned before seeking funding, rather than making up projects to fit whatever funds happen to be available. However, it is also important to be flexible and ready to take advantage of new opportunities.

Ethics

See Chapter 6 for discussion of this issue.

Management and sustainability

Funding bodies now require rigorous project management. Even if funders do not require this, using project management methods helps keep projects on track and ensures they do what they are intended to. If not well planned, projects can be completed without leaving a lasting legacy. Nowadays grant-giving bodies are more aware of this issue and will expect libraries to create projects that have long-term value.

Is your fund-raising really necessary?

It is easy to think that any worthwhile activity beyond business as usual needs external fund-raising. This is not necessarily the case. Interesting new projects in Special Collections can be created using existing resources. Witness a project created by the author, celebrating 100 Objects Bradford, which has successfully reached new audiences internally and externally by repackaging information via an existing popular message (the British Museum's 100 Objects) and using the power of social media – with no extra funding.

Sources of external funding for Special Collections

Here are the main ways that Special Collections can raise external funds. They overlap and complement each other, but it is useful to look at them separately.

Before going into detail, a reminder: the application or request for funding needs to be aimed at the right audience and in the right form to persuade them. The applicant needs to understand why that funder might fund them, what the funder will gain and why their project fits. There is no point in sending out applications or appeals that are not suited to the funder concerned.

Public project funding

Many government and non-government organizations exist to distribute funding to worthwhile activities, including Special Collections. The grant information may not mention Special Collections, libraries or archives; look out for headings like education, humanities, arts, culture, heritage, conservation, access or skills. Grants can cover substantial projects in acquisitions, preservation, digitization, cataloguing or outreach.

There are many advantages in applying to such bodies:

1   They have funding available and they exist to channel it to activities relevant to Special Collections.
2   Decision making and timetables are clear and publicly available: it will be immediately obvious which organizations and projects are eligible and when and how they can apply.
3   The award of funding is rational rather than emotional (though it is important for applicants to build relationships with the funding body throughout the process).
4   They often support libraries in writing applications and managing their projects, to achieve better results.

However, there are issues to consider before embarking on large project bids. Competition can be fierce and it can be hard for smaller libraries to get started as funding may be directed to those with stronger track records. Core costs are unlikely to be met. Applications may require substantial investment from the library, because funders may:

- have complex application procedures, sometimes requiring pre-applications
- require formal project management techniques and evidence of planning around risk and sustainability
- demand significant levels of match funding
- require evidence about the impact of the funding, especially for new audiences. This requires research in advance (though funders may support this too).

To cope, Special Collections need to ensure that their investment in the process is likely to be worthwhile. They need to consider what the funder is seeking and how to make their application stand out. As we mentioned above, partnerships may help share the load and strengthen applications.

The funding available from these organizations fluctuates as the political and economic situation changes: previous programmes are suspended, new opportunities are offered. Librarians can keep in touch through the listservs and 'Useful websites' (below). Here are some organizations that have offered significant funding to Special Collections recently. Some are government organizations but many of these initiatives include funding from major trusts.

Some UK funders:

1 Heritage Lottery Fund, offers range of funding programmes from £3000 to £5 million, to preserve UK heritage, with emphasis on involving people and building skills.
2 JISC funds innovative digital technologies in UK universities and colleges, via calls for applications for specific activities.
3 National Cataloguing Grants Programme, administered by the National Archives, offers funding to tackle cataloguing backlogs for archives in the UK.
4 National Heritage Memorial Fund, 'financial assistance towards the acquisition, preservation and maintenance of heritage treasures', including manuscripts and archives, a fund of last resort to buy material that might otherwise be lost to UK public collections. The Fund gave almost £2 million towards the Broadlands Archives, discussed in Chapter 4.
5 National Manuscripts Conservation Trust, 'to help preserve manuscripts of historical or educational value by awarding grants for their conservation'.
6 PRISM Fund, supports 'acquisition and/ or conservation of any object or group of objects illustrating the history of any branch of science, industry or technology.'
7 Research Councils UK, especially the Arts and Humanities Research Council and the Economic and Social Research Council, supporting academic research, which can involve Special Collections activities.
8 The Art Fund, helps buy and raise funds for art for public collections (libraries and archives, artworks and objects are eligible).

Some US funders:

1 CLIR Cataloging Hidden Special Collections and Archives (funded by the Mellon Foundation), offers 'grants to support innovative, efficient description' of uncatalogued collections.
2 Institute of Museum and Library Services grants cover conservation, leadership and outreach activities.
3 Library of Congress Teaching with Primary Sources grants support educational bodies in developing primary sources work for teachers, using LoC digitized material alongside local collections.
4 National Endowment for the Humanities, 'an independent grant-making agency of the United States government dedicated to supporting research, education, preservation, and public programs in the humanities'. Grants have supported preservation surveys and treatment.

5 National Historical Publications and Records Commission offers grants to 'preserve, publish, and encourage the use of documentary sources' relating to US history.

Charitable trusts and foundations

Trusts and foundations are bodies set up to channel funding to charitable purposes. Some also channel individual giving, witness the Friends of the National Libraries, below. Trusts and foundations vary considerably in size and scope. Some are relatively little known, often having a precise geographical or other remit. Larger trusts operate more like the government bodies mentioned above and, as mentioned, may help to fund government schemes. They may have more flexibility to develop libraries over a longer period rather than a focus on projects, witness the Andrew W. Mellon Foundation, which wishes 'to build, strengthen and sustain institutions and their core capacities, rather than be a source for narrowly defined projects' (www.mellon.org).

Again, trusts exist to channel funding to good causes and their missions often overlap with Special Collections aims, for example education, arts, culture. However, trusts are limited by the scope of their original trust deed, and can rarely support core costs. They may meet only once a year, meaning a delay in decision making. Smaller trusts are often shy of publicity (many do not have websites), which makes it hard to find out how to apply and how decisions are reached. However, this can be positive, as it may mean less competition for a library with a good case for support.

Other major trusts with a track record of supporting Special Collections include:

- Wolfson Foundation, emphasis on capital build, history, education and the arts
- Rothschild Foundation, Jewish heritage
- Alfred P. Sloan Foundation, science history and education
- Wellcome Trust, history and education in medicine and biology
- Pilgrim Trust, preservation, scholarship and access
- Esmée Fairbairn Foundation, arts, education, learning (including conservation and digitization).

A note on associations and societies

Many professional associations and other societies offer small grants for staff development, preservation, publications, etc. These grants are often well suited to Special Collections and have straightforward application procedures. For example, the Association for Manuscripts and Archives in Research Collections (AMARC) offers 'modest funding' to 'promote the accessibility, preservation and study of manuscripts and archives' (www.amarc.org.uk), for example the conservation and rehousing of the Rabanus Maurus Commentaries manuscript at University College London (UCL) Special Collections. Organizations that are unable to offer direct grants may support Special Collections in other ways such as offering bursaries to attend their conferences.

Individual giving

Special Collections can also benefit from funding given by individuals. Such giving is often known as **philanthropy**, especially when talking about larger sums. Individual givers to Special Collections may have a connection with the organization: alumni, local businesspeople, collections users, trustees. They may give for general purposes, for a particular item, collection, subject or activity. They give because they care about the subject or heritage, wish to return something or are concerned about a threat.

Individual gifts offer many benefits: they may be unrestricted and offer unlimited scope and possibilities (providing capacity is available to manage the process). It can be rewarding for librarians and donors to work together to improve collections and services.

However, there are issues to consider when seeking individual gifts. See also Chapter 4 on materials donors: issues and motivations are similar. Key points:

1 **Competition**. Libraries seeking donations from individuals are competing not only with other libraries and charities, but also with all the other calls on those individuals' finances.
2 **Perception**. Individuals may perceive universities and other organizations hosting Special Collections as rich (though recent cuts may change this perception). Some may be, but many, certainly in the UK, are not; and such funding does not necessarily reach Special Collections.
3 **Mission creep**. Mission creep can happen when dealing with individuals, if services, dazzled by large sums available, take funding for an unsuitable purpose or allow donors to dictate policy. However, donors of large sums expect to have a say in how those are to be spent. A balance is needed, to encourage individual givers to donate in a way that is helpful to the service and satisfies their motives. See Browar (2004) on the growth of venture philanthropy and a donation that went very wrong.
4 **Ethics**. As we discussed in Chapter 6, organizations need to decide where they will draw the line in accepting donations. They will also need to decide how much policy and practice can be influenced by funders.
5 **Up the triangle**. Donors rarely give without prior contact with Special Collections. Their involvement and giving moves up a similar pyramid to the marketing one in Chapter 8. Fund-raisers try to move donors up the triangle from small gifts to major bequests and donations, using techniques outlined below. Patience is needed: asking for too much too early in the relationship (e.g. a bequest from someone who has never given before) may deter the individual from further involvement.

Channelling individual givers

Here are some useful channels for Special Collections giving. These are not ends in themselves; they are ways that have reached donors: not all will work for every library or giver.

Alongside these campaigns, infrastructures are needed:

1 To manage and spend gifts. This involves working with finance staff to ensure that the system can cope.
2 To keep track of donations and ensure good communication with donors. This can be complex: specialist fund-raising software such as Raiser's Edge should be considered for large programmes. See Chapter 8 on legal issues for mailing lists.
3 To attract other one-off and ongoing donations, for example persuasive text on Special Collections web pages with details of how to give and tax advantages, donations box if building type permits.

Making the ask
Donors give to people rather than libraries. Usually someone (the librarian, the fund-raiser, a senior member of the organization) has to **make the ask**. When dealing with large sums or an eminent donor, the ask is better made by a peer of the person concerned, for example a famous trustee, chancellor or honorary graduate. Thus librarians need support from senior management and other stakeholders to raise significant funding from individual givers. Sometimes the ask can be made by other people, for example telethons could use students or volunteers who care about collections.

Social giving
There is a strong social element to giving: people are more likely to donate at an auction or event where others are doing so. Leab (2010) is interesting on past networks of philanthropy in the US. Invoking influential people who have given is an excellent way to encourage others. These can be well-known contemporaries or even historic figures (Trinity College Dublin mention Beckett and Ussher as past donors). Getting people involved who can encourage others is one of the most important aspects of fund-raising: these could be influential local businesspeople, actors, artists. They might become trustees or sponsors of the appeal, but could also work well out of the limelight.

Friends' organizations
Many Special Collections have 'Friends of the Library', who help raise funds from individual givers (the friends themselves and their contacts). Friends' fund-raising tends to concentrate on purchasing and conservation, as these tend to appeal to individual givers.

Friends can be mobilized quickly for urgent appeals, for example if deposited material is under threat of sale. The great efforts made to keep the Macclesfield Psalter (which we met in Chapter 3) in England included contributions from the Fitzwilliam Museum's Friends. Friends also encourage gifts of material, act as advocates for the service, and attract and work with volunteers. The Aberdeen case study below shows how valuable Friends can be in raising funds.

Typically, Friends pay an annual subscription and receive benefits, for example newsletters, special lectures, exhibition previews, tours behind the scenes, borrowing rights from the main library, the chance to socialize with like-minded people, and above all the knowledge that they are supporting the Special Collections they value. Many Friends organize themselves with little input required from the library; other libraries find that the benefits of Friends justify the use of staff to manage and develop the group.

Special Collections lacking a Friends' group need to plan carefully before setting one up and ensure there is sufficient enthusiasm among key benefactors to make it work. Otherwise the library risks creating an ongoing administrative burden in exchange only for a few subscriptions in return, not the substantial benefits noted above. Herring (2004) advises on working with Friends.

Other important Friends include the Friends of the National Libraries (UK), which can support any appropriate library, archive or museum in making a purchase, via grants, encouraging and channelling individual giving, and helping with appeals. They have helped purchase many significant items, for example the Codex Sinaiticus (see Chapter 3).

Adoption and naming

Special Collections lends itself to this kind of fund-raising because it is so concerned with material objects and spaces. Adopt a Book is a common method, usually centred on conservation needs of treasures. Lambeth Palace Library has a scheme called 'Back-a-Book', to pay for conservation work.

When creating new spaces, naming a brick or chair or other part of the build offers donors a way to become involved. The charge does not necessarily have to be the actual cost of a brick, but an amount that a donor would see as fair for the benefits received. Donors could also adopt/name a member of staff, a room or even the whole service.

The 'shopping list'

A variant on the above and familiar from charity appeals, this approach allows givers at all levels to feel they are making a difference, but also lets them see the difference a larger gift would make, for example Lambeth Palace Library's Back-a-Book Scheme suggests that:

£30 will rebind a small volume in buckram

£150 will restore a leather binding

£250 helps conserve a volume requiring paper and binding conservation.

(www.lambethpalacelibrary.org/content/backabook)

Tiered approaches

These recognize different levels of giving with coherent packages of benefits, allowing donors to feel rewarded while at the same time showing the possible benefits from larger gifts. Variants on bronze, silver and gold are often used, though it is possible to brand the tiers more creatively, for example the Derry and Raphoe Diocesan Library Project at the University of Ulster called its levels the Rare Books Guild and the Bishops' Circle (fitting for a project aimed at conserving and sharing 5000 rare books).

Legacies

A legacies programme aims to encourage existing donors to leave bequests and to let the library know that they have done so. Donors benefit because they know their ideas and values will live on. Libraries benefit because:

1 Legacies arrive in a more managed way rather than occasional 'pennies from heaven' that are not expected (or no legacies at all).
2 People are more likely to make it clear which library is intended if they have had recent contact: wills where a beneficiary cannot be identified cause many problems.

These are challenging programmes to run, requiring sensitivity in writing and mailing. However, if the capacity to run a legacies programme is available, it can bring in significant funding.

A note on tax

As mentioned when discussing Special Collections materials donations, it helps to be aware of tax arrangements from which donors can benefit if they give to Special Collections.

The best-known is the 501(c) (3) tax-exempt status in the USA. This allows certain types of non-profit organizations exemption from federal income tax and makes them eligible to receive tax-deductible charitable contributions. The status is also useful for other reasons, for example making organizations eligible for certain federal grants. Special Collections in US universities, museums and other organizations are often covered by this status. Those based in other countries can also benefit by setting up a separate 501(c) (3) organization, for example UK universities are increasingly setting up such groups to channel gifts from their American alumni and Friends.

Company giving

Firms might give money or goods to Special Collections without expectations of a direct return to show support (this may of course have indirect benefits). Examples are sometimes seen after disasters when local businesses may offer space and supplies.

Organizations may pay to have their name associated with Special Collections, to gain exposure to relevant audiences and positive associations from links with a worthwhile organization (also known as sponsorship). The term 'sponsor' is also often used for a patron or donor, such as a grant-giving body or an individual.

Advantages of sponsorship to the library:

- unrestricted: it does not have to be spent on whatever is being sponsored
- quick, business/rational decision.

However, ethical issues must be considered (see Chapter 6) and the library must be able to deliver whatever has been promised. Good relations are vital: happy sponsors will sponsor again. Always thank the sponsors at launch events!

More points about business sponsors:

1 Any organization with a budget and an interest in Special Collections work or audiences could become a sponsor: not just commercial ventures.
2 Special Collections sponsors generally prefer to be associated with an exhibition, project, space or event rather than the whole service. These are easier for them to understand and can be presented with more clearly defined audiences and objectives.
3 Channels and structures used for individual giving, for example the tiered approach can often be useful for corporate sponsors and givers.

The amount sponsors should be charged is the value of the exposure, not what it costs the library to provide whatever is sponsored. It may cost a tiny amount to put a logo on an exhibition catalogue, for example, but if it is then seen by thousands of people in the sponsor's target market, it will be worth far more to the sponsor.

It is not always easy to interest businesses in Special Collections unless the library or institution is a well-known name, particularly in the regions and when dealing with smaller firms. A link with the nature of the sponsor's business can be productive, as we see below at Aberdeen. Occasionally the connection may be with a whole industry rather than a particular firm, for example the Utah Ski Archives at the University of Utah are supported by corporate sponsors from local ski resorts and related businesses.

Case study: a library for a sixth century

The University of Aberdeen has been raising major funds for a new library (£57 million), opening in 2011. Preservation of and access to the University's historic collections is a 'major purpose' of the new build and clearly has been a significant factor in the fund-raising. The project shows how a major programme requires funding to be brought together from all the sources mentioned above. Note in particular the input of:

1 Local industries, for example Aberdeen Harbour Board are supporting the photographic archive room, home to 6000 glass plate negatives documenting the Harbour's history.
2 The Friends of the Library. A significant group with over 200 members worldwide, they have given £200K from donations and legacies for a room for group work with Special Collections and £60K for public engagement events.
3 A major national scheme (Heritage Lottery £875K for the conservation suite) and one open to projects in certain locations: Biffaward, funded by landfill tax credits from Biffa Waste Services, offers grants to projects within a certain distance of a

Biffa site – Aberdeen received £45K for a listening room for oral history sound recordings.

Income generation

Special Collections can raise income from commercial transactions in which individuals or businesses pay for services or goods. Income generation is more straightforward than the emotional complexities of individual giving, and offers the benefits of unrestricted funds and (sometimes) quick return on investment. However, there is stiff competition from the private sector and activities may not be truly cost-effective, especially when staff time is properly costed. In order to generate income, services must be run in a business-like way, draw on appropriate legal and other expertise, and focus on customer needs.

Special Collections must also keep in mind collections care issues. Income generation may increase risk of damage to collections either directly (location shooting and hospitality, which put pressure on collections and spaces) or indirectly via increased fire risk. Effective risk assessment, policies and procedures are needed. Another risk is that services such as conservation will spend time generating income instead of working on the collections. Some income generation may impinge on user services, for example filming may lead to closure of the reading room; others, for example catering, may improve the user experience.

The potential for income generation in Special Collections depends on many factors, including visitor footfall, size of building, control over building, type of collections and nature of staffing. Here are some possibilities:

1 **Reprographics charges**. This income stream may have a captive audience, if Special Collections is the only holder of particular material. Historically reprographics has been a vital source of unrestricted income for libraries. However, these services take up considerable staff time and put pressure on the collections, and it may not be possible or appropriate to charge users the true cost of making copies, which limits the scope for generating income. This source is also affected by matters outside the control of Special Collections: changes in copyright law that may limit what can be copied and new technologies, for example the impact of digital photography (see Chapter 7). Making digitized material freely available via the web may cut income, but not necessarily: it may bring in more requests for commercial use. It will have benefits in reducing staff time spent on individual reprographics requests, and above all in making collections more widely available.

2 **Image licensing and publication charges**. To what extent it is possible for an individual service to generate significant income in this way depends on the kinds of collections held and (crucially) whether the library holds rights in them. Cost and convenience are critical: prospective buyers must be able to search for images easily, see what is available and buy quickly. This requires investment in appropriate image

library software. Special Collections will be competing with established picture libraries with huge collections and infrastructure and will need to promote the unique selling points of their images and other resources available. Mahurter (n.d.) is a useful case study on the processes involved in setting charges.

3 **Research services**. As discussed in Chapter 7. Whether these can make profit as opposed to covering costs and providing a service is questionable: if the price is set too high, enquirers will not use the service or will have unrealistic expectations.

4 **Conservation and digitization**. Special Collections with appropriate equipment, staff and space may be able to raise income by offering services externally (although note the risk mentioned above). In the past, binding services could also offer an income stream; it is unlikely that this would raise income now that libraries are buying e-journals and cutting binding budgets.

5 **Location shooting**. Broadcasters and film-makers may be interested in using historic or quirky libraries as locations. More modern libraries (e.g. as examples of 1960s campus architecture) might also appeal. This could bring in substantial income and raised profile. However, shoots can be disruptive to services and put collections at extra risk. Libraries need clear policies and procedures and must be assertive to ensure that the arrangement works for all parties.

6 **Retail**. As discussed under 'Merchandizing' in Chapter 8. If well managed, this, along with catering and hospitality, may bring people to the building who would not otherwise use it.

7 **Catering**. From vending machines to cafes and restaurants. This is also a service to visitors, particularly if the location is far from other eating places. Often catering in libraries is run by an external firm who pay for the privilege: ideally one that shares the values of the service, for example fairtrade. The presence of catering increases the risk of fire and other damage to collections.

8 **Hospitality**, for example weddings, conferences, banquets, etc. Again, beautiful historic libraries are more likely to attract such customers. Unlike regular catering, which can usually be confined to non-collections parts of the building, functions will wish to use the most impressive spaces, so care will be needed to ensure that collections and building are not damaged. As with location shoots, policies, procedures and information are needed to minimize damage.

Developing a fund-raising strategy

Special Collections have many options for fund-raising but none offers a simple answer. All require investment, and time, and have pitfalls to avoid. It is therefore important to think strategically and develop a programme that works for the organization, rather than leaping into random activities that may not be cost-effective.

The needs of Special Collections should be part of the parent organization's fund-raising strategy. If different people within an organization are fund-raising, good communication is vital to ensure that the same funders are not approached for multiple projects.

A fund-raising strategy, as with any strategy, needs to:

1 **Understand the present financial situation and sources of funding**. If the organization is already fund-raising from a range of sources, analyse these existing funding streams. Which are bringing in funding? Which are in need of attention? Which are not working?
2 **Have clear objectives**. Why is funding needed? When? How much? The purpose for which funding is being raised and the timescale in which it is needed affect how funds are raised. Targets need to be realistic based on the capacity available, both in amounts and timescales.
3 **Establish who is to do the fund-raising**. Raising large sums requires time and skills that it may be better to buy in from external specialists. If library staff are to do the fund-raising alongside their other work, then targets must reflect this.
4 **Decide which funding streams to use**. As our Aberdeen case study shows, large projects require funding from most of the income streams we mentioned, put together like a jigsaw. It is usual to find one large grant and fill the gaps with individual giving and smaller grants: the Derry and Raphoe Project illustrates this well. This mix of methods brings money in at different times and mitigates the disadvantages of individual income streams. The skill lies in getting the mix right and being open to new possibilities that arise during a long programme of fund-raising.

Conclusion

Without influence and understanding at a high level in their parent organizations, Special Collections are vulnerable to cuts, even closure. Marketing to influential people (advocacy) is essential, both in times of threat and as ongoing good practice. Like advocacy, fund-raising is about building relationships and connections. Special Collections can raise funds in several ways, including grants from funding bodies, individual giving, sponsorship and commercial ventures. All require investment, time and understanding of the pitfalls, but if properly put together, can enable services to bring collections to life in ways that would never have been possible from core funding alone.

Further reading

Like marketing, there is a huge publishing industry around fund-raising. Note in particular the extensive range of directories of funding sources and textbooks produced by the Directory of Social Change, which is particularly helpful for tracking down smaller trusts. On advocacy, Hackman (2011) includes case studies on US Special Collections.

Examples and case studies

100 Objects Bradford, http://100objectsbradford.wordpress.com
Aberdeen University's new library, www.abdn.ac.uk/newlibrary
Derry and Raphoe Diocesan Library, www.derryraphoelibrary.org/index.html

Designation Scheme, www.mla.gov.uk/what/raising_standards/designation

Lambeth Palace Library Back-a-Book, www.lambethpalacelibrary.org/content/backabook

Mingana Collection of Middle Eastern Manuscripts, Designation and link to the Virtual
     Manuscript Room, www.special-coll.bham.ac.uk/highlights/mingana/designation.shtml

Philadelphia Area Consortium of Special Collections Libraries (PACSCL), www.pacscl.org

Rabanus Maurus manuscript at UCL, www.ucl.ac.uk/library/special-coll/news.shtml

Utah Ski Archives, www.lib.utah.edu/collections/ski-archives/

Useful websites
Selected bodies offering funding

Andrew W. Mellon Foundation, www.mellon.org

AMARC, www.amarc.org.uk

Art Fund, www.artfund.org

CLIR Cataloging Hidden Collections, www.clir.org/hiddencollections/index.html

Esmée Fairbairn Foundation, www.esmeefairbairn.org.uk

Friends of the National Libraries, www.friendsofnationallibraries.org.uk/index.shtml

Heritage Lottery Fund, www.hlf.org.uk

Institute of Museum and Library Services, www.imls.gov/index.shtm

JISC, www.jisc.ac.uk/fundingopportunities.aspx

Library of Congress Teaching with Primary Sources, www.loc.gov/teachers/tps

National Cataloguing Grants Scheme, www.nationalarchives.gov.uk/information-
     management/our-services/cataloguing-grants-programme.htm

National Endowment for the Humanities, www.neh.gov

National Heritage Memorial Fund (UK), http://search.hlf.org.uk/nhmfweb/aboutthenhmf

National Historical Publications and Records Commission, www.archives.gov/nhprc

National Manuscripts Conservation Trust (UK), www.nmct.co.uk/index.html

Pilgrim Trust, www.thepilgrimtrust.org.uk/index.php

PRISM Fund, www.mla.gov.uk/what/support/grants/PRISM

Research Councils UK, www.rcuk.ac.uk/Pages/Home.aspx

Rothschild Foundation, www.rothschildfoundation.eu

Sloan Foundation, www.sloan.org

Wellcome Trust, www.wellcome.ac.uk

Wolfson Foundation, www.wolfson.org.uk

Help, advice and advocacy

501(c) (3) information, www.irs.gov/charities/charitable/article/0,,id=96099,00.html

ALA advocacy bibliography,
     www.ala.org/ala/mgrps/divs/acrl/issues/marketing/advocacy%20bibliograph.pdf

Arts and Business (UK), http://artsandbusiness.org.uk

CILIP RBSCG advocating the role of a rare books librarian, www.cilip.org.uk/
     filedownloadslibrary/groups/rbsc/advocating%20the%20role%20of%20a%20
     rare%20books%20librarian.pdf

Directory of Social Change (UK), www.dsc.org.uk/Home

Grants.gov (guide to US federal grants), www07.grants.gov

Heritage Funding Directory, www.heritagelink.org.uk/fundingdirectory/main/fundinghome.php

Voices for the Library, www.voicesforthelibrary.org.uk/wordpress

Afterword:
Special Collections futures

These are indeed challenging times for Special Collections. Special Collections contain a wealth of wonderful materials and librarians who care about bringing those collections and people together. This is shown by the many examples of good practice in this book (and I could have included so many more). But services are often underfunded, undervalued, under threat, beset with hidden collections and other inherited problems. A 'perfect storm' of pressure on public sector and higher education resources and the perception that everything is or soon will be digitized means that Special Collections must defend their very existence.

However, there are also tremendous opportunities. I hope this book will help librarians to see the power of new technologies to make collections available in ways unimaginable before, to make connections, to share ideas and to show their value to their host organizations. In a world flattened and homogenized by digital technologies, there is a demand for the power of objects and fresh narratives that Special Collections can offer.

Moving beyond the next few years, what of the future for Special Collections? Are they, or the library, dying, as is often predicted thanks to the digital age?

Many possible futures exist for Special Collections and their parent libraries, depending on developments in the 'ecosystems' of which they are part. The study of 'scenarios' can stimulate Special Collections librarians to reflect on likely developments and build strategies to shape and respond to these possibilities. See for example:

- Libraries of the Future: UK university libraries in 2050
- Staley and Malenfant (2010): trends affecting ACRL libraries in 2025
- Association of Research Libraries (2010b): looking to 2030.

Though these all focus on higher education, these developments will also affect Special Collections in other sectors.

The deciding factors, already noticeable now, will be:

1 **Academia open or closed**. Openness will encourage non-traditional learners, collaboration between expert hubs and sharing of digital resources, offering exciting possibilities for bringing Special Collections to the world. Closure will see

universities protecting their IP and market share by restricting access and sharing. Contrast Staley and Malenfant's 'Archives on Demand' and 'Renaissance Redux' and Futures' 'Walled Garden', but note that in either case Special Collections has a role, for instance in the latter as sources of expertise and unique selling points.

2 **Role of market and/or state**. The former pushes services into more marketing, management and aggressive fund-raising to survive, for example Staley and Malenfant 'This class brought to you by –'. Though ethically troubling, this world is one in which Special Collections may find a niche, as discussed in Chapter 10. The state might encourage outreach and openness, or push higher education towards a narrow focus on employability, which could be the most difficult scenario for Special Collections (witness the Libraries of the Future 'Beehive' scenario): survival might involve great emphasis on transferable skills in handling information.

Thinking about these possibilities helps us see how we might respond to them. The future is open-ended, and at least partly in our own hands: making the case for Special Collections and their value with everything we do, making openness happen by sharing and collaborating, campaigning for more sensible copyright law ... It is probably safe to predict the following as features of whatever futures we find:

1 More emphasis on the management of Special Collections materials as artefacts, less on their informational content, which will be available via other routes.
2 Changing ideas about ownership, for example focus on expertise, curation, metacollections, networks and selection, and less on ownership of a given object – especially concerning digital materials.
3 Possibly fewer visitors in person, but many more virtual ones, using exciting new technologies to bring collections to huge new audiences.
4 Changes in cataloguing and metadata, with emphasis on use and sharing.
5 More emphasis on management techniques, marketing, fund-raising and making the case for continued support within the organization.
6 Working more closely within the parent organization, for example in support of marketing or teaching.
7 Much more sharing and collaboration between Special Collections services, and convergence between the heritage and information professions.

Useful websites

ARL 2030 scenarios, www.arl.org/rtl/plan/scenarios/index.shtml
Libraries of the Future, www.futurelibraries.info/content

Appendix A: Key reference resources for Special Collections

Every Special Collections librarian needs to be aware of the following core reference resources. They are invaluable for helping users, and also for management activities, for example assessing rarity for acquisitions or insurance or assistance with cataloguing. Many are short-title catalogues (STCs), which abbreviate the very long titles characteristic of early printed books. The resources are freely available online unless otherwise noted. See the Chapter 3 'Further reading' for more resources on these subjects.

Union catalogues

These are vast catalogues combining records from many libraries.

1 **WorldCat**. Managed by OCLC, records for 1.5 billion items from 70,000 national, academic and public libraries worldwide. Particularly useful for accessing Special Collections in North American universities, www.worldcat.org
2 **COPAC**. Managed by MIMAS at Manchester University, 36 million catalogue records from UK and Irish research libraries, very rich in Special Collections records. MIMAS also manage COPAC's sister service, the Archives Hub, a database of archive collections from these libraries, http://copac.ac.uk
3 **Karlsrüher Virtueller Katalog** (KVK). Via the Karlsrüher Institut für Technologie, 500 million records from libraries in Germany, Austria, Switzerland and worldwide, useful for European early printed books, www.ubka.uni-karlsruhe.de/kvk_en.html.

Catalogues of incunabula

Gesamtkatalog der Wiesendrucke (GW) is the most detailed but far from complete; Incunabula Short Title Catalogue (ISTC) records are shorter and cover more titles: the editors estimate that 90% of the relevant material is now included. The British Museum catalogue (BMC) is essential for the works covered.

1 **Incunabula Short Title Catalogue** (ISTC). On the British Library website, a catalogue of pre-1501 European items printed with movable type. Records for

30,000 editions held at the British Library and elsewhere,
www.bl.uk/catalogues/istc

2 **Gesamtkatalog der Wiesendrucke** (GW). A union catalogue of incunabula held
   in libraries worldwide, based on a printed edition (1925–). Published in author
   order, 11 volumes so far (to H),
   www.gesamtkatalogderwiegendrucke.de/GWEN.xhtml

3 **British Museum catalogue of books published in the fifteenth century**
   (BMC). British Museum, Department of Printed Books (1908–2007). Printed
   catalogue of copy-specific detail about the incunabula held at the British Museum
   Library (now the British Library). Divided by country of printing, 13 parts have
   been published.

Other catalogues of hand-press era books

1 **Short-title catalogue (STC) and Wing**: short-title catalogues listing books printed
   in Britain, Ireland and the colonies or printed in English elsewhere. The STC, by
   Pollard et al. (1986), covers 1475–1640, and Wing et al. (1982–1998) continues to
   1700. STC and Wing numbers are often encountered in published works.

2 **English Short Title Catalogue** (ESTC). On the British Library website, catalogue
   of over 460,000 books, mainly in English and printed in the British Isles and North
   America, held by the British Library and 2000 other libraries. Began as the
   Eighteenth Century Short Title Catalogue covering 1701–1800, later extended to
   cover 1473–1700, including every entry in STC and Wing, http://estc.bl.uk

3 **Heritage of the Printed Book Database** (HPB). Formerly the Hand Press Book
   Database, hosted by OCLC, available online to CERL members and publicly in
   CERL libraries. Three million catalogue records from research libraries in Europe
   and North America for books printed in Europe during the hand-press era,
   www.cerl.org/web/en/resources/hpb/main

4 **Nineteenth Century Short Title Catalogue** (NSTC). Available by subscription
   via ProQuest. The 19th century explosion of print means a comprehensive
   catalogue would be immense. This one includes 1.2 million records for books
   printed 1801–1919 from certain national and major research libraries,
   http://nstc.chadwyck.com

5 An interesting new project hosted by the University of St Andrews: the **Universal
   Short Title Catalogue** (USTC) will create bibliographies of early printed books for
   European countries lacking them and create a searchable resource for all Europe,
   www.ustc.ac.uk.

Digitized books

In addition to books digitized by individual libraries and large-scale digitization initiatives
(LDSIs) like Google Books and Archives.org, two major resources are available by
subscription from ProQuest:

1 **Early English Books Online** (EEBO). Over 100,000 digitized images of English printed books up to 1700. It will eventually contain everything in STC and Wing. The Text Creation Partnership is creating searchable full text versions of the books, http://eebo.chadwyck.com

2 **Eighteenth Century Collections Online** (ECCO). Digitized images of over 180,000 editions, 26 million pages, from books printed in the UK 1701–1800, mostly in English. Based on ESTC, cross-searchable with EEBO, http://mlr.com/DigitalCollections/products/ecco.

Provenance

Useful tools from the Consortium of European Research Libraries (CERL):

1 **Index Possessorum Incunabulorum** (IPI), by Paul Needham of Princeton University, 32,000 entries concerning owners of incunabula and which volumes they owned, http://ipi.cerl.org

2 **Material Evidence in Incunabula** (MEI). Database of incunabula provenance: 'ownership, decoration, binding, manuscript annotations, stamps, prices, etc', www.cerl.org/web/en/resources/mei/main

3 **Can You Help?** Site for librarians and scholars to post details of provenance queries and offer help, www.cerl.org/web/en/resources/provenance/main.

Latin

Latin place name resources

1 *Orbis Latinus*, Grässe, Benedict and Plechl (1971) and online, www.columbia.edu/acis/ets/Graesse/contents.html

2 RBMS/Bibliographic Standards Committee Latin Place Names File, http://net.lib.byu.edu/~catalog/people/rlm/latin/names.htm

3 Places search in the CERL Thesaurus, http://thesaurus.cerl.org/cgi-bin.

More Latin

Hillyard (2009) includes seven pages of vocabulary likely to be seen in rare book work plus useful references. Hillyard recommends using the dictionary Lewis and Short (1879) as it includes post-classical Latin vocabulary.

Appendix B:
Careers and skills in Special Collections

Special Collections work remains a popular career choice; new entrants are drawn to the mixture of fascinating material and varied opportunities. It is therefore a competitive sector, a problem compounded by low turnover (staff tend to stay in jobs they enjoy for many years) and lack of opportunities at senior level. As in all job sectors, prospective Special Collections librarians are advised to monitor the market, see and try to fill their skills gaps, reflect on their own practice and strengths, and produce high quality applications. Engaging with the profession at events and via the listservs and social media will help. Many of the skills required can be developed in other aspects of library or other work, for example customer care and project management.

This book gives a flavour of the core skills for Special Collections work. Of course many Special Collections librarians have specialist roles, but this work needs to be informed by understanding of the basics, for example collections care. The professional associations have produced skills frameworks to help Special Collections librarians and employers assess training needs: CILIP Rare Books and Special Collections Group (2007b) and Rare Books and Manuscripts Section (2008).

It is becoming more difficult for many Special Collections librarians to seek training, as cuts affect training budgets or short-staffed services cannot spare them. However, skills can be built in other ways even if external paid-for courses are not possible. Trainers may offer sessions in-house to meet the library's training needs (and why not share the cost with local partners?). There are many free events and roadshows; professional bodies and other groups offer bursaries and grants to support librarians in learning new skills.

Above all, new media open up all kinds of free networking and training possibilities, for example the specialist listservs, social media, and the many reports, research and toolkits freely available online. New professionals in libraries and archives are forming networks and creating teachmeets and other events to share experiences. Don't forget also the mentoring schemes offered, for example by CILIP.

Suggestions for external training

1 **Rare Books Schools**. Intensive courses on the history of manuscripts, books and other formats, including bindings, illustrations and printing, book dealing. Rare Book School, Virginia, www.rarebookschool.org and the London Rare Books School, Institute of English Studies, University of London, http://ies.sas.ac.uk/cmps/events/courses/LRBS/index.htm.

2 **Library associations**, RBSCG and RBMS. Training and courses on all aspects of Special Collections librarianship. Other sections of the professional bodies may offer useful training, for example CILIP Cataloguing and Indexing Group (CIG) on cataloguing, CILIP Local Studies Group (LSG) on working with communities. See also the organizations of archivists and museum staff for common concerns like collections care or outreach.

3 **Specialist groups** based around common interests in particular formats, subjects or types of libraries, for example AMARC for manuscripts, Historic Libraries Forum for the concerns of historic libraries, Group for Literary Archives and Manuscripts (GLAM) for literary archives, Cathedral Libraries and Archives Association and RLIS for visual arts, architecture and design.

4 **Library and archive schools**, for example UCL or Centre for Archive and Information Studies (CAIS) at Dundee offer relevant continuing education, based on course modules.

5 **Consultancies and groups** offer a range of relevant courses, notably the Archive-Skills Consultancy Ltd and Creating Capacity.

Online learning

1 Preservation 101 from the NEDCC, http://unfacilitated.preservation101.org/loggedin.asp

2 Strategic Content Alliance created an e-learning resource for intellectual property and licensing, www.web2rights.com/SCAIPRModule

3 Online tutorials from the National Archives: Beginners' Latin 1086–1733 and Advanced Latin tutorials, www.nationalarchives.gov.uk/latin and Reading Old Handwriting 1500–1800 tutorial, www.nationalarchives.gov.uk/palaeography

4 Cambridge University on palaeography, http://scriptorium.english.cam.ac.uk/handwriting.

Bibliography

All works cited in the text, and some other recommended texts. Many core texts have appeared in several editions: the latest is cited, but earlier ones often remain useful. Note, for further reading, the bibliographies mentioned in Chapter 3 and elsewhere include more detail than is possible here.

Alexander, J. J. G. (1992) *Medieval Illuminators and their Methods of Work*, Yale University Press.

Allen, S. M. (1999) Rare Books and the College Library: current practices in marrying undergraduates to Special Collections, *Rare Books & Manuscripts Librarianship*, **13** (2), 110–119.

ARL Working Group on Special Collections (2009) *Special Collections in ARL Libraries: a discussion report*, www.arl.org/bm~doc/scwg-report.pdf

Artim, N. (2007) *An Introduction to Fire Detection, Alarm, and Automatic Fire Sprinklers*, NEDCC, www.nedcc.org/resources/leaflets/3Emergency_Management/02IntroToFireDetection.php

Association of College and Research Libraries (1992) *Standards for Ethical Conduct for Rare Book, Manuscript, and Special Collections Librarians, with Guidelines for Institutional Practice in Support of the Standards*, 2nd edn, www.ala.org/Template.cfm?Section=speccollections&template=/ContentManagement/ContentDisplay.cfm&ContentID=8969

Association of College and Research Libraries (2000a) Getting Ready for the Nineteenth Century: strategies and solutions for rare book and special collections librarians: *proceedings of the Thirty-Ninth Annual Preconference of the Rare Books and Manuscripts Section, Association of College and Research Libraries, Washington, DC, 23–26 June, 1998*, ACRL.

Association of College and Research Libraries (2000b) *Information Literacy Competency Standards for Higher Education*, www.ala.org/ala/mgrps/divs/acrl/standards/informationliteracycompetency.cfm

Association of College and Research Libraries (2003) *Code of Ethics for Special Collections Librarians*, www.rbms.info/standards/code_of_ethics.shtml.

Association of College and Research Libraries (2004) *Guidelines for the Interlibrary Loan of Rare and Unique Materials*, www.ala.org/ala/mgrps/divs/acrl/standards/rareguidelines.cfm.

Association of College and Research Libraries (2005) *Guidelines for Borrowing and Lending Special Collections Materials for Exhibition*, ww.ala.org/ala/mgrps/divs/acrl/standards/borrowguide.cfm.

Association of College and Research Libraries (2006) *The Power of Personal Persuasion: advancing the academic library agenda from the front lines*, www.ala.org/ala/mgrps/divs/acrl/issues/marketing/advocacy_toolkit.pdf.

Association of College and Research Libraries (2008) *Guidelines on the Selection and Transfer of*

Materials from General Collections to Special Collections, 3rd edn, www.ala.org/ala/mgrps/divs/acrl/standards/selctransfer.cfm.

Association of College and Research Libraries (2009a) *ACRL/RBMS Guidelines Regarding Security and Theft in Special Collections*, www.ala.org/ala/mgrps/divs/acrl/standards/security_theft.cfm.

Association of College and Research Libraries (2009b) *Joint Statement on Access to Original Research Materials,* www.ala.org/ala/mgrps/divs/acrl/standards/jointstatement.cfm.

Association of College and Research Libraries (forthcoming) *The Past is Portal: teaching undergraduates using special collections and archives.*

Association of College and Research Libraries and Library of Congress (2007) *Descriptive Cataloging of Rare Materials (Books)*, Library of Congress.

Association of College and Research Libraries and Library of Congress (2008) *Descriptive Cataloging of Rare Materials (Serials)*, Library of Congress.

Association of Moving Image Archivists (n.d.) *Storage Standards and Guidelines for Film and Videotape*, www.amianet.org/resources/guides/storage_standards.pdf

Association of Research Libraries (2010a) *Principles to Guide Vendor/Publisher Relations in Large-Scale Digitization Projects of Special Collections Materials*, www.arl.org/bm~doc/principles_large_scale_digitization.pdf

Association of Research Libraries (2010b) *The ARL 2030 Scenarios: a user's guide for research libraries*, www.arl.org/bm~doc/arl-2030-scenarios-users-guide.pdf

Attar, K. (2007) Rare Books Librarianship. In Bowman, J. H. (ed.), *British Librarianship and Information Work 2001–2005*, Ashgate.

Australian Libraries Copyright Committee and Australian Digital Alliance (n.d.) *Information for Organisations Seeking to be Prescribed as a 'Key Cultural Institution'*, www.digital.org.au/alcc/documents/Key_cultural_institutions.pdf

Baca, M., et al. (2006) *Cataloging Cultural Objects: a guide to describing cultural works and their images*, American Library Association.

Baker, C. A. and Silverman, R. (2005) Misperceptions about White Gloves, *International Preservation News*, **37**, 4–16.

Barnes, M. Kelly, R. G. and Kerwin, M. (2010) Lost Gems: identifying rare and unusual monographs in a university's circulating collection, *Library Collections*, **34** (2), 57–65.

Bastian, J. A. and Alexander, B. (2009) *Community Archives: the shaping of memory*, Facet Publishing.

Behrnd-Klodt, M. L. (2008) *Navigating Legal Issues in Archives*, Society of American Archivists.

Belanger, T. (1977) Descriptive Bibliography. In Peters, J. (ed.) *Book Collecting: a modern guide*, Bowker, excerpt at www.bibsocamer.org/bibdef.htm.

Bendix, C. (2005) *Packing and Moving Library and Archive Collections*, NPO, www.bl.uk/blpac/pdf/moving.pdf.

Bendix, C. and Walker, A. (2011) *Cleaning Books and Documents*, rev. edn, BLPAC, www.bl.uk/blpac/pdf/clean.pdf.

Birrell, D. et al. (2011) The Discmap Project: digitisation of Special Collections: mapping, assessment, prioritisation, *New Library World*, **112** (1), 19–44.

Bodleian Library (1971) *The John Johnson Collection: catalogue of an exhibition.*

Bond, T. J. and Butler, T. (2009) A Dialog on Teaching an Undergraduate Seminar in Special

Collections, *Library Review*, **58** (4), 310–316.

Bowers, F. (1994) *Principles of Bibliographical Description*, new edn, St. Paul's Bibliographies.

British Museum, Department of Printed Books (1908–2007) *Catalogue of Books Printed in the 15th century now in the British Museum*, Trustees of the British Museum.

British Standards Institution (2000) *Recommendations for Storage and Exhibition of Archival Documents*, BS: 5454.

British Standards Institution (2002) *Repair and Allied Processes for the Conservation of Documents – Recommendations*, BS: 4971.

Browar, L. (2004) Paving the Road to Hell? Cultural institutions and the new philanthropy, *RBM*, **5** (1), 52–72.

Brown, K. E. (2007) *Worksheet for Outlining a Disaster Plan*, NEDCC, www.nedcc.org/resources/leaflets/3Emergency_Management/04DisasterPlanWorksheet.php.

Brown, M. (1990) *A Guide to Western Historical Scripts from Antiquity to 1600*, British Library.

Brown, M. (1994) *Understanding Illuminated Manuscripts: a guide to technical terms*, J. Paul Getty Museum in association with the British Library.

Brown, M. (1998) *The British Library Guide to Writing and Scripts: history and techniques*, British Library.

Bülow, A. E. and Ahmon, J. (2011) *Preparing Collections for Digitization*, Facet Publishing.

Bureau of Canadian Archivists (2008), *Rules for Archival Description*, rev. edn, www.cdncouncilarchives.ca/RAD/RADComplete_July2008.pdf.

Burnley, D. and Wiggins, A. (eds) (2003) *The Auchinleck Manuscript*, National Library of Scotland, auchinleck.nls.uk/index.html

Bury, S. (1995) *Artists' Books: the book as a work of art, 1963–1995*, Scolar Press.

Carter, H. G. and Mosley, J. (2002) *A View of Early Typography up to About 1600*, Hyphen.

Carter, J. and Barker, N. (2004) *ABC for Book Collectors*, rev. edn, Oak Knoll Press.

Cave, R. (1983) *The Private Press*, 2nd edn, Bowker.

Cave, R. (2001) *Fine Printing and Private Presses: selected papers*, British Library.

Center, C. and Lancaster, D. (2004) *Security in Special Collections*, ARL Spec Kit, executive summary, www.arl.org/bm~doc/spec284web.pdf

Chappell, W. (1999) *A Short History of the Printed Word*, 2nd edn, Hartley & Marks Publishers.

Child, R. E. (2011) *Mould Outbreaks in Library and Archive Collections*, NPO, www.bl.uk/blpac/pdf/mould.pdf.

CILIP Rare Books and Special Collections Group (2007a) *Guidelines for the Cataloguing of Rare Books*, www.cilip.org.uk/get-involved/special-interest-groups/rare-books/bibliographic-standards/guidlines-for-cataloguing-rare-books/pages/index.aspx.

CILIP Rare Books and Special Collections Group (2007b) *Skills of a Rare Books and Special Collections Librarian*, www.cilip.org.uk/filedownloadslibrary/groups/rbsc/skills%20of%20a%20rare%20books%20librarian.pdf.

CILIP Rare Books and Special Collections Group (2009a) *Disposals Policy for Rare Books and Manuscripts*, www.cilip.org.uk/get-involved/special-interest-groups/rare-books/policy/pages/policy_sales.aspx.

CILIP Rare Books and Special Collections Group (2009b) *Theft of Books and Manuscripts from Libraries: an advisory code of conduct for booksellers and librarians*, www.cilip.org.uk/get-involved/special-interest-groups/rare-books/policy/pages/policy_theft.aspx.

CILIP Working Party on Ephemera (2003) *Ephemera: the stuff of history*, www.cilip.org.uk/filedownloadslibrary/policy%20and%20advocacy/ephemera.pdf.

Clark, S. (2009) *Photographic Material*, BLPAC, rev. edn, www.bl.uk/blpac/pdf/photographic.pdf.

Clark, S. and Frey, F. (2003) *Care of Photographs*, ECPA, www.ica.org/?lid=5735&bid=744.

Clemens, R. and Graham, T. (2007) *Introduction to Manuscript Studies*, Cornell University Press.

Clement, R. W. (2004) Editor's Note, *RBM*, **5** (2), 82–83.

Cornish, G. P (2009) *Copyright: interpreting the law for libraries, archives and information services*, 5th edn, Facet Publishing.

Crosby, C. (2010) *Effective Blogging for Libraries*, Facet Publishing.

Darbey, N. and Hayden, H. (2008) Special Collections for Beginners, *New Library World*, **109** (5/6), 258.

De Hamel, C. (1992) *Scribes and Illuminators*, University of Toronto Press.

De Hamel, C. (1994) *A History of Illuminated Manuscripts*, 2nd edn, BCA.

De Saëz, E. E. (2002) *Marketing Concepts for Libraries and Information Services*, 2nd edn, Facet Publishing.

Deegan, M. and Tanner, S. (2006) *Digital Preservation*, Facet Publishing.

Dewe, M. (2009) *Renewing our Libraries: case studies in re-planning and refurbishment*, Ashgate.

Dewey, B. I. and Parham, L. (2006) *Achieving Diversity: a how-to-do-it manual for librarians*, Neal-Schuman.

Dooley, J. M. and Luce, K. (2010) *Taking our Pulse: the OCLC research survey of Special Collections and archives*, OCLC, www.oclc.org/research/publications/library/2010/2010-11.pdf.

Dowding, G. (1998) *An Introduction to the History of Printing Types: an illustrated summary of the main stages in the development of type design from 1440 up to the present day*, new edn, British Library.

Dowell, E. (2008) Web Site Usability for Rare Book and Manuscript Libraries, *RBM: A Journal of Rare Books, Manuscripts and Cultural Heritage*, **9** (2), 168–182.

Driggers, P. F. and Dumas, E. (2011) *Managing Library Volunteers*, 2nd edn, American Library Association.

Drucker, J. (2004) *The Century of Artists' Books*, 2nd edn, Granary Books.

East, D. and Myers, W. G. (1998) Get the Thief 'Out of the Business': diary of a theft, *Rare Books & Manuscripts Librarianship*, **13** (1), 27–47.

Eisenstein, E. L (2005) *The Printing Revolution in Early Modern Europe*, 2nd edn, Cambridge University Press.

Erway, R. (2010) *Defining Born Digital: an essay*, OCLC, www.oclc.org/research/activities/hiddencollections/borndigital.pdf.

Erway, R. (2011) *Rapid Capture: faster throughput in digitization of Special Collections*, OCLC, www.oclc.org/research/publications/library/2011/2011-04.pdf.

Falk, P. K. and Hunker, S. (2009) *Cataloguing outside the Box: a practical guide to cataloguing special collections materials*, Chandos.

Farman, N. (2008) Artists' Books: managing the unmanageable, *Library Management*, **29** (4/5), 319.

Feather, J. (2004) *Managing Preservation for Libraries and Archives: current practice and future developments*, Ashgate.

Febvre, L. P .V. (2010) *The Coming of the Book: the impact of printing, 1450–1800*, Verso.

Finch, L. and Webster, J. (2008) *Caring for CDs and DVDs*, NPO, www.bl.uk/blpac/pdf/cd.pdf.

Florian, M.-L.E. (2002) *Fungal Facts: solving fungal problems in heritage collections*, Archetype.

Foot, M. (2001) *Building Blocks for a Preservation Policy*, NPO. www.bl.uk/blpac/pdf/blocks.pdf.

Foot, M. (2006) *Bookbinders at Work: their roles and methods*, British Library.

Forde, H. (2007) *Preserving Archives*, Facet Publishing.

Ford-Smith, A. (2010) 'Is this a Fortune that I See Before Me?' the sale of Dr Williams's First Folio, *Rare Books Newsletter*, **87**, 12–14.

García-Ontiveros, D. (2010) Retrospective Cataloguing: the forgotten projects, *Catalogue & Index*, **161**, 21–25.

Gardner, J. (2006) *Report on GLAM Survey, Delivered at Manuscripts Matter: collecting modern literary archives: a conference at the British Library, 19–20 October 2006*, www.literary.org.uk/pdfs/Jessica_Gardner.pdf.

Gardner, J. and Pavelich, D. (2008) Teaching with Ephemera, *RBM*, **9** (1), 86–92.

Gascoigne, B. (2004) *How to Identify Prints: a complete guide to manual and mechanical processes from woodcut to ink jet*, 2nd edn, Thames & Hudson.

Gaskell, P. (1995) *A New Introduction to Bibliography*, new edn, Oak Knoll Press.

Gluibizzi, A. and Glassman, P. (2010) *The Handbook of Art and Design Librarianship*, Facet Publishing.

Gorman, G. E. and Shep, S. J. (2006) *Preservation Management for Libraries, Archives and Museums*, Facet Publishing.

Gorman, M. and Winkler, P. W. (1978) *Anglo-American Cataloguing Rules*, 2nd edn, Library Association.

Grässe, J. G. ., Benedict, F. and Plechl, H. (1971) *Orbis Latinus: Lexikon lateinischer geographischer Namen Handausgabe*, 4, rev. und erw. Aufl., Klinkhardt & Biermann. 1909 edition online, www.columbia.edu/acis/ets/Graesse/contents.html.

Greene, M. and Meissner, D. (2005) More Product, Less Process: revamping traditional archival processing, *American Archivist*, **68** (2), 208–263.

Griffey, J. (2010) *Mobile Technology and Libraries*, Facet Publishing.

Grob, J. (2003) RBMS, Special Collections and the Challenge of Diversity: the road to the diversity Action Plan, *RBM*, **4**, 74–107.

Hackman, L. J. (2011) *Many Happy Returns: advocacy and the development of archives*, Society of American Archivists.

Hammond, H. (1996) Norfolk and Norwich Central Library: the emerging phoenix, *New Library World* **97**, 6.

Hargreaves, I. (2011) *Digital Opportunity: a review of intellectual property and growth*, IPO, www.ipo.gov.uk/ipreview-finalreport.pdf.

Harris, N. (2004) *An Alternative Prospectus*, Institut d'histoire du livre, http://ihl.enssib.fr/siteihl.php?page=55&aflng=fr

Harris, N. (2009) Tribal Lays and the History of the Fingerprint. In Shaw, D. (ed.), *Many into One:*

problems and opportunities in creating shared catalogues of older books, CERL.

Harthan, J. (1997) *The History of the Illustrated Book: the Western tradition*, Thames and Hudson.

Harvey, D. R. (2010) *Digital Curation: a how-to-do-it manual*, Facet Publishing.

Hastings, R. (2010) *Microblogging and Lifestreaming in Libraries*, Facet Publishing.

Henderson, J. (2010) *Environment*, rev. edn, BLPAC, www.bl.uk/blpac/pdf/environment.pdf.

Herring, M. Y. (2004) *Raising Funds with Friends Groups*, Neal-Schuman.

Hillyard, B. (2009) *Latin for Rare Book Librarians*, RBIS, www.nls.uk/media/778068/latin-words-list.pdf.

Hirtle, P. (2011) *Copyright Term and the Public Domain in the United States*, Cornell Copyright Information Centre, copyright.cornell.edu/resources/publicdomain.cfm.

Hirtle, P. B., Hudson, E. and Kenyon, A. T. (2009) *Copyright and Cultural Institutions: guidelines for digitization for U.S. libraries, archives, and museums*, Cornell University Library.

Hubbard, M. A. and Myers, A. K. D. (2010) Bringing Rare Books to Light: the state of the profession, *RBM*, **11** (2), 134–151.

Hudson, G. S. (2008) *The Design and Printing of Ephemera in Britain and America, 1720–1920*, British Library.

Hughes, S (2001) *Preserving Library and Archive Collections in Historic Buildings*, Resource: the Council for Museums, Archives and Libraries.

Hughes, S. (2002) *Managing the Preservation of Library and Archive Collections in Historic Buildings*, NPO Preservation Guidance, NPO, www.bl.uk/blpac/pdf/historic.pdf.

Hults, L. C (1996) *The Print in the Western World: an introductory history*, University of Wisconsin Press.

Hunter, D. (1978) *Papermaking: the history and technique of an ancient craft*, Dover Publications.

Hunter, N. C. Legg, K. and Oehlerts, B. (2010) Two Librarians, an Archivist, and 13,000 Images: collaborating to build a digital collection, *The Library Quarterly*, **80**, 81–103.

Institut de recherche et d'histoire des textes (1984) *Fingerprints*, in association with the National Library of Scotland, edit16.iccu.sbn.it/web_iccu/info/en/Impronta_regole.htm.

International Association of Sound and Audiovisual Archives (2005) *The Safeguarding of the Audio Heritage: ethics, principles and preservation strategy*, Version 3, www.iasa-web.org/sites/default/files/downloads/publications/TC03_English.pdf.

International Council on Archives (2000) *ISAD(G): General International Standard Archival Description adopted by the Committee on Descriptive Standards, Stockholm, Sweden, 19–22 September 1999*, 2nd edn, International Council of Archives, www.icacds.org.uk/eng/ISAD%28G%29.pdf.

International Council on Archives (2004) *ISAAR (CPF): International Standard Archival Authority Record For Corporate Bodies, Persons and Families*, www.icacds.org.uk/eng/ISAAR%28CPF%292ed.pdf.

International Federation of Library Associations and Institutions (2007) *International Standard Bibliographic Description (ISBD)*, preliminary consolidated edn, IFLA, K. G. Saur.

International Federation of Library Associations and Institutions. Study Group on the Functional Requirements for Bibliographic Records and International Federation of Library Associations and Institutions (1998) *Functional Requirements for Bibliographic Records: final report*,

K. G. Saur, http://archive.ifla.org/VII/s13/frbr/frbr1.htm.

Johnstone, C. (n.d.) *All Together Now. [Yorkshire Rapid Response Network]*, available from www.shcg.org.uk/scripts/resources_training.asp.

Joint Steering Committee for Development of RDA (2010) *Resource Description & Access: RDA*, American Library Association.

Jones, B. M. (2003) *Hidden Collections, Scholarly Barriers: creating access to unprocessed Special Collections materials in North America's research libraries: a White Paper for the Association of Research Libraries Task Force on Special Collections*, www.arl.org/bm~doc/hiddencollswhitepaperjun6.pdf.

Kahn, M. (2008) *The Library Security and Safety Guide to Prevention, Planning, and Response*, American Library Association.

Khan, A. (2009) *Better by Design: an introduction to planning and designing a new library building*, Facet Publishing.

Kidd, P. (2004) Cutting Up Manuscripts for … Profit, *AMARC Newsletter*, **42**, 9–10.

Kingsley, H. (ed.) (2001) *Integrated Pest Management for Collections: Proceedings of 2001: A Pest Odyssey*, James & James.

Kitching, C. J. (2007) *Archive Buildings in the United Kingdom, 1993–2005*, Phillimore.

Kitching, C. J., Edgar, H. and Milford, I. (2001) *Guide to the Interpretation of BS 5454:2000, 'Recommendations for the Storage and Exhibition of Archival Documents'*, BSI.

Kommission für den Gesamtkatalog der Wiegendrucke (ed.) (1925–) *Gesamtkatalog der Wiegendrucke*, K. W. Hiersemann.

Korn, N. (2009) *In from the Cold: an assessment of the scope of 'orphan works' and its impact on the delivery of services to the public*, Strategic Content Alliance, www.jisc.ac.uk/media/documents/publications/infromthecoldv1.pdf.

Krause, M. G. (2010) 'It Makes History Alive for Them': the role of archivists and Special Collections librarians in instructing undergraduates, *Journal of Academic Librarianship*, **36** (5), 401–411.

Krizack, J. D (2007) Preserving the History of Diversity: one university's efforts to make Boston's history more inclusive, *RBM*, **8** (2), 125–132.

Lambert, S. (2008) *Making the Most of Your Plastics*, Plastics SSN, www.collectionslink.org.uk/subjects/plastics/962-making-the-most-of-your-plastics.

Lawson, A. (1990) *Anatomy of a Typeface*, Hamish Hamilton.

Leab, K. K. (2010) Collecting, Auctions, and the Book Trade, *RBM*, **11** (1), 47–60.

Lee, D. M. (2009) *Film and Sound Archives in Non-specialist Repositories*, Best Practice Guideline, Society of Archivists, www.archives.org.uk/images/Film_BPG.pdf.

Levy, D. M. (2005) *Contemplating Scholarship in the Digital Age*, RBM, **6**, 69–81.

Lewis, C. T. and Short, A. (1879) *A Latin Dictionary : founded on Andrew's edition of Freund's Latin dictionary ; revised, enlarged and in great part rewritten*, Clarendon.

Lindsay, H. (2011) *Volunteering in Collections Care*, Best Practice Guide, ARA, www.archives.org.uk/images/documents/VOLUNTEERING_in_COLLECTIONS_CARE_-_GUIDE-1.pdf.

Lindsay, J. (2009) *Fine Bookbinding: a technical guide*, British Library.

Lundy, M. (2008) Provenance Evidence in Bibliographic Records: demonstrating the value of best practices in Special Collections cataloging, *Library Resources & Technical Services*, **52** (3), 164.

Lundy, M. W. and Hollis, D. R. (2004) Creating Access to Invisible Special Collections: using participatory management to reduce a backlog, *Journal of Academic Librarianship*, **30** (4), 466–475.

Mahurter, S. (n.d.) *Charging for Reproduction Services*, VADS, Look-Here! Project Case Studies www.vads.ac.uk/lookhere/UALCaseStudy.pdf.

Mandel, C. (2004) Hidden Collections: the elephant in the closet, *RBM*, **5** (2) 106–113.

Mander, D. (2008) *A Standard for Access to Archives*, NCA/PSQG, www.nca.org.uk/materials/access_standard_2008.pdf.

Martin, S. K. (2002) *Insuring and Valuing Research Library Collections*, ARL Spec Kit, ARL, executive summary, www.arl.org/bm~doc/spec272web.pdf.

Matthews, G., Smith, Y. and Knowles, G. (2009) *Disaster Management in Archives, Libraries and Museums*, Ashgate.

Mazella, D. and Grob, J. (2011) Collaborations between Faculty and Special Collections Librarians in Inquiry-Driven Classes, *portal: Libraries and the Academy*, **11** (1), 467–487.

McCarthy, R. C. (2007) *Managing your Library Construction Project: a step-by-step guide*, American Library Association.

McCoy, M. (2010) The Manuscript as Question: teaching primary sources in the archives: the China Missions Project, *College & Research Libraries*, **71** (2010), 49–62.

McIntyre, J. et al. (2000) *Guidance for Exhibiting Library and Archive Materials*, NPO, www.bl.uk/blpac/pdf/exhibition.pdf.

McKerrow, R. B. (1994) *An Introduction to Bibliography for Literary Students*, St Paul's Bibliographies.

McKnight, O. M. (n.d.) *Bibliographical Fingerprints*, http://users.ox.ac.uk/~bodl0842/fingerprints/.

Meyer, L. (2009) *Safeguarding Collections at the Dawn of the 21st Century: describing roles and measuring contemporary preservation activities in ARL Libraries*, ARL, www.arl.org/bm~doc/safeguarding-collections.pdf.

Miller, J., Spitzmueller, P. J. and Jones, J. W. (2010) *Books will Speak Plain: a handbook for identifying and describing historical bindings*, Legacy Press.

Miller, L., Galbraith, S. K. and the RLG Partnership Working Group on Streamlining Photography and Scanning (2010) *'Capture and Release': digital cameras in the reading room*, OCLC Research, www.oclc.org/research/publications/library/2010/2010-05.pdf.

Miller, W. and Pellen, R. M. (2006) *Dealing with Natural Disasters in Libraries*, Haworth Information Press.

Millett, T. (ed.) (2011) *The Copyright Act 1994 and Amendments: guidelines for librarians*, Standing Committee on Copyright of the Library and Information Association of New Zealand, 7th edn, www.lianza.org.nz/sites/lianza.org.nz/files/lianza_copyright_guidelines_may_2011.pdf.

Milne, C. and McKie, A. (2009) *Displays and Exhibitions in Art Libraries*, ARLIS.

Minow, M. and Hirtle, P. (2010) *Factoids*, blog.librarylaw.com/librarylaw/2010/03/index.html.

Myers, R., Harris, M. and Mandelbrote, G. R. (eds) (2005) *Owners, Annotators and the Signs of Reading*, Oak Knoll Press.

National Archives (2004) *Standard for Record Repositories*, www.nationalarchives.gov.uk/documents/information-management/standard2005.pdf.

National Archives (2005) *Guidance on Assessing whether Deposited Private Archive Collections are Covered by the Freedom of Information Act (FOI) 2000*, www.nationalarchives.gov.uk/documents/information-management/guidance_private_archives.pdf.

National Archives (2006) *Guidance for Record Repositories on Loan (Deposit) Agreements for Privately-Owned Archives*, www.nationalarchives.gov.uk/documents/information-management/loanagreement.pdf.

National Archives (n.d.) *Purchasing Archives and Manuscripts: a checklist for archivists*, www.nationalarchives.gov.uk/documents/information-management/information-management/purchasing-archives-and-manuscripts-checklist.pdf.

National Archives et al. (2007) *Code of Practice for Archivists and Records Managers under Section 51 (4) of the Data Protection Act 1998*, www.archives.org.uk/images/documents/DP_codeofpractice_Oct_2007.pdf.

National Council on Archives (1997) *NCA Rules for the Construction of Personal, Place and Corporate Names*, www.nationalarchives.gov.uk/documents/information-management/naming-rules.pdf.

National Preservation Office (2000a) *Good Handling Principles and Practice for Library and Archive Materials*, www.bl.uk/blpac/pdf/handling.pdf.

National Preservation Office (2000b) *Photocopying of Library and Archive Materials*, www.bl.uk/blpac/pdf/photocopy.pdf.

National Preservation Office (n.d.) *Glossary*, www.bl.uk/blpac/pdf/glossary.pdf.

Nicholson, J. R. (2010) Making Personal Libraries More Public: a study of the technical processing of personal libraries in ARL institutions, *RBM*, **11** (2), 106–133.

North East Document Conservation Centre (2007) *The Book Shoe: description and uses*, rev. edn, NEDCC leaflets, www.nedcc.org/resources/leaflets/4Storage_and_Handling/07BookShoe.php.

Nyberg, S. (n.d.), *Invasion of the Giant Mold Spore*, rev. edn, cool.conservation-us.org/byauth/nyberg/spore.html.

O'Gara, G., Walters, E. and Putirskis, C. (2010) Articulating Value in Special Collections: are we collecting data that matter? *In the Library with the Lead Pipe*, www.inthelibrarywiththeleadpipe.org/2010/articulating-value-in-special-collections-are-we-collecting-data-that-matter.

Ogden, S. (ed.) (1999) *Preservation of Library and Archival Materials: a manual*, NEDCC, 3rd edn.

Ogden, S. (2007) *Conservation Treatments for Bound Materials of Value*, NEDCC, www.nedcc.org/resources/leaflets/7Conservation_Procedures/06BoundMaterials.php.

Pacifico, M. F. and Wilsted, T. P. (2009) *Archival and Special Collections Facilities: guidelines for archivists, librarians, architects, and engineers*, Society of American Archivists.

Padfield, T. (2010) *Copyright for Archivists and Records Managers*, 4th edn, Facet Publishing.

Panitch, J. (2000) *Special Collections in ARL Libraries: results of the 1998 survey sponsored by the ARL Research Collections Committee*, ARL.

Paris, J. (2010) *Choosing and Working with a Conservator*, NEDCC, www.nedcc.org/resources/leaflets/7Conservation_Procedures/07ChoosingAConservator.php.

Parkes, M. B. (1991) *Scribes, Scripts, and Readers: studies in the communication, presentation, and dissemination of medieval texts*, Hambledon Press.

Pass, G. A. (2003) *Descriptive Cataloging of Ancient, Medieval, Renaissance, and Early Modern Manuscripts*, ACRL.

Patkus, B. (2003) *Assessing Preservation Needs: a self-survey guide*, NEDCC, www.nedcc.org/resources/downloads/apnssg.pdf.

Pavelich, D. (2010) Lighting Fires in Creative Minds: teaching creative writing in Special Collections, *College & Research Libraries News*, **71**, 295–297.

Pearson, D. (1998) *Provenance Research in Book History: a handbook*, British Library.

Pearson, D. (2005) *English Bookbinding Styles, 1450–1800: a handbook*, British Library.

Pearson, D. (2011) *Books as History: the importance of books beyond their texts*, rev. edn, British Library.

Pearson, D., Mumford, J. and Walker, A. (2010) *Understanding and Caring for Bookbindings*, BLPAC, rev. edn, www.bl.uk/blpac/pdf/bookbindings.pdf.

Pedley, P. (2007) *Digital Copyright*, 2nd edn, Facet Publishing.

Pedley, P. (2008) *Copyright Compliance: practical steps to stay within the law*, Facet Publishing.

Peters, J. (2010) Rare Books Collection to find New Home at Cardiff University Library, *SCONUL Focus*, (2010), 54–56.

Pettegree, A. (2010) *The Book in the Renaissance*, Yale University Press.

Pinniger, D. (2009) *Pest Management: a practical guide*, Collections Trust.

Pollard, A. W. et al. (1976–1986) *A Short Title Catalogue of Books Printed in England, Scotland and Ireland and of English books Printed Abroad 1475–1640*, 2nd edn, Bibliographical Society.

Potter, S. and Holley, R. (2010) Rare Material in Academic Libraries, *Collection Building*, **29** (4), 148–153.

Pritchard, S. (2009) Special Collections Surge to the Fore, *Portal: Libraries and the Academy*, **9** (2), 177.

Procter, M. and Cook, M. (2000) *Manual of Archival Description*, 3rd edn, Gower.

Public Services Quality Group (2003) *Towards Generic and Universal PIs for Archives, Phase 1: performance indicators for access and usage*, NCA/PSQG, www.nca.org.uk/materials/performance_measures.pdf.

Randeria, P. and Foot, M. (2004) *Eloquent Witnesses: bookbindings and their history*, Bibliographical Society.

Rare Books and Manuscripts Section (2006) *Your Old Books*, rev. edn, www.ala.org/ala/mgrps/divs/acrl/publications/digital/youroldbooks.pdf.

Rare Books and Manuscripts Section (2008) *Guidelines: competencies for special collections professionals*, www.ala.org/ala/mgrps/divs/acrl/standards/comp4specollect.cfm.

Rare Books and Manuscripts Section (2009) *Digitization of Special Collections: RBMS principles for digital content*, www.rbms.info/committees/task_force/digitization/digprinciples.html.

Ray, L. (2009) *Volunteering in Archives: a report for the National Council on Archives*, NCA, www.archives.org.uk/images/documents/volunteeringinarchivesfinal.pdf.

Reed, C. (2009) *Revisiting Archive Collections*, 3rd edn, MLA, www.collectionslink.org.uk/programmes/revisiting-collections..

Resource: The Council for Museums, Archives and Libraries (2003) *Security in Museums, Archives and Libraries: a practical guide*, www.collectionslink.org.uk/programmes/museums-accreditation/923-security-in-museums-archives-and-libraries-a-practical-guide.

Rhys-Lewis, J. (2007) *Specifying Library and Archive Storage*, NPO, www.bl.uk/blpac/pdf/storage.pdf.

Rickards, M. and Twyman, M. (2001) *The Encyclopedia of Ephemera: a guide to the fragmentary documents of everyday life for the collector, curator and historian*, British Library.

Rieger, O. Y. (2010) Enduring Access to Special Collections: challenges and opportunities for large-scale digitization initiatives, *RBM*, **11** (2010), 11–22.

Robb, J. E. (2009) The Opper Project: collaborating with educators to promote the use of editorial cartoons in the social studies classroom, *RBM*, **10** (2), 70–94.

Sannwald, W. W. (2009) *Checklist of Library Building Design Considerations*, 5th edn, American Library Association.

Schaffner, J., Snyder, F. and Supple, S. (2011) *Scan and Deliver: managing user-initiated digitization in Special Collections and archives*, OCLC, www.oclc.org/research/publications/library/2011/2011-05.pdf.

Shashoua, Y. (2008) *Conservation of Plastics: materials science, degradation and preservation*, Elsevier, 2008

Sheehan, J. K (2009) Making the Most of What We Have: a framework for preservation management in rare book collections, *RBM*, **10** (2), 111–121.

Silverman, E. (2010) A Place for Books: fundraising for collections, *The Bottom Line*, **23** (2), 70–73.

Simes, L. (2008) *A User's Guide to the Flexible Dealing Provision for Libraries, Educational Institutions and Cultural Institutions*, ALCC, www.digital.org.au/alcc/resources/documents/FlexibleDealingHandbookfinal.pdf.

Smyth, E. B. (1999) A Practical Approach to Writing a Collection Development Policy, *Rare Books and Manuscript Librarianship*, **14**, 27–31.

Society of American Archivists (2004) *Describing Archives: a Content Standard*, SAA.

Society of American Archivists (2005) *Glossary of Archival and Records Terminology*, www.archivists.org/glossary/index.asp.

Staley, D. J. and Malenfant, K. J. (2010) *Futures Thinking for Academic Librarians: higher education in 2025*, ACRL, www.ala.org/ala/mgrps/divs/acrl/issues/value/futures2025.pdf.

Starmer, M. E., McGough, S. H. and Leverette, A. (2005) Rare Condition: preservation assessment for rare book collections, *RBM*, **6** (2), 91–107.

Steinberg, S. H (1996) *Five Hundred Years of Printing*, new edn, British Library.

Stewart, C. (2010) *The Academic Library Building in the Digital Age: a study of construction, planning, and design of new library space*, ACRL.

Stewart, D. (2009) *Fire*, Canadian Conservation Institute, www.cci-icc.gc.ca/crc/articles/mcpm/chap04-eng.aspx

Sudduth, E., Newins, N. and Sudduth, W. (2005) *Special Collections in College and University Libraries*, ACRL.

Summerfield Hammerman, S. et al. (2006) College Students, Cookies and Collections: using holiday study breaks to encourage undergraduate research in Special Collections, *Collection Building*, **25** (4), 145.

Tabb, W. (2004) 'Wherefore are These Things Hid?' A report of a survey undertaken by the ARL Special Collections Task Force, *RBM*, **5** (2), 123–126.

Tanselle, G. T. (2009) *Bibliographical Analysis: a historical introduction*, Cambridge University Press.

Taraba, S. (2003) Now What Should we Do with Them? Artists' books in the curriculum, *RBM*, **4** (20) 109–120.

Terras, M. M. (2008) *Digital Images for the Information Professional*, Ashgate.

Theimer, K. (2010) *Web 2.0 Tools and Strategies for Archives and Local History Collections*, Neal-Schuman.

Tidy, S. (2008) Travelling Treasures: a touring rare book roadshow, *International Preservation News*, **45**, 30.

Torre, M. E. (2008) Why Should not they Benefit from Rare Books?, *Library Review*, **57** (1), 36.

Traister, D. (2000) Is there a Future for Special Collections? And should there be? *RBM*, **1** (1), 54–76.

Traister, D. H. (2003) Public Services and Outreach in Rare Book, Manuscript, and Special Collections Libraries, *Library Trends*, **52** (1), 87–108.

Turcotte, F. and Nemmers, J. (2006) *Public Services in Special Collections*, ARL, www.arl.org/bm~doc/spec296web.pdf.

UNESCO (1995) *UNESCO Thesaurus: a structured list of descriptors for indexing and retrieving literature in the fields of education, science, social and human science, culture, communication and information,* www2.ulcc.ac.uk/unesco.

Various Authors (1986) In the News: LA Public Library burns, *WAAC Newsletter*, **8** (3), 12–13, cool.conservation-us.org/waac/wn/wn08/wn08-3/wn08-307.html.

Visser, M. (2006) Perspectives on… Special Collections at ARL Libraries and K-12 Outreach: current trends, *Journal of Academic Librarianship*, 32 (3), 313–319.

Walton, D. L. (2008) *Manuscript Collections on the Web*, ARL, SPEC Kit 307, executive summary, www.arl.org/bm~doc/spec307web.pdf.

Ward, A. (2003) *Is your Oral History Legal and Ethical?* Oral History Society, www.oralhistory.org.uk/ethics/index.php.

Waters, P. (1993) *Procedures for Salvage of Water Damaged Library Materials*, Library of Congress, cool.conservation-us.org/bytopic/disasters/primer/waters.html.

Watson, R. (2003) *Illuminated Manuscripts and their Makers*, V&A Publications.

Welburn, W. C., Welburn, J. and McNeil, B. (eds) (2010) *Advocacy, Outreach, and the Nation's Academic Libraries: a call for action*, ACRL.

White, M. Perratt, P. and Lawes, L. (2006) *Artists' Books: a cataloguers' manual*, ARLIS.

Whitley, K. P. (2010) *The Gilded Page: the history and technique of manuscript gilding*, 2nd edn, Oak Knoll Press.

Whittaker, B. (2008) Using Circulation Systems for Special Collections: tracking usage, promoting the collection, and addressing the backlogs, *College & Research Libraries*, **69** (1), 28.

Whittaker, B. M. and Thomas, L. M. (2009) *Special Collections 2.0: new technologies for rare books, manuscripts, and archival collections,* Libraries Unlimited.

Wilkie, E. C. (2006) Weighing Materials in Rare Book and Manuscript Libraries as a Security Measure against Theft and Vandalism, *RBM,* **7** (2), 146–164.

Wilkinson, F. C. (2010) *Comprehensive Guide to Emergency Preparedness and Disaster Recovery,* ACRL.

Wing, D. G. et al. (1982–1998) *Short-title Catalogue of Books Printed in England, Scotland, Ireland, Wales, and British America, and of English books Printed in other Countries, 1641–1700,* 2nd edn, Modern Language Association of America.

Winsor, P. (2002) *Benchmarks in Collection Care for Museums, Archives and Libraries: a self-assessment checklist,* Resource, www.collectionslink.org.uk/programmes/benchmarks-for-collections-care/961-benchmarks-in-the-collection-care-for-museums-archives-and-libraries.

Yakel, E. (2005) Hidden Collections in Libraries and Archives, *OCLC Systems & Services,* **21** (2), 95–99.

Yakel, E. and Tibbo, H. (2010) Standardized Survey Tools for Assessment in Archives and Special Collections, *Performance Measurement and Metrics,* **11** (2), 211.

Index

Individual objects, collections and libraries are listed only where they feature as case studies or detailed examples; references to Special Collections, books, archives, libraries, research and the other subjects of this book are indexed selectively.